The Origins of Modern Mexico

Laurens Ballard Perry,
General Editor

Church Property and the Mexican Reform, 1856–1910

Robert J. Knowlton

Northern Illinois University Press   DeKalb 1976

About the artist: The scenes depicted on the jacket, frontispiece, and in the details throughout the book are from original artwork created by Mario Pérez Orona especially for the Origins of Modern Mexico series. Mario Pérez has exhibited his paintings, collages, and drawings in more than 25 exhibitions throughout Mexico in the past 15 years. He is a professor of painting, drawing, and graphics in the art department of the University of the Americas in Puebla, Mexico.

Library of Congress Cataloging in Publication Data

Knowlton, Robert J   1931–
    Church property and the Mexican Reform, 1856–1910.
    (The Origins of Modern Mexico)
    Bibliography: p.
    Includes index.
    1. Secularization—Mexico—History. 2. Church
property—Mexico—History. 3. Mexico—History—
1867–1910. I. Title. II. Series.
HD325.K56   333.1′4   74-28897
ISBN 0-87580-055-6

For Barbara

Contents

Preface

The Reform represented a national peak in the lengthy nineteenth–century struggle of Mexican liberals to "modernize" their country. The years of the Reform were ones of especially protracted violence and conflict between liberalism and conservatism in Mexico—opposing forces which had been present at least since the birth of the independent state in 1821. The upheaval of these years at mid-century obscures the accommodation achieved, if not the complete resolution of conflicting principles in the post-Reform period, during the long "neo-conservative" rule of Porfirio Díaz. The attainment of liberal objectives signified an assault on colonial corporate structures and institutions, an assault in which conflict with the Catholic Church was inevitable. The success of the liberal program increasingly hinged on victory over the political Church and proclerical forces.

The first major property law, the disamortization law of 25 June 1856 forced corporations, civil and ecclesiastical, to dispose of their real estate but permitted them to retain income from the property in the form of mortgages. The second major law, at the height of the War of the Reform in 1859, nationalized all Church property and was aimed principally at capital invested in real estate.

The government's rationale for the first law was primarily economic; it believed that real estate in mortmain stagnated to the detriment of economic prosperity, while disentailment would promote economic progress and foster democracy by creating a large body of "middle-class" proprietors. The basis for nationalization in 1859 was primarily political, to deprive the Church of the means to challenge the authority of civil government. In the case of both laws, financial considerations also figured prominently. In operations of disamortization the government charged a 5 percent tax for the transfer of ownership of property. In nationalization operations, purchasers paid the government partly in specie and partly in bonds of the internal debt. The expectation was that, in this way, important resources would be obtained to carry out further reforms in the country and to retire the bulk of the large national debt. Political upheaval, however, largely defeated the financial objectives. The government of necessity condoned many irregularities and disposed of property at low rates in order to obtain funds to combat its enemies.

The liberals achieved power in the latter part of 1855 in a broadly supported revolution against Antonio López de Santa Anna. Over the next two years they faced intense divisions and successfully coped with sporadic revolts in the country against their authority. In December 1857 a conservative rebellion provoked a three-years' Civil War dividing the republic into two opposing governments, conservatives based in Mexico City and liberals headquartered in Veracruz. The liberal victory late in 1860 was soon followed by foreign intervention, with the French ultimately gaining control of large parts of the country and establishing an empire under the Austrian Archduke Maximilian. This intervention ended only in mid-1867 with the withdrawal of the French and the collapse of the Empire. For some years thereafter, the federal government faced periodic and sporadic challenges to its authority that diverted resources and attention from various problems.

Irregularities, concealment of property, and constant clerical opposition made it extremely difficult to carry out nationalization. Chaotic records and the loss or destruction of important files added to the difficulties. To correct the worst abuses, revisions of operations were authorized. The government also concerned itself with collecting all sums due from former ecclesiastical debtors and making redemption payments on mortgages easy enough to be realistic. Also, to make certain that all ecclesiastical property came under its control, the government permitted denunciations. This policy led to lengthy and costly litigation by proprietors in defense of their ownership, often against unfounded claims. The result was insecurity of ownership and depreciation in the value of real estate, making it of scant worth in sales or as surety for loans. Available published cases and contemporary accounts amply attest to the confusion and conflict arising from the extraordinary conditions under which the laws were implemented—conflicts between individuals, between individuals and the federal government, and between state and federal authorities, as well as between Church and State. The government intended to resolve these conflicts with justice and in strict accordance with the laws, but all too often the intent of the laws and the objectives of the government had to be subordinated to political necessity, an expediency which defeated the best intentions.

As operations dealing with nationalization dragged on, frustration over the inability to conclude the process replaced the confusion of the early, politically unstable years. Nationalization had changed from a political and economic necessity into an obstacle to economic stability and progress. A definitive settlement did not occur, however, until the turn of the century, late in the Díaz period. By that time, security for property owners was more important to the government than the meager amounts that the treasury received from nationalization.

Various facets of the Reform have been studied, but comparatively little attention has focused on the many ramifications of the attack on Church wealth. Nearly all writers dealing with the period touch on the expropriation of ecclesiastical property. Some briefly summarize major laws and estimate Church wealth, while their emphasis remains on political events. Other writers, more specifically concerned with economics, stress the failure of the laws to benefit the propertyless masses. Recently, scholars have begun to analyze in detail the transfer of property.

This study serves in some ways as a counterpoint to the excellent monograph by Jan Bazant—the one complements the other.[1] Bazant and I ask many of the same questions and agree on many points where our labors overlap. But this duplication of two researchers working independently strengthens the validity of conclusions regarding such things as motives of the reformers, objectives of the property legislation, total value of ecclesiastical wealth,[2] and certain results.[3] Bazant's scope, however, is narrower, his focus more pointed than that of the present study. He selected for examination a few territorial entities which he considered the most important,[4] and he

1. *Alienation of Church Wealth in Mexico. Social and Economic Aspects of the Liberal Revolution, 1856–1875*, ed. and trans. Michael P. Costeloe (Cambridge: The University Press, 1971).

2. Bazant's $100,000,000 estimate, however, represents a maximum, while I suggest it as a minimum figure. See Appendix 1 at end of this work.

3. For example, the long-run failure of the reformers to achieve their goals with anticorporate property laws.

4. Federal District and states of San Luis Potosí, Michoacán, Jalisco, Puebla, Veracruz.

sampled notarial records in those states. He concentrated on the well-to-do, those who adjudicated property and redeemed mortgages in greatest amounts. Bazant's analysis is limited primarily to the 1856–1867 period; it is highly statistical and devoted rather explicitly to property transfer.

This study, on the other hand, is more broadly framed. While the focus is on the impact of the anticorporate property legislation, this specific is placed in the context of the total Reform movement and of Church-State relations. It deals more extensively with continuing problems associated with property legislation and their final termination late in the Porfirian period. While the core of study is the same period, relatively more space is devoted here to the later years. Furthermore, attention is given to the meaning of the reform legislation for ordinary Mexicans and for individual ecclesiastical corporations and their members, as well as the significance for Church and State in general. Finally, while Bazant's is a selective social-economic study, the present work is more broadly legal and political. Needless to say, I owe much to the Bazant book and to other recent researchers as well.

This monograph, then, deals with the operation and administration of the laws, their alteration over the years, and the many problems that plagued their effectiveness, some of which were beyond the anticipation or best intentions of the reformers. It encompasses the history of the successful liberal assault on Church property from disamortization at the beginning of the Reform in 1856 to the liquidation of nationalization in the later years of the Porfirian regime.

Acknowledgments

Many individuals have assisted me in this study through the years of research, writing and rewriting, and editing. Several generously contributed their expertise in methodically reading the manuscript and making perceptive suggestions. The enduring confidence and encouragement of friends and colleagues have been no less important. I gratefully acknowledge my debt to: Charles Gibson, Jan Bazant, Charles Hale, Asunción Lavrin, Richard Greenleaf, Laurens B. Perry, Charles Berry, Michael Costeloe, Robert Gold, Benjamin Keen, and Donald Cooper. Without the patience, constant encouragement, and the secretarial, editorial, and intellectual skills of Barbara, the work would never have been completed.

Nettie Lee Benson and the staff of the Latin American Collection at the University of Texas made available the incomparable resources of the collection, brought to my attention many materials, and cheerfully endured the demands of one more researcher in 1961–1962 and 1966–1967. Lic. Jorge Ignacio Rubio Mañé and his staff made available and assisted me with materials in the Archivo General de la Nación in Mexico City.

A University Fellowship from the University of Iowa in 1961–1962 and a Teacher Improvement Leave from the University of Wisconsin–Stevens Point in 1966–1967 supported the research. Mario Pérez improved on the quality of the cartoons in the book.

Chapter 1
Prelude to Reform

A panacea for Mexico's ills or a godless attack on religion and God-given rights? These two extremes of opinion, liberal and clerical, greeted the measures against ecclesiastical property. A brutal civil war flared from the inflexibility of the extremes. The uncompromising dedication of each to principles and the increasingly fanatical adherence to positions taken sundered Mexican society. The wound opened by the conflict remained unhealed and festered. The struggle embittered political life for many years. Those who sought compromise, who spoke for moderation, were cast aside, consumed by extremism.

In retrospect, the results of reform seem not to justify the high cost. The Mexican experience with property-related reform was not a happy one nor a striking success: it largely failed as an attempted land reform, in both its civil and ecclesiastical aspects; it was disappointing as a financial measure; it succeeded temporarily in eliminating the economic and political power of the Church. Yet, within the larger context of the Reform movement and the still larger one of Mexican history, such an appraisal must be tempered; and the results of reform were by no means entirely negative nor the efforts unnecessary.

An assault on corporate property was inherent in liberal ideology. It was fundamental to a reordering of Mexican institutions and society; the goal signified a clash with colonial institutions and practices, notably with the Church over its dominant position in Mexican life.

An attack on Church wealth was not untried or unique in the middle of the nineteenth century. It formed part of Spanish royal policy under Charles III and Charles IV in the late colonial period. Clerical wealth, like the Church's position in general, was scrutinized and attacked during the Independence movement and on into nationhood. Mexico was not unique in nineteenth-century Latin America in the problems it faced. Liberal ideas emanating principally from eighteenth-century France found their way to America, where they inspired colonials, especially the white Creole elite, and gave impetus to their discontent with peninsular commercial, political, and social domination. The influence of French ideas in the Independence movements is generally recognized; the Spanish impact is only in-frequently appreciated. The representative body, the Cortes, con-voked by the opposition to the French occupation of Spain, included delegates from the colonies. It is apparent that the liberal ideas ex-pressed there and the experience gained by the colonial deputies in the Cortes were influential in determining later Mexican acts toward the Church.[1]

Notions of popular sovereignty, liberty, equality, and economic freedom might serve as a catalyst for Mexican Independence, but once independence had been achieved, basically little had changed. Liberty might mean an end to slavery and royal authority, but it did not mean improvement for the lowest classes of society, the workers of the land; indeed, the end of royal authority probably worsened their lot by removing royal restraints. Liberty did not mean untram-meled freedom of speech or the press—the freedom to criticize reli-gion. Equality in Mexico meant equality of Creoles with peninsulars, not actual equality for all. The old corporate structure remained; the narrow, stringent class system continued. With the winning of politi-cal independence, the promoters of independence became defenders of the social and economic *status quo*.

By no means did all Mexicans belong to the privileged elite, nor were all of the articulate and educated population satisfied; for many, the revolution was incomplete. In Mexico, in contrast to most of Latin America, a social revolution had been attempted. This early move-ment was crushed, and independence was eventually won under the leadership of Agustín de Iturbide, representing conservative-Creole interests—those of the landed aristocrats, Church hierarchy, and mili-tary. Liberal ideas favoring economic and social change remained, however, and gained in strength. In both ideological camps, conserva-tive and liberal, there were men not at all inspired by ideas, but simply interested in power, wealth, and fame; they supported one or the other faction as expediency warranted. Thus, there were opportunists like Iturbide and Antonio López de Santa Anna, but there were also

1. James Breedlove, "Effect of the Cortes, 1810–1822, on Church Reform in Spain and Mexico," in *Mexico and the Spanish Cortes, 1810–1822. Eight Essays*, ed. Nettie Lee Benson (Austin: University of Texas Press, 1966), p. 133. See also the other articles on Spanish influence.

the sincere constructive conservatives like Lucas Alamán and liberals like Valentín Gómez Farías and Benito Juárez.

Iturbide, at the head of a regency while a Spanish prince was sought for Mexico, convoked a Constituent Congress in 1822. Ideas aired in that body on the issues of property and the Church exemplified liberal thought at the time and foreshadowed their successors' thinking at mid-century as well.[2] Carlos María Bustamante believed that property rights derived from a social contract and urged the government to promote a broad distribution of landholding and circulation of wealth to foster prosperity and the well-being of the masses. Bustamante set forth two significant points of the liberal ideology: that government had to force the changes necessary to secure the benefits of liberalism and that prosperity and democracy required broad distribution of landholding. For Deputy Manuel Terán, history showed that corporations were not the best proprietors. Corporate lands were condemned, if not to perpetual sterility, at best to careless cultivation, yielding little benefit to the public; the individual proprietor exploited the land to fullest advantage. Terán expressed a view that reformers repeated again and again to justify their assault on corporate property, civil as well as ecclesiastical. This view stemmed from a profound belief in individualism and in the baleful effects of corporate ownership of real property. A colonization bill submitted to Congress in August 1822 reflected this belief in the desirability of achieving the greatest possible equality in the distribution of property. A year later a decree ended the entailment of property. The liberals, for all their ardor to distribute property broadly, recognized that too great fractioning of the land would result in misery. This recognition and the belief in the sanctity of private property contributed to the ambivalence in their actions and to the defeat of their aim to equalize property ownership.

The deputies also discussed a broad range of ecclesiastical matters. Speeches revealed dissatisfaction with existing conditions and foreshadowed reform.[3] Criticism of tithes and first fruits, of parish

2. These comments on the Congress follow Jesús Reyes Heroles, *El liberalismo mexicano*, vol. 1, *Los orígenes* (Mexico: Editorial Cultura, 1957), pp. 128–46.

3. See Juan Porras Sánchez, *Orígenes y evolución de la Reforma en México:*

fees and ecclesiastical entailment by such eminent figures as Joaquín Fernández de Lizardi and Manuel Crescencio Rejón were as much a reflection of concern with the poverty of the masses and the miserable existence of the lower clergy as with the great wealth of the Church. Both recommended State financial support of the Faith. A more radical suggestion of José María Covarrubias would have separated Church and State. This deputy maintained that Christ's dictum to render unto Caesar the things that were Caesar's supported the opinion that the Church should be strictly limited to the spiritual order. Liberals also discussed freedom of conscience and the ecclesiastical privilege to maintain separate courts with jurisdiction over clerical and some lay offenses. They did not secure the former or restrict the latter, however.

Clearly, liberal ideas about property and the Church, prominent later in the century, received a hearing at the time of Independence. Independence was, however, primarily a conservative achievement. The Constitution drafted by a new Congress in 1824 declared Catholicism the exclusive religion and guaranteed the clergy's privileges (*fueros*) and property. Personal rights and private property were guaranteed, and expropriation of individual or corporate property was permitted only in case of general need and with compensation. Liberals did not necessarily oppose these provisions; they, like the conservatives, believed in the sanctity of private, if not corporate, property and generally accepted the desirability of Catholicism as the sole religion. Although anticlerical in their determination to limit the role of the Church to the purely spiritual, liberals considered themselves good Catholics.

In the years after Independence, a coalition of the upper clergy, aristocratic landowners, and military chiefs defended their privileges and the traditional social and economic structure. In opposition to these defenders of the *status quo* was a liberal group of reformers scattered throughout the states, of professionals, journalists, lesser officials, lower clergy, and lower-ranking military officers.[4] The con-

Antecedentes ideológicos y legislativos con un apéndice sobre la debatida cuestión del Patronato; 1800–1834 (Puebla: n.p. 1949), pp. 35–52; and Reyes Heroles, 1:285, 344–53.

4. Leopoldo Zea, "La ideología liberal y el liberalismo mexicano," in Medina et al., *El liberalismo y la Reforma en México* (Mexico: Editorial Cultura,

servatives supported centralized government, the continuance of close Church-State ties, the restriction of individual liberties, and the maintenance or increase in legal privileges. Liberals favored federalism as the system best assuring individual rights and as the means to achieve power, equality before the law, and amplification of individual liberties.

After Independence, chaos, confusion, and disillusion descended on Mexico. Liberals experienced many defeats and few successes in challenging the conservatives. In the decades prior to the Reform, however, there were some attacks on Church position and property at both the national and state levels. In the state of Mexico in the late 1820s and early 1830s, a liberal governor, Lorenzo de Zavala, acted to break up latifundia and to redistribute land to benefit poor Indians and mestizos. The governor's efforts struck specifically at lay- and Church-owned properties whose income left the country.

As encouraging as such acts might be, probably of greater influence and importance for the generation of mid-century reformers were the ideas of José María Luis Mora. The Zacatecan Congress in 1831 offered a prize, which Mora won, for the best dissertation on ecclesiastical income.[5] Mora's extensive analysis of Church wealth—its foundation and justification, sources and uses—and his recommendations revealed his historical and theological knowledge, as well as his liberal orientation and commitment to social and economic progress. He acknowledged the moral and social importance of religion but denied the divine origin and hence the untouchability of ecclesiastical property. Church wealth was nothing more than property destined to sustain the Faith; it was temporal by nature, ecclesiastical in application. The Church was an institution established by Christ and was, as such, eternal, perfect, and independent of secular authority. But the Church was also a political association whose privileges could be altered or abolished by civil government. Mora cited Church authorities

---

1957), pp. 498–505; and Reyes Heroles, vol. 2, *La sociedad fluctuante* (Mexico: Editorial Cultura, 1958), p. xiv.

5. José María Luis Mora, *Disertación sobre la naturaleza y aplicación de las rentas y bienes eclesiásticos* (Mexico, 1833; reprint ed., Mexico: Talleres de la Secretaría de Hacienda y Crédito Público, 1957). For an excellent study of Mora and liberalism in this period, see Charles Hale, *Mexican Liberalism in the Age of Mora, 1821–1853* (New Haven, Conn.: Yale University Press, 1968).

and laws drawn from history to defend his contention that ecclesiastical property was subject to civil law. He was not unique in such references, for, typically, both critics and defenders of the Church used them to support their respective cases. Proclericals disputed Mora's analysis. Critics, citing historical "chapter and verse" as Mora had, reached different conclusions: Church rights were superior to the rights of individuals and the civil corporations because the origin of the former was divine; the latter derived from civil law.[6]

Mora did not deny the Church's civil right to own property, but he insisted that in origin and intent it was a corporate right as distinct from an individual right. This distinction, not an unusual one, was fundamental for liberal reformers. Property rights of an individual were natural rights, antedating society. Society could not tamper with those rights. A corporation's right to property, however, was a civil right, postdating society. Society could, consequently, limit that right and deprive a corporation of its property as public necessity demanded. Moreover, the commonweal required restriction due to the perpetual nature of corporations, whose property tended to increase indefinitely, and, conversely, because the maximum utilization of property resulted from a distribution among many individuals who had direct personal interest in productivity and efficiency. Corporations lacked this interest.

Mora's concern extended beyond the property issue; it included the clergy's pervasive influence and intervention in the civil order. He believed this influence inimical to representative government, freedom, and the country's progress. As interested as Mora was in eliminating what he believed to be a dangerous influence, he was also concerned that the clergy enjoy adequate income, be well trained, and be more equitably distributed throughout the country to meet the spiritual needs of the people. Mora recognized the equally noxious influence of military intervention in civil affairs and urged restriction of both the military and the Church as essential for Mexico to achieve stability, representative government, and progress.[7]

6. *Rentas eclesiásticas, o sea impugnación de la disertación que sobre la materia se ha publicado de orden del honorable congreso de Zacatecas* (Guadalajara, 1834), pp. 11–26.

7. José María Luis Mora, "Revista política," in *Obras sueltas* (Paris, 1837), 1:xcv, cvi–cx, and cxxv; and Mora, *Ensayos, ideas y retratos* (Mexico: Ediciones

The presence of these two institutions—the Church and the military, with their privileges and power—was, then, the prime cause of Mexico's backwardness. The liberals' determination to restrict both drew those privileged groups together in a common interest to preserve their influence. The liberals faced formidable enemies indeed. In addition, they were weakened by internal disagreements. The division into radical (*puro*) and moderate (*moderado*) factions arose principally, though not exclusively, over the rate at which reforms should be effected rather than over the issue of the temporal role of the Church. As will be seen, the moderates were cautious and hesitant; they were reluctant to appropriate ecclesiastical property, for example. The moderates favored gradual reform rather than the more abrupt changes and frontal assault favored by radicals such as Mora.

In the early 1830s liberals had an opportunity to implement their ideas. The election of Antonio López de Santa Anna to the presidency in 1832 brought the radical liberal Valentín Gómez Farías to the vice-presidency. Santa Anna quickly wearied of humdrum administrative duties, retired to his estate, and left Gómez Farías a free hand to run the government. In the national Congress that convened in March 1833, liberal deputies brought the full weight of argument and action against conservative interests to carry out a comprehensive program. The liberal-dominated Congress and government in 1833 and 1834 enacted some measures, and considered still more, against both Church and military establishments.[8]

Financial as well as ideological motives inspired liberal acts against these institutions. The treasury was chronically empty; servicing the large national debt was a perennial problem, one which seemed easily soluble with Church wealth. Several proposals were discussed to liquidate the public debt by appropriating some or all ecclesiastical

---

de la Universidad Nacional Autónoma en la Imprenta Universitaria, 1941), pp. 111, 116.

8. See Lucas Alamán, *Historia de México* (4th ed.; Mexico: Editorial Jus, 1942), vol. 5; Agustín Cue Cánovas, *Historia social y económica de México*, vol. 2, *La revolución de independencia y México independiente hasta 1854* (Mexico: Editorial América, 1947); Porras Sánchez, *Orígenes*; Enrique Olavarría y Ferrari, *México independiente, 1821–1855*, vol. 4 of *México a través de los siglos*, ed. Vicente Riva Palacio (Mexico, n.d.); and Niceto de Zamacois, *Historia de Méjico desde sus tiempos más remotos hasta nuestros días* (Barcelona, 1880), vol. 12.

property; none of these proposals was approved, however. Among the measures passed, one in 1833 prohibited religious orders and *cofradías* (sodalities or confraternities) from alienating their real estate in the Federal District without government approval and nullified all such transfers since 1821. A *cofradía* was an association, generally of laymen, established in a parish for the purpose of honoring a saint or carrying on pious activities such as conducting a festival for a saint or maintaining a church in good repair. These church-related corporations often amassed considerable property, especially in villages, and the government was concerned about the wealth in general and the monopolization of village property in particular. The next year a decree required government approval for the establishment of *cofradías*. A proposal to nationalize the real estate of vacant *cofradías* and *capellanías* (chaplaincies) in which the line of succession was extinct reflected similar interest. In accord with a policy of nationalizing all pious funds with income leaving Mexico, the government confiscated the property of the Philippine missions. The California missions, long declining in efficiency, were secularized and the lands distributed to the Indians working them.

Of greater significance was termination of the use of government authority in the collection of tithes and in the fulfillment of monastic vows. Liberal dedication to freedom and individual liberty doubtless motivated both actions, but the law on tithes had important financial and economic repercussions as well. The government customarily received a portion of the tithes, so the measure affected not only Church income but government revenue as well. In addition, the end of this compulsory tax, ideally of 10 percent of the gross agricultural and pastoral product, freed landowners of a burden and should have promoted rural development.

These measures were a few of those that in 1833 and 1834 sought to limit the fiscal independence of ecclesiastical corporations and reflected the government's desire to gain some authority over Church wealth. For their part, to protect their wealth, especially real estate, from liberal attack—confiscations, loans, taxes—some corporations undertook an apparently deliberate policy of disposing of real estate, converting to relatively more secure investments, mortgages.[9]

9. Michael P. Costeloe, *Church Wealth in Mexico: A Study of the 'Juzgado de*

The government struck at the Church in other respects. Questions about the value and political implications of clerical-controlled education led to the suppression of the venerable University of Mexico, founded in 1551, and the inauguration of a public school system under a Bureau of Public Instruction. Furthermore, the government clearly interfered in religious matters by establishing government supervision of worship, even within churches, and by converting some churches to other purposes, such as theaters and circuses. Some states even regulated the expenses of the Faith.[10]

Late in 1833 government moves against that other powerful, privileged institution, the military, included the retirement of all troops that had revolted against it and a reduction in the size of the army. Unfortunately for the liberals, a proposal to create a civil militia especially frightened the regular army, uniting it with supporters of the clerical cause.

Discontent with the aggressive liberal regime increased throughout 1833 and early 1834. Nevertheless, the government continued with its program until, in the spring of 1834, a conservative rebellion gained President Santa Anna's support. He returned to Mexico City and dissolved the Congress. He then revoked most of the reform legislation, leaving only the laws abolishing the use of civil power in the collection of tithes and the fulfillment of monastic vows. To demonstrate his solidarity with the Church, the President appointed the Bishop of Michoacán, Juan Cayetano Portugal, Minister of Justice and Ecclesiastical Affairs. Reaction seemed complete with a new constitution, *Las Siete Leyes*, in December 1836, replacing the federalist document of 1824. The new constitution was centralist in character, and it reaffirmed clerical *fueros*. Like the earlier one, it also understandably declared Catholicism the exclusive religion of Mexico.

The liberal defeat, however, did not signify the end of government

---

Capellanías' in the Archbishopric of Mexico, 1800–1856 (Cambridge: The University Press, 1967), pp. 117–26. Asunción Lavrin has pointed out that many clerical corporations, including nunneries, continued to prefer real estate as the primary source of income. Apparently, the yield from real estate was better than that from other invested capital. "Mexican Nunneries from 1835 to 1860: Their Administrative Policies and Relations with the State," *The Americas* 28 (January 1972): 298, 305–6.

10. Zamacois, 12:44.

acts against Church property, though a need for money rather than ideology motivated the measures. Thus, in 1842 a conservative government annulled an 1836 decree and assumed the administration and investment of the Pious Fund of the Californias, which had sustained the California missions, and then absorbed the Fund into the public treasury. Former Jesuit property was also auctioned off at this time. Early in 1843 another conservative act prohibited alienation of property of all pious establishments without government permission.[11]

In this period a perceptive, leading moderate liberal, Mariano Otero, analyzed Mexico's depressing condition.[12] The rural and urban economies were in a shambles, unrelieved by any signs of hope. Stagnation or backwardness characterized all sectors, agriculture and mining, business and industry. The causes of the deplorable situation were many: an inadequate transportation system, backward agricultural techniques, high taxes and expenses. Excessive mortgages and bankruptcies characterized landed estates. Even more disastrous, a few families monopolized the land; the masses worked it in virtual slavery. It was vital to alter this situation by ending concentration of property ownership and the agricultural backwardness which tended to maintain this concentration. Otero believed that economic progress was the key to political development and to the achievement of a just social order in which liberty would replace servitude, equality would replace privilege, and the will of all would replace brute force.

As a moderate, Otero balanced criticism of the Church's wealth and influence with praise for clerical good works and valuable services, such as its charities and lenience as a creditor. Furthermore, the Church had suffered extensive losses of wealth and influence since Independence. Continual political crises, forced and voluntary loans, and the termination of civil authority to collect tithes had all reduced Church wealth, while the spread of freedom of thought and the loss of its monopoly of education had reduced clerical influence. The

11. Alfonso Toro, *La iglesia y el estado en México, estudio sobre los conflictos entre el clero católico y los gobiernos mexicanos desde la independencia hasta nuestros días* (Mexico: Publicaciones del Archivo General de la Nación, 1931), pp. 166, 174.

12. Mariano Otero, *Ensayo sobre el verdadero estado de la cuestión social y política que se agita en la República Mexicana* (Mexico, 1842); and Reyes Heroles, 2:125–29.

failure to secure the annulment of all liberal legislation of 1833–1834 exemplified the extent of the Church's decline. As was also true of Mora, Otero did not dispute the absolute necessity of religion for society, but religion was not, as Church leaders argued, incompatible with individual security, equality, education, and freedom of thought, all of which were essential for stability and progress.

The depressing condition of the country was not destined to improve soon, for war with the United States loomed on the horizon. The war did, however, provide an opportunity for liberal action once again at the national level, though the circumstances were inauspicious. In the crisis the impecunious government looked to the Church for funds as was customary. Months of negotiation between the government and the Church, decrees, protests, and more negotiations throughout the last half of 1846 did not relieve the situation; by the beginning of 1847 the financial situation was desperate.[13] Santa Anna was once more president and Gómez Farías was vice-president, as in 1833. Santa Anna, conducting a military campaign in the north, needed funds badly and initially supported a loan guaranteed by Church property.

On 11 January 1847 the Congress, with radical and moderate liberals divided on the issue, narrowly passed a law authorizing the government to raise $15,000,000 by mortgaging or auctioning Church property. The clerical protest was immediate. On 12 January the Metropolitan Chapter of the Archbishopric protested that the Church was sovereign and could not be deprived of its property by any authority. The Bishop of Michoacán added that there were two temporal sovereigns in Mexico, one of which was ecclesiastical. The Bishop of Sonora, Lázaro de la Garza y Ballesteros, issued one of the noteworthy protests.[14] A decade later de la Garza was Archbishop of

13. See Michael P. Costeloe, "Church-State Financial Negotiations in Mexico during the American War, 1846–1847," *Revista de Historia de América*, no. 60 (July-December, 1965), pp. 91–101; Zamacois, 12:553–54; and Olavarría y Ferrari, p. 601–3.

14. *Despojo de los bienes eclesiásticas, apuntes interesantes para la historia de la iglesia mexicana* (Mexico, 1847), pp. 7–8, 33–36, pastoral letter dated 5 April 1847.

Throughout this study, the symbol "$" will indicate pesos; one peso equals eight *reales* or one hundred *centavos*. In the nineteenth century, a peso

Mexico, and this same pastoral letter was recirculated in response to the 1856 law that deprived corporations of their real property. Like other defenders of the Church, the Bishop maintained that ecclesiastical property did not derive from secular authority but was a natural right granted to the Church at its inception by Christ. This divine right to acquire, administer, alienate, and invest property in full authority was, therefore, not dependent on or subject to any other authority.

The furor over the law continued until, on 26 February 1847, national guard units in the capital, supporting the sanctity of clerical property, revolted to overthrow Gómez Farías. The rebellion failed, but conflict continued, and in March Santa Anna, the legal president, returned to Mexico City. He restored peace, undertook negotiations with the clergy for a loan, and suppressed the office of vice-president, thereby removing Gómez Farías from the scene. Very quickly Santa Anna revoked the objectionable law of 11 January in return for an agreement that the Archdiocese would guarantee a $1,500,000 loan.[15]

All efforts failed, and Mexico met defeat, a defeat which impressed upon liberals most dramatically the urgency of transforming their country into a modern nation. The trauma of the war helped widen the gulf between liberals and conservatives, but the tone of the national government in the following years was conciliatory. Moderate liberal presidents sought to heal the political and ideological fissures.[16] The Church, favored by the government, gained in wealth and influence, though the patronage question remained troublesome. Still, the clergy and conservatives in general were not satisfied, and they labored for the establishment of a monarchy. In 1853 they restored Santa Anna to the presidency as a temporary expedient until a foreign prince could be found to rule. When death removed the restraining hand of Lucas Alamán, the most influential member of

equalled one United States dollar. During the first decade of the twentieth century, one peso was equal to fifty United States cents.

15. Costeloe, "Chuch-State Financial Negotiations," p. 108.

16. General José Joaquín de Herrera served as president from 1848 to 1851. His legally elected successor was General Mariano Arista. For a good biography of the eminent moderate Herrera, see Thomas Cotner, *The Military and Political Career of José Joaquín de Herrera, 1792–1854* (Austin: University of Texas Press, 1949, reprint ed., New York: Greenwood Press, 1969).

the cabinet and a proponent of monarchy, Santa Anna lost no time in first throwing favors to the privileged groups and then erecting a dictatorship.

In the midst of his repressive and arbitrary rule, on 1 March 1854, the Plan of Ayutla was proclaimed, initiating the revolution that would topple Santa Anna from power for the last time and inaugurate the Reform. Mexico, at the time of the Reform, presented as depressing a picture as it had earlier in the century: politics was chaotic, transportation inadequate, bank credit and monetary policy nonexistent. Agriculture was backward; mining prostrate; foreign commerce negligible. Besides all this, the nation was experiencing trauma from the loss of more than half the national territory. The population consisted of a well-organized, traditionalist, and aggressive clergy, an illiterate and undernourished people, and a weak middle class that was impotent to bridge the chasm between the privileged few and the forsaken many. Mexico, on the eve of the Reform, was indeed ripe for change.

The Catholic Church in Mexico occupied center stage and wielded a pervasive influence. The narrative of events from Independence to the Reform provides some understanding of the growing conflict between forces of change and defenders of the socio-economic system. A more detailed examination of conditions that prompted reform and of the Church's role in Mexican life is appropriate as background for the central concern of this study, the impact of the liberal expropriation of Church property.

The Church was the wealthiest proprietor in Mexico. As an institution, it consisted of a multiplicity of corporations or perpetual bodies. These included monasteries and nunneries, sodalities, chaplaincies, churches, brotherhoods, hospitals, charitable and educational establishments, and a staggering number of other foundations for pious works, *obras pías*. From meager beginnings in the early post-Conquest years of the sixteenth century, ecclesiastical corporations accumulated increasingly more wealth. The original few plots of land given to the first friars to found their monasteries grew into vast urban and rural holdings of real estate through donations from pious individuals and in other ways. Of even greater value than the religious buildings, houses, mills, mines, and farms was capital, notably mortgages held by the corporations on real estate. The nineteenth-century historian and statesman, Lucas Alamán, estimated that at the end of the colonial period the Church owned or held mortgages on fully one-half of the real estate of the viceroyalty of New Spain with a value of about $300,000,000. Estimates of Church property vary widely, but without question, the income from the property amounted to millions annually. The clergy derived income from other sources, such as parish fees charged for the performance of baptisms, marriages, burials, confirmations, and masses as well as from tithes and first fruits. The latter was a tax of from one-sixtieth to one-fortieth of the first harvest, used to support the parish priest. The tithe was a gross tax, levied on agricultural and pastoral produce, supposedly 10 percent of the value, though the amount varied with the product and was often less.[17] Tithes and first fruits, collected in kind, tended to depress agricultural prices because the collector sold surplus produce cheaply on the open market, thus reducing the price for products the rural populace wished to sell. When the tithe became voluntary in 1833, Church revenue dropped drastically, by as much as one-third or one-half. Thereafter, the parish priests became more dependent on, and thus more careful about exacting, the fees for baptisms, marriages, and burials, thereby increasing the burden on the population.

Fees charged for the various religious services varied among bishoprics, and rates differed too, depending on the type of service desired—simple or lavish—and on the status of the individual involved—whites paid the most, mestizos and mulattoes less, Indians the least.[18] There is abundant evidence of evasion of the established

17. In the early nineteenth century the tithe was divided in half: 50 percent of one-half went to the bishop and 50 percent to the Cathedral Chapter, or *cabildo*, the governing body of a see. The other half was divided into ninths with three-ninths destined for the maintenance of the Cathedral and hospitals, two-ninths for the government, and four-ninths for the parish priests to defray the cost of administering the sacraments and other works. Manuel Rivera Cambas, *Historia de la reforma religiosa, política, y social en México* (Mexico, 1875), 1:71; and Costeloe, *Church Wealth*, p. 16.

18. For the fees and differences, see *Colección de los aranceles de obvenciones y derechos parroquiales que han estado vigentes en los obispados de la República Mexicana y que se citan en el supremo decreto de ll de abril de 1857* (Mexico, 1857), pp. 2–7; or Emilio del Castillo Negrete, *Apéndice al tomo XXVI de "México en el Siglo XIX"* (Mexico, 1892), pp. 407–547.

fees and exploitation of the poor in other ways, through exaction of special fees and personal services.[19]

Furthermore, glaring contrasts between some clerical and lay incomes and between upper and lower clergy, along with reported abuses, added to the liberals' arsenal of charges against the Church. Income for the clergy, as for the laity, varied widely. Prelates enjoyed handsome incomes, while the lower clergy often eked out a bare existence, living on a level with their poor parishoners. Many parish priests earned $100 to $200 a year, while bishops received more than $10,000 and the archbishop of Mexico perhaps over $100,000. In the same period, the president of the Republic earned $36,000, cabinet ministers $6,000, senators $3,500, and deputies $3,000 annually.[20]

Despite great disparities of income and property, the Church as a whole was immensely wealthy. Abuses aside, the Church did much good with its wealth, and it was a responsible and usually sympathetic landlord. The Church sustained hospitals, schools, asylums, orphanages, missions—all manner of works for the common good. Individual clergy—wealthy prelates and poor priests—performed extensive charitable works. Ecclesiastical corporations rented their properties at reasonable rates, within reach of the poor, and lent money to needy families, miners, landowners, and merchants. The Church served as a bank, charging modest interest, generally 5 percent a year, in contrast to private lenders who might demand 2 percent or more a

19. Paul V. Murray, *The Catholic Church in Mexico. Historical Essays for the General Reader*, vol. 1 (Mexico: Editorial E. P. M., Imprenta Aldina, 1965), p. 118; del Castillo Negrete, pp. 458–68; see also Mario de la Cueva et al., *Plan de Ayutla, conmemoración de su primer centenario* (Mexico: Talleres de Impresiones Modernas, 1954), p. 14; Luis de la Rosa, *Observaciones sobre varios puntos concernientes a la administración pública del estado de Zacatecas* (Baltimore, 1851), p. 95; *Colección de los aranceles*, pp. 102–103; and Rivera Cambas, *Historia de la reforma*, 1:414.

20. For these and other estimates, see William Parish Robertson, *A Visit to Mexico, by the West India Islands, Yucatan and United States* (London, 1853), 2:18–19; Jacinto Pallares, ed., *Legislación federal complementaria del derecho civil mexicano* (Mexico, 1897), p. xl; Lucio Mendieta y Núñez, "La Revolución de Ayutla desde el punto de vista sociológico," in de la Cueva et al., pp. 15–16; and Andrés Molina Enríquez, *Juárez y la Reforma* (Mexico: Editora Ibero-Mexicana, 1956), p. 86.

month. As a creditor, the Church demanded back rent and interest only in unusual circumstances. It was not uncommon for individuals to be very much behind in their payments to ecclesiastical creditors because of unstable conditions, natural disasters, or simply their style of living. A property might even be mortgaged for a sum equal to or greater than its actual value and with interest in arrears nearly equal to the value of the mortgage itself, representing many years' payments. The most important of the ecclesiastical lending institutions, the *Juzgado de Capellanías* (Chaplaincy Court), required that at least two-thirds of a property to be mortgaged be unencumbered, but this corporation, too, was plagued by the common problem of non-payment of interest.[21]

While ecclesiastical corporations performed many useful and necessary services with their wealth and continued to accumulate more with each passing year, they had also suffered losses since before Independence. Depreciation in property values resulted from unsettled conditions during and after Independence. The expulsion of the Jesuits in 1767, the abolition of the Inquisition at Independence, and the sale of the properties of these institutions were serious losses. Most severe, however, was the order of King Charles IV in 1804 for the disposal of the property of various pious foundations and religious establishments to help pay off the national debt; this alone cost the Church in New Spain at least $10,000,000.[22] The ever-

21. Rivera Cambas, *Historia de la reforma*, 1:73–74; and Costeloe, *Church Wealth*, p. 77.

22. On this and other losses, see Pallares, p. xxxvii; Porras Sánchez, p. 99; Mariano Cuevas, *Historia de la iglesia en México* (El Paso: Editorial "Revista Católica," 1928), 5:40–41; "Documentos para la historia. La desamortización eclesiástica en tiempo de Carlos IV," *Boletín de la Sociedad de Geografía y Estadística de la República Mexicana*, 2nd epoch (Mexico, 1869), 1:495; "Escrito presentado a D. Manuel Sixtos Espinosa del consejo de estado y director único del Príncipe de la Paz en asuntos de real hacienda, dirigido a fin de que se suspendiese en las Américas la real cédula de 26 de diciembre de 804, sobre enagenación de bienes raíces, y cobro de capitales píos para la consolidación de vales," in Manuel Abad y Queipo, *Colección de los escritos más importantes que en diferentes épocas dirigió al gobierno D. Manuel Abad y Queipo, obispo electo de Michoacán* (Mexico, 1813), pp. 95–100; and Asunción Lavrin, "The Execution of the Law of *Consolidación* in New Spain: Economic Aims and Results," *Hispanic American Historical Review* 53 (February 1973): 27–49.

needy post-Independence governments, too, considered the Church an inexhaustible source of financial aid; the Church usually complied, opening its coffers sometimes graciously, sometimes reluctantly.

Despite losses and the general economic stagnation of the country, the churches and convents themselves often presented a sumptuous appearance. The adornment and appointments of some were lavish, for example, the Convents of La Concepción and La Encarnación in Mexico City and the Cathedrals of Mexico City, Puebla, and Morelia. Other churches, too, were richly decorated and offered a striking contrast to the majority of worshippers who were poor, ragged, and dirty.[23]

In addition to great material wealth, the Church occupied a privileged position in society. Privileges included exemptions from the tax on transfers of property, from personal property taxes, and from personal taxes on such things as lodging and the repair or construction of walls, bridges, or fountains. Clergy were exempt from the jurisdiction of secular courts and could not even testify in a civil case without the bishop's permission. Cases of simony, sacrilege, adultery, divorce, legitimacy of children, and perjury were reserved to Church courts; crimes committed by clerics fell under the jurisdiction of their own courts. Moreover, the ecclesiastical judge decided whether a person belonged to the clerical state and, hence, should enjoy the *fuero*. Even though there had been some encroachments on the *fuero* by Independence, by and large the privileges remained intact.[24]

Clerical subjection to special courts might be justified for religious matters, but liberals insisted that the clergy, as citizens, should be subject to secular courts in civil issues such as debts and contracts. The

23. See Brantz Mayer, *Mexico as It Was and Is* (New York, 1844), pp. 40–41; Madame Frances Calderón de la Barca, *Life in Mexico, during a Residence of Two Years in That Country* (London, 1843), pp. 107, 114–16; and Robertson, 2:288ff.

24. In 1795 a 15 percent tax was levied on ecclesiastical real estate in an attempt to restrict the accumulation of land by the Church, and beginning in 1820 clergy were required to testify in criminal cases. Rivera Cambas, *Historia de la reforma*, 1:352–55. An excellent study of the late colonial restriction of ecclesiastical immunity and the impact of Caroline reforms in Mexico is N. M. Farriss, *Crown and Clergy in Colonial Mexico 1759–1821. The Crisis of Ecclesiastical Privilege* (London: The Athalone Press of the University of London, 1968).

corporate spirit weakened the national spirit because the *fuero* permitted perpetrators of civil crimes to evade and be immune from public authority; the special courts seemed to punish members only for failure in their obligations to the corporation. The Church felt dishonored by the clergy's crimes and feared the reflection on religion, so the inclination was to hide such acts. Still, the Church was not the only institution with special courts or a special position in the State. The military, the university, sodalities, entailed estates, guilds—a multitude of corporate entities—enjoyed a separate and privileged status.[25] Liberals struck at all of them.

The economic wealth of the Church and the *fuero*, the intervention of the Church in all acts of life, its dominant role in printing and education, its authority over conscience, the home, and social activities—all, in effect, made the institution a public power, independent of civil authority. It often used that authority and wealth wisely and beneficially by any standards. Nevertheless, the Church's ideas, practices, and position were contrary to the secularism of the nineteenth century and were obstacles to current notions of economic and social progress. The Church represented a potent rival to civil government, a rival that the liberals had to reduce and limit to strictly spiritual functions in order to carry out successfully a program of national reconstruction. Crucial to this program was ecclesiastical wealth.

25. Rivera Cambas, *Historia de la reforma,* 1:356–70.

Chapter 2
The Onset of the Reform: Disamortization and Its Early Impact, 1856–1857

The Plan of Ayutla, proclaimed 1 March 1854, called for rebellion against the despotism of "His Most Serene Highness," the dictator Antonio López de Santa Anna. This Plan initiated the Reform. The wording of the Plan, however, scarcely revealed the far-reaching reforms that were in the offing. The avowed aim of the revolutionaries was the overthrow of the dictator, to be followed by the establishment of popular, representative government. There was little that presaged fundamental economic or social reform. If the Plan's concept was not very inspiring, neither was its origin: the old caudillo Juan Alvarez, master of Guerrero, fearing that his power might be threatened by Santa Anna's centralizing tendencies, took up arms against him; Colonel Florencio Villareal, fearing punishment for abuse of authority, fathered the Plan; and Colonel Ignacio Comonfort, recently demoted by Santa Anna, adhered to the Plan after securing minor revisions in Acapulco on 11 March to make it attractive to a wider audience. Outbreaks against the dictatorship soon followed elsewhere in the country. The Revolution was a truly popular rising, probably because the Santa Anna despotism was equally oppressive to conservatives and liberals.[1]

From the beginning, the Revolution was a hybrid. Villareal, a conservative, proclaimed the Plan. Comonfort, a moderate, reformed it. Alvarez, frankly liberal, led the fight and was joined by radicals like Benito Juárez, Melchor Ocampo, and Ponciano Arriaga. Despite the almost universal character of the Revolution, the rebels were by no

1. Alberto Trueba Urbina, ed., *Centenario del Plan de Ayutla* (Mexico: Biblioteca Campechana, Librería de Manuel Porrúa, S.A., 1954), pp. 13–33; Richard A. Johnson, *The Mexican Revolution of Ayutla, 1854–1855* (Rock Island, Ill.: Augustana Book Concern, 1939), p. 43; and Fernando Lizardi, Sr., "Ley de desamortización del 25 de junio de 1856," and Mendieta y Nuñez, "La Revolución de Ayutla," in de la Cueva et al., pp. 323,27. The following summary is based on Johnson.

means united behind Alvarez and the Plan of Ayutla: in May 1855 the caudillo of Nuevo León, Santiago Vidaurri, proclaimed the Plan of Monterrey; in Mexico City the garrison, supported by bureaucrats, moderate liberals, and some conservatives, chose General Martín Carrera to replace Santa Anna; and in August 1855 the moderate Manuel Doblado raised a revolt in Guanajuato. Santa Anna resigned in the same month. In September the Mexico City revolutionaries, having failed to win wide support, accepted the Plan of Ayutla, as did the Doblado group. On 4 October a provisional government was formed in Cuernavaca with Alvarez as president.

The new government, to which Vidaurri adhered, reflected the division in the liberal ranks that had existed for many years; the moderates favored gradualism, while radicals urged a frontal assault on the existing system. The new cabinet included the radicals Ocampo, Minister of Relations, Juárez, Minister of Justice, Miguel Lerdo de Tejada, Minister of Development, and Ponciano Arriaga, Minister of Government. Guillermo Prieto, an independent liberal, became Minister of Finance and Comonfort, a moderate, Minister of War and Commander of the Army.

The dawn of the Reform had arrived. The reformers' program, in general, paralleled that of European liberalism of the nineteenth century, with modifications for Mexican peculiarities. Goals included the promotion of capitalism, the subordination of the autonomous and privileged Church and military to civil authority, the establishment of legal equality, and a general elimination of the corporate strictures on the individual. More specifically, a proposal in 1855 called for the army's subjection to civil authority and its reduction in size to ten or twelve thousand men, a number deemed adequate to provide security and yet not overburden the budget. The proposal favored a federal system of government, improvements in education and in the condition of agricultural workers, who were virtual slaves of the *hacendados*. Finally, the author proposed a better distribution of priests throughout the country, reduction in Church wealth to a level sufficient for it to perform its functions, and religious toleration as an inducement to foreign commerce and immigration.[2] In effect, the liberal program

2. Y.O. [Manuel Payno], *La reforma social de Méjico deducida del aspecto político que él presenta, y fundada en la esperiencia de cuarenta y cinco años* (Mexico, 1855),

of the 1850s was substantially the same as that outlined a generation before, a program that the Reform laws attempted to implement. It is worth emphasizing that the liberals' collision with the Church developed not from a desire to attack religion but because they viewed the Church's position as an obstacle to the modernization of the country.

The first measure of the Reform, called the Juárez law after the Minister of Justice and Ecclesiastical Affairs, was issued on 23 November 1855 with the aim of judicial reorganization.[3] The law provided for a Supreme Court of Justice, District and Circuit courts, a Superior Court of the Federal District, and District and Territorial civil and criminal courts. What created controversy, however, was the partial suppression of *fueros*. All special tribunals were abolished except for ecclesiastical and military courts; these lost jurisdiction over civil crimes of their members. Military courts thereafter could try only cases involving military crimes. Ecclesiastical courts had jurisdiction only over common crimes of members of the clergy, but an accused cleric could renounce the *fuero* and be tried in a civil court. More importantly, the law removed laymen from ecclesiastical court jurisdiction. Equality before the law demanded this kind of law, yet it could have been more extreme. Nationhood as well as equality dictated the measure. The privileges enjoyed by diverse special interests fragmented the country, promoting individual loyalty to a corporation over loyalty to the nation.

Clerical opposition to the Juárez law was swift and strenuous. Without doubt, one of the most articulate, intelligent, and forceful defenders of the Church's privileges was the Bishop of Michoacán, Clemente de Jesús Munguía. He protested to Minister Juárez barely a

pp. 8–32. See also Walter V. Scholes, "A Revolution Falters: Mexico, 1856–1857," *Hispanic American Historical Review* 32 (February 1952): 1–21, which presents opposing liberal and conservative solutions to Mexico's economic problems.

3. Manuel Dublán and José María Lozano, eds., *Legislación mexicana o colección completa de las disposiciones legislativas expedidas desde la independencia de la república* (Mexico, 1878), 7:598–606.

Technically, the Reform laws refer only to those measures issued in Veracruz in 1859 and 1860, but more generally the laws from the Juárez law to the end of the civil war in 1860 were reform measures that should fall under that heading.

week after the issuance of the law. The Bishop found the law pernicious in its effects on society and in its attack on the Church. The law deprived the Church of a right inherent in its mission and essential to its disciplinary authority. It also interfered with the sacraments, such as marriage. Furthermore, bringing clerical abuses before the public view in civil courts could only endanger public morals and lessen respect for the clergy.[4]

The day following the Bishop's communication, on 1 December, Alexis de Gabriac, the French Minister to Mexico, prophetically wrote to his chief:

> The abolition [*sic*] of ecclesiastical *fueros* constitutes an act of incalculable rashness, as a measure of a government whose weakness, ineptitude, and disorders lead, or must lead, inevitably to ruin. To struggle against an enemy as powerful as the clergy, without possessing sufficient power to contain it or conquer it, is madness.[5]

Indeed, the clerical reaction to the law was vigorous and comprehensive. Protest issued from the pulpit, in pastoral letters, even through overt acts. A conspiracy led by Father Francisco Javier Miranda and General José Uraga, symbolizing the conservative-clerical alliance in defense of *fueros*, planned the deposition of Alvarez, a defense of clerical property and rights, and the restoration of the 1824 Constitution. In fact, on 12 December 1855 Alvarez resigned, not unwillingly. The long-standing factionalism between moderate and radical liberals plus conservative opposition led to the reorganization of the cabinet. The moderate and conciliatory Comonfort replaced Alvarez at the head of a moderate-dominated government.[6] Nevertheless, this government was responsible for major reform measures.

4. 30 November 1855, Clemente de Jesús Munguía, *Defensa eclesiástica en el Obispado de Michoacán desde fines de 1855 hasta principios de 1858* (Mexico, 1858), 1:2–14.

5. 1 December 1855, Lilia Díaz López, ed. and trans., *Versión francesa de México. Informes diplomáticos* (Mexico: El Colegio de México, 1963–1967), 1:234. Unless otherwise noted, all citations from this work are from de Gabriac to the French Minister of Foreign Affairs.

6. The new cabinet contained: Luis de la Rosa, Minister of Relations; José María Lafragua, Government; Juan Soto, War; Manuel Siliceo, Development;

The new executive immediately faced a serious revolt in Puebla on 19 December under the banner "Religión y Fueros." At the very least, the clergy provided financial support and perhaps prompted this rebellion led by conservatives. After the costly suppression of the revolt, calculated at $1,200,000, Comonfort, because of alleged clerical involvement, ordered the appropriation of sufficient property of the Puebla diocese to indemnify the government for the cost of defeating the rebels and to pay for other losses.[7]

Pelagio Antonio Labastida, Bishop of Puebla and future Archbishop of Mexico, protested this "unjust and cowardly and hypocritical" law. Denying complicity in the revolt, he admitted that the Church had recognized and given resources to the rebels. This aid he justified on the ground that the Church was required to obey the existing government in temporal matters, regardless of what kind of government it was. The government rejected Bishop Labastida's explanation; when he continued to protest and delivered hostile sermons, the government expelled him from the country on 13 May 1856.[8] Still clergy continued with seditious sermons and new conspiracies, prompting a new government decree in June. This decree established a subtreasury of the national government in Puebla for the deposit of all income from ecclesiastical property in the diocese. The treasury made disbursements to maintain the Faith and to pay for losses from the rebellion.[9] The Church responded in a way that soon became common—with threatened excommunication and denial of the sac-

and Manuel Payno, Finance, who was replaced on 20 May 1856 by Miguel Lerdo de Tejada, a radical.

7. James Gadsden to William L. Marcy, 26 January 1856, *Despatches from United States Ministers to Mexico, 1823–1906* (Washington, D.C.: National Archives, Microcopy File no. 97) roll 20, vol. 19 (cited hereafter as *Despatches from Ministers*); and Law of 31 March 1856, in Manuel Payno, ed., *Colección de las leyes, decretos, circulares y providencias relativas a la desamortización eclesiástica, a la nacionalización de los bienes de corporaciones, y a la reforma de la legislación civil que tenía relación con el culto y con la iglesia* (Mexico, 1861), 1:3–5. Cited herafter as Payno, *Leyes*.

8. Justo Sierra, *Obras completas del Maestro Justo Sierra*, vol. 12, *Evolución política del pueblo mexicano* (Mexico: Imprenta Universitaria, 1948), p. 284; and *Secretaría de Estado y del despacho de Gobernación*, 18 April 1856 (Mexico, n.d.), pp. 6–7, 16–23.

9. Payno, *Leyes*, 1:10–18.

raments to anyone directly or indirectly contributing to fulfillment of the decrees. Nonetheless, implementation proceeded.

Meanwhile, the anticlerical measures continued with the suppression of the Society of Jesus and the revocation of an 1854 decree that had reestablished civil coercion in the fulfillment of monastic vows. The second major act of the Reform came with stunning impact on 25 June 1856. Three days later the Constituent Congress overwhelmingly approved (87 to 11) the Law of Disamortization, or the Lerdo Law, named after the Minister of Finance, Miguel Lerdo de Tejada.[10] The measure ordered all real estate owned or administered by ecclesiastical or civil corporations adjudicated, that is, sold, to the tenants with the rent considered as 6 percent of the value of the property for purposes of the sale. Real estate not being rented was to be publicly auctioned to the highest bidder. The term "corporation" included all religious communities, *cofradías, archicofradías*, congregations, brotherhoods, educational establishments, and, in general, all organizations or foundations of perpetual or indefinite duration. The only exceptions to this order were buildings destined immediately and directly to the object of the corporation, such as churches themselves and municipal buildings. The law allotted three months for adjudications and auctions. After that period, the tenant forfeited his rights to subtenants. Lacking a subtenant, the property could be denounced by anyone. As a safeguard against rent increases, the new owners of the property were to respect the terms of the previous contracts and not alter the rent. New owners could, however, alienate the property and even divide it and rent or sell it in parts, as long as the mortgage and interest on the property were proportionately distributed.

Viewing it as a panacea for Mexico's economic ills, proponents of the law expected it to benefit all interests, including those of the Church. Although the act required ecclesiastical corporations to dispose of their real estate and prohibited future ownership or administration, they could continue to possess capital. The measure, therefore, simply forced conversion of clerical wealth in real estate into capital, usually mortgages. Some corporations had in fact been

10. "Desamortización de fincas rústicas y urbanas propiedad de corporaciones civiles y religiosas," *Leyes de Reforma: Gobiernos de Ignacio Comonfort y Benito Juárez (1856–1863)*, (Mexico: Empresas Editoriales, S.A., 1947), pp. 25–36.

pursuing this policy voluntarily for years. The intent of the law was not to deprive the Church of its material wealth, but only to alter the character of part of that wealth. The stated reasons were economic and financial, not political or antireligious. In fact, the corporations would benefit because they would no longer have to bear litigation for collection of overdue rent, expenses of repairs and upkeep, or losses from lack of tenants; they would not have to tolerate lazy renters; they would be relieved of property taxes and salaries for administrators and managers. Not only would the corporations be better off, but the populace in general and the economy would benefit by dividing property among thousands of individuals and by placing capital in circulation, ending the alleged stagnation of mortmain.The government would benefit by the receipt of the 5 percent transfer-of-ownership tax, or *alcabala*.

Customarily, the Church accepted a 5 percent return on its investment or loans and considered real estate rental as the equivalent of 5 percent of the property's value. But presumably the Church evaded taxes by low property valuations and by accepting low rents openly and additional sums secretly. The liberals, in using 6 percent instead of 5 to compute property values, sought to establish truer values and to punish the Church for its alleged dishonesty.

Liberal faith in the individual and in the importance of individual private proprietorship justified the law and promised a solution to Mexico's retardation.[11] Indeed, government leaders were highly optimistic about what the law would accomplish, if not about the government's chances of surviving its implementation. The Minister of Finance, Miguel Lerdo, acknowledged as one of the most intelligent men in the administration, emphasized as did others the economic virtues of the law.[12] Acting President Comonfort wrote Governor Jesús Terán of Aguascalientes that the law was a new testimonial of the government to the nation, showing that without vacillating it was following the path of reform and progress indicated in the Plan of Ayutla. He hoped the clergy would understand their true interests

11. See, for example, Anselmo Portilla, *Méjico en 1856 y 1857, gobierno del General Comonfort* (New York, 1858), pp. 69–70; and *El Constituyente, Periódico Oficial del Gobierno de Oaxaca*, 13 July 1856, p. 3.

12. Circular 1, 28 June 1856, Payno, *Leyes*, 1:57–58; and 23 May 1856, Díaz López, 1:285.

and the needs of the times and would facilitate the execution of the decree.[13] Manuel Siliceo, Minister of Development, believed:

> if we achieve this, we will do immense good for the country; if not, we will fall; but we will fall for something worthwhile . . . and though falling, we will leave the seed of good, which in the future will be able to grow.[14]

The Mexican newspaper *The Herald* termed the law the basis of the regeneration of the country.[15] *El Republicano* believed the law would open a thousand sources of public wealth that would give impetus to agriculture, industry, commerce, and crafts, placing immense capital in circulation. All classes of people, the clergy, the rich, and the poor, should thank the government for the law.[16]

Sabino Flores, an associate of Governor Doblado in Guanajuato, eloquently analyzed the Lerdo law and clerical wealth. Flores concluded in much the same vein as newspapers that the measure was useful and just to the nation and to the Church and clergy. The law promised to create many new proprietors who would be dedicated to peace and stability, thus reducing revolutions. Political stability and economic prosperity would be achieved. The law maintained the rights of the nation without violating its duties. The Church would be purified and abuses ended, the clergy returned to their true mission.[17]

Miguel Lerdo, reporting to President Comonfort on the operation of his Ministry early in 1857, was confident of the law's results.[18] The

13. 28 June 1856, in Jesús Terán, Correspondencia y papeles, 1855–65 1:5, Latin American Collection, University of Texas, Austin.

14. Letter of M. Siliceo to Manuel Doblado in Guanajuato, 25 June 1856, in Genaro García, ed., *Documentos inéditos o muy raros para la historia de México*, vol. 31, *Los gobiernos de Alvarez y Comonfort según el archivo del general Doblado* (Mexico: Librería de la Vda. de Ch. Bouret, 1910), p. 211.

15. Cited in *El Siglo Diez y Nueve* (Mexico), 1 July 1856, p. 1. Cited hereafter as *Siglo*.

16. Issue of 1 July, cited in *Siglo*, 3 July 1856, p. 2. See also *El Constituyente*, 10 and 13 July 1856, pp. 1–2.

17. *La Nacionalidad. Periódico Oficial del Estado de Guanajuato*, 24 August 1856, p. 4.

18. *Memoria presentada al Exmo. Sr. Presidente Sustituto de la República por el C. Miguel Lerdo de Tejada dando cuenta de la marcha que han seguido los negocios de la Hacienda Pública en el tiempo que tuvo a su cargo la Secretaría de este ramo* (Mexico, 1857), pp. 9–11.

law had, in large part, been consummated, he confidently announced: through 31 December 1856, $23,000,000 worth of corporate real estate, of which $20,667,000 was ecclesiastical, had been adjudicated and auctioned. The true value of the property, however, was easily $45,000,000 or $50,000,000 because of the abnormally low prices at which transactions occurred due to clerical opposition. The Church often did lose by the sale of its property, as Lerdo suggested. The Puebla government reported, for example, that urban properties of corporations sold between 11 August and 31 October 1856 represented capital of $572,180.66, but the sale price was $342,277.65, resulting in a loss to the corporations of $229,903.01.[19] The Minister asserted that even though the law had been laxly implemented in some states, more than 9,000 proprietors had been created, a sufficient response to those who claimed that only a few individuals had been enriched.

This official enthusiasm was by no means a universal sentiment. The United States Secretary of Legation was uncertain of the government's ability to sustain the law, while the French Minister believed that the government and congress were pursuing a course bordering on socialism.[20] Among liberals themselves dissension developed. Two well-known figures exchanged words on the measure's merits in the Constituent Congress on 28 June 1856. Francisco Zarco defended the law in the customary way as a great economic and financial reform benefiting virtually everyone and despoiling no one. Ignacio Ramírez, on the other hand, with great insight maintained that the majority of tenants lacked the funds to buy the properties. Moreover, fear that a revolution would annul the sales would act as a restraint on many. Furthermore, disentailment was attainable under earlier laws, including canon law that recognized civil authority over property and permitted the clergy to sell their real estate. Not only was the law unnecessary and imperfect, it was dangerous; leaving capital untouched benefited only the clergy and provided them with large resources to promote conspiracies. Zarco rebutted, citing the ineffectiveness of earlier legislation and the broadening of proprietorship through sub-

19. Archivo General de la Nación de México (cited hereafter as AGN), Justicia eclesiástico, vol. 176, fols. 275–76.

20. John S. Cripps to Marcy, 5 July 1856, *Despatches from Ministers*, roll 20, vol. 19; and 29 June 1856, Díaz López, 1:290.

tenants and auctions, thus increasing liberal adherents and weakening reactionary forces. The congress overwhelmingly approved the Lerdo law, but events bore out Ramírez' prophetic words.[21]

The reformers' economic reasons for individualizing proprietorship rested more on ideological conviction than on reality. Sincere revolutionaries are often excessively optimistic, even utopian, about the benefits that will flow from their reforms. They are equally blind to any virtues in the system or institutions they are seeking to overthrow. Mexican radical liberals were no different. Thus, their belief that the Lerdo law would work a virtual "miracle" reflected their utopianism, while the liberals' insistence that corporate proprietorship prevented economic progress and prosperity revealed their blindness toward corporations. Reality was rather a different matter. Clerical property did circulate; corporations could and, under certain conditions, did sell real estate. Furthermore, following the liberal attack on property in 1833 and 1834, it apparently became deliberate policy for some corporations to convert wealth from real estate to mortgages, an investment relatively safer from use by impecunious governments. The circulation of clerical property was not completely unrestricted, however, because contracts prohibited borrowers from disposing of the encumbered property without permission of the creditor.[22] In any event, the relative mobility of clerical property did not satisfy liberal aims, and the Church viewed the law as pernicious.

At the time and since, the clergy and its defenders generally condemned the law as destructive of property rights and of religion, the cement holding society together. The measure, they maintained, attacked natural rights and invaded the spiritual realm.[23] With some

21. Francisco Zarco, *Historia del congreso estraordinario constituyente de 1856 y 1857* (Mexico, 1857), 1:598–609.

22. Costeloe, *Church Wealth*, pp. 91–93. Other corporations, such as nunneries, continued their preferences for real estate as the principal source of income. Lavrin, "Mexican Nunneries," pp. 288, 305–6.

23. See Silvestre Bordonova, *Conducta del obispo de Puebla, Licenciado Don Pelagio Antonio de Lavastida, manifestada en las notas que dirigió al gobierno de Méjico inmediatamente antes y después de su destierro ejecuatado el 12 de mayo de 1856* (Paris, 1857), pp. 6–7; Regis Planchet, *La cuestión religiosa en México o sea vida de Benito Juárez* (Rome: Librería Pontificias de Desclée, Lefebvre & Cía., 1906), p. 42; Mariano Cuevas, *Historia de la nación mexicana*, 2nd ed. (Mexico: Buena Prensa, 1952), 2:49; Munguía, 1:98–105; and Robert J. Knowlton, "Clerical

notable exceptions, the Mexican bishops protested the Lerdo law. Apparently the Bishop of Guadalajara, Pedro Espinosa, did not initially view the law as an attack on Church wealth, for he undertook to alienate some properties. In Oaxaca, Bishop José Agustín Domínguez said nothing, and the clergy did not publicly protest. The corporations, however, did not generally surrender the title deeds to new owners.[24] In any case, acquiescence was isolated and short-lived. As will be seen, protests became increasingly strenuous and opposition more intransigent. The government responded by expelling offending priests and confiscating episcopal circulars and pastorals that attacked the government.

Meanwhile, on 30 July 1856, the government issued a regulatory law on the Lerdo law. In Miguel Lerdo's opinion, the law of disamortization contained all the regulations necessary for its execution, but the ignorance and malice of opponents aroused doubts over diverse matters. The 30 July law sought to remove these doubts and clarify the measure's intentions. The new law specified which corporations were included and excluded, how renters should proceed, and what the rights of subtenants and denouncers were. It established procedures for auctions and lawsuits as well as many other particulars.[25] Despite the detailed regulations, the government found it necessary to issue numerous circulars, resolutions, and decrees dealing with particular points. It almost seemed that the Minister of Finance had to settle each case individually.

There were, indeed, many problems and much confusion over the operation of the laws; these arose from "ignorance and malice" but also from defects in the law. For example, the inclusion or exclusion of property caused some confusion. Despite provisions of the laws to make this distinction clear, at least two circulars, in September and November 1856, stated that the laws referred only to real estate of

Response to the Mexican Reform, 1855–1875," *Catholic Historical Review* 50 (January 1965): 509ff.

24. José M. Vigil, *La reforma*, vol. 5 of *México a través de los siglos*, ed. Vicente Riva Palacio (Mexico, n.d.), p. 159; and Charles R. Berry, "The Reform in the Central District of Oaxaca, 1856–1867. A Case Study" (Ph.D. diss., University of Texas, 1967), p. 81.

25. "Reglamento de la ley de 25 de junio de 1856," Payno, *Leyes*, 1:36–53; and *Memoria . . . por . . . Lerdo*, p. 9.

corporations, not to capital.[26] The exemptions allowed under the Lerdo law occasioned a great many special resolutions. Confusion in this respect was perhaps understandable, for Article VIII stated:

> The only exceptions to alienation are the buildings destined immediately and directly to the service or object of the institution of the corporations, even when a part, not separate from them, is rented, such as convents, episcopal and municipal palaces, schools [colegios], hospitals, hospices, markets, correctional and charitable houses. Considered included in this exemption will be a house which is attached to one of the buildings and inhabited by reason of the office of those serving the object of the institution, such as parish priests' houses and those of chaplains of the nuns. . . .[27]

Thus, it was necessary to assure the rector of the school of San Juan de Letrán that a building attached to the school was exempt, even though it was rented and had a separate entrance. The head of the school of San Ildefonso was told that the building being constructed at the rear of the school and attached to it, destined to be the rector's home, was exempt. A special order affirmed the exemption of tithe collection houses. The national government even found it necessary to clarify the meaning of the prohibition against "administering" real estate for the political chief of the Sierra Gorda territory.[28]

Minor matters of "confusion" aside, there were those who tried to take advantage of the laws by illegal means despite the law's prohibition. Some demanded increased rents from tenants of former ecclesiastical property. New owners also allegedly evicted tenants without giving them the required forty days' notice. Still others, perhaps inadvertently, perhaps deliberately, but in any case illegally,

---

26. Luis G. Labastida, ed., *Colección de leyes, decretos, reglamentos, circulares, órdenes y acuerdos relativos a la desamortización de los bienes de corporaciones civiles y religiosas y a la nacionalización de los que administraron las últimas* (Mexico, 1893), p. 49.

27. *Leyes de Reforma*, pp. 25–36.

28. 5 and 6 September 1856, Narciso Bassols, *Leyes de reforma que afectan al clero, publicadas por orden cronológico por Narciso Bassols* (Puebla: Imp. del Convictorio, 1902), pp. 20–21; and 26 July and 26 September 1856, Payno, *Leyes*, 1:84–85, 101–105.

sought to denounce and thus acquire at a reduced price properties already adjudicated.[29]

Furthermore, the laws contained certain defects that contributed to the liberals' failure to achieve their goals. A number of the weaknesses were financial in nature; the required 5 percent transfer-of-property tax, or *alcabala*, aroused the greatest controversy and concern. All purchasers of corporate property either by adjudication, at auction, or by denunciation, paid this tax. The initial and all subsequent transfers of the property were subject to the tax. Such was the opposition to the *alcabala* that the government decreed that tax evaders forfeited the property and that it would then be resold.[30] Melchor Ocampo declared in 1859, albeit with the benefit of three years' hindsight, that the *alcabala* flouted the axiom of political economy that the principal, not the income from it, should be taxed. The 5 percent tax, disregarding this axiom, was a gross injustice to the individual purchaser, while the wealth of the clergy remained intact and was even likely to increase. Thus, the act of disamortization greatly burdened former tenants with taxes, interest payments, and maintenance costs, while the Church became richer.[31]

The important resolution of 9 October 1856 reflected governmental awareness of at least some of these problems. The resolution noted the adverse impact of the *alcabala* on the poor, especially those in communal villages. A principal aim of the law was being defeated if rural lands did not pass to tenants, so the government abolished all fees on adjudication of lands worth less than $200. In addition, tenants had to renounce their rights expressly before anyone else could acquire the land. A later order explicitly included poorer urban inhabitants in these benefits.[32] Nevertheless, in many rural areas the

29. *Siglo*, 3 February 1857, p. 3; document 46, 15 October 1856 and document 89, 24 October 1856, *Memoria . . . por . . . Lerdo*, pp. 61, 103.

30. 13 November and 26 December 1856, Labastida, pp. 86–87, 89–90; and 13 August 1856, and 15 September 1857, Payno, *Leyes*, 1:69–70 and 2:369–72.

31. Melchor Ocampo, *Obras completas*, vol. 2, *Escritos políticos*, ed. F. Vásquez (Mexico: Imp. y encuadernación de Jesús M. Valdés, 1901), pp. 161–63.

32. Labastida, pp. 13–14 and Resolution of 7 November 1856, pp. 105–106; and Manuel López Gallo, *Economía y política en la historia de México* (Mexico: Ediciones Solidaridad, 1965), pp. 145–46.

Indians either did not understand or appreciate individual ownership of lands and evaded the intent of the law by turning their titles over to a single person and continuing as before, or they were defrauded by local officials, caciques, and others.[33]

Preoccupation with the *alcabala* and the stringent measures to prevent evasion, far from being of minor importance, signified serious weakness in a law that intended to mobilize real estate and create a great new class of proprietors. It is certain that, in this matter, necessity—the lack of money to pay the tax—dictated apparent evasion of the law. Furthermore, large estates were too expensive for most to acquire, except for the already wealthy. The liberals wished to subdivide the large ecclesiastical rural estates, but they did not insist that this subdivision be done prior to adjudication or that the property be distributed among a number of purchasers. The law did allow estates to be fractioned and adjudicated to the several tenants, while mortgages encumbering estates were to be proportionately distributed among the tenants. In addition, for a conventional sale to a person other than the tenant to be valid, the tenant had to renounce his rights explicitly.

The *alcabala*, interest payments to the corporation on mortgages that usually resulted from adjudication, and the costs of maintenance, cultivation, and development of the land—all of these factors placed rural property beyond the reach of most of those the law sought to benefit. The same was true of urban properties: the *alcabala*, interest payments, and costs of maintenance constituted a great burden for tenants, the would-be adjudicators. And under the law, if the tenant or subtenant did not adjudicate, anyone else could denounce the property, receiving for the trouble a one-eighth reduction in price. This provision again favored the wealthy and those lacking in moral

33. See, for example, *La población del Valle de Teotihuacán. El medio en que se ha desarrollado. Su evolución étnica y social. Iniciativas para procurar su mejoramiento. Por la dirección de Antropología, Manuel Gamio, director* (Mexico: Dirección de Talleres Gráficos, 1922), 2:569–70; 5 January 1861 and 23 October 1868, *Colección de acuerdos, órdenes y decretos, sobre tierras, casas y solares de los indígenas, bienes de sus comunidades, y fundos legales de los pueblos del estado de Jalisco* (Guadalajara, 1849–1880), 3:113–14 and 4:69–70; Luis González y González, "El agrarismo liberal," *Historia Mexicana* 7 (April–June 1958): 485ff.; and Moisés González Navarro, *Vallarta y su ambiente político jurídico* (Mexico: Talleres Mayela, 1949), pp. 151–52.

scruples, who could buy extensive blocks of real estate. Many who had accumulated wealth in mining, commerce, contraband, and usury wanted to invest in real estate but had been unable to prior to the Lerdo law because there was little available. The law provided them an opportunity and thus created a new class of latifundists. Moreover, poorer elements, often mestizos, turned as denouncers to property they could afford, primarily communal lands. Thus, the law failed to force the breakup of ecclesiastical estates, it failed to take into consideration the large private properties that, in effect, constituted a true entailment, but it did include communal village property—a disaster for such communities.

Just as the law did little about the maldistribution of rural property, it did little to end monopolization of urban real estate—the owners changed, but the concentration did not. There was no limit placed on acquisition of property by a single individual. One inhabitant in Puebla, the recognized tenant of seventeen houses owned by the Asylum for the Poor, could legally acquire all of them.[34] This case was an unusual one, to be sure. Generally, a person was the tenant of only one property so that adjudication under the Lerdo law itself scarcely promoted concentration of property. Auctions and denunciations, however, definitely did. Special companies were formed for the purpose of denunciation that "in their zeal denounced the same property up to three and four times." Circumstances contrived to concentrate property in a few hands. The tenants' lack of resources to acquire property initially or to retain it permanently led to forfeitures, auctions, and denunciations. The unlimited number of properties any single person could acquire and the failure to insist on division of estates both contributed to the concentration. Clerical opposition deterred the devout from taking advantage of the law, leaving the way clear for those unconcerned about eternal damnation, often foreigners, to obtain large amounts of property.[35]

Recent research by Charles Berry on the Central District of Oaxaca

34. Circular 10, Lerdo to Governor of Puebla, 9 September 1856, Payno, *Leyes*, 1:86–87.

35. Jan Bazant, "La desamortización de los bienes corporativos de 1856," *Historia Mexicana* 16 (October–December 1966):193–212; 1 July and 12 October 1856, Díaz López, 1:304–5, 346–47; and Forsyth to Lewis Cass, 1 March 1858, *Despatches from Ministers*, roll 22, vol. 21.

indicates that generalizations for the Republic as a whole may not apply in specific local cases. In that district most of the property sold was purchased by middle or lower class people, and there was little speculation in the properties—the resale price generally was the same as that at the initial sale. In that locality, then, the liberals to a certain extent achieved their goal of creating a sizeable number of small land-holdings. In addition, village lands were individualized with little difficulty; the Indians apparently welcomed the change from com-munal to private ownership.[36] In northern Mexico, also, the law ap-parently created many new mestizo proprietors. The recent mono-graph of Jan Bazant, which deals with the core area of Mexico, the states of greatest population and ecclesiastical wealth, concludes as well that the immediate result of the Lerdo law was large-scale trans-fer of property. Elsewhere Bazant describes the subdivision of several ecclesiastical estates in the state of Guanajuato.[37] Immediate transfer, however, did not signify that in the long run the reformers achieved their goals. Clerical anathemas, the economic incapability of tenants, and defects in the legislation all defeated the liberals' intentions.

Berry acknowledges, for example, despite his conviction that the Reform achieved its goals as they applied to corporate property in the Central District of Oaxaca, that there was a "certain frequency" of resale by original purchasers and that of 1,380 pieces of property disamortized and offered for sale, 639 were sold during the 1856–1867 period; the other 741, a majority, remained unsold during those years.[38]

Minister Lerdo himself despite a general glow of optimism, re-vealed in February 1857 that all was not well.[39] Clerical efforts to

36. Charles R. Berry, "The Fiction and Fact of the Reform: The Case of the Central District of Oaxaca, 1856–1867," *The Americas* 26 (January 1970):277–90.

37. Jan Bazant, *Alienation of Church Wealth in Mexico. Social and Economic Aspects of the Liberal Revolution, 1856–1875*, ed. and trans. Michael P. Costeloe (Cambridge: The University Press, 1971), pp. 41–134; Bazant studied Mexico City and the Federal District and the states of San Luis Potosí, Michoacán, Jalisco, Puebla, and Veracruz. See also Jan Bazant, "The Division of Some Mexican *Haciendas* during the Liberal Revolution, 1856–1860," *Journal of Latin American Studies* 3 (1971):25–37.

38. Berry, "Fiction and Fact," pp. 284, 286–87.

39. *Memoria . . . por . . . Lerdo*, pp. 10–11.

persuade the people of the heretical and antireligious nature of the law, plus the threat of damnation to anyone who took advantage of it, slowed transactions considerably. Reportedly, in Puebla few people acted under the law because of devotion and respect for the clergy and because they lacked confidence in the permanence of the law. The threat of excommunication and the denial of sacraments caused great agitation, and many annulled their purchase contracts. Even convinced liberals hesitated; the Governor of Oaxaca, Benito Juárez, adjudicated a property in the city of Oaxaca to inspire others to follow his example.[40] Despite Lerdo's confidence early in 1857 that the law had in large part been consummated, barely a month earlier he had admitted that in some states the greater share of corporate property remained to be disamortized. He attributed this lack of action to reactionary movements which, by upsetting public order, prevented many from acting within the stipulated time limit.[41] For example, through 31 December 1856 the value of ecclesiastical property disamortized in the state of Puebla was $2,386,626, while the value of real estate operations in that state submitted for revision to Emperor Maximilian's authorities in 1865–1866 was more than $5,435,000.[42] Thus, the evidence on the implementation of the law is decidedly mixed. On the one hand, transactions occurred regularly, and in a matter of a few months amounted to millions of pesos. On the other hand, clerical attitudes, defects in the law, ignorance, malice, disturbances, and monetary considerations affected the implementation and permanence of property transfer.

It is too simple to sum up the official Church attitude and position

40. Juan de la Portilla, *Episodio histórico del gobierno dictatorial del Señor Ignacio Comonfort en la República Mexicana, años de 1856 y 1857. Escrito en propia defensa por el Lic. J. de la Portilla* (Mexico, 1861), pp. 81–82; 17 and 31 October 1856, Díaz López, 1:348, 357–58; and "Apuntes para mis hijos (de 1806 a 1857)," *Archivos privados de D. Benito Juárez y D. Pedro Santacilia*, prologue by J. M. Puig Casauranc (Mexico: Publicaciones de la Secretaría de Educación Pública, 1928), 1:252.

41. 2 January 1857, document 148, *Memoria . . . por . . . Lerdo*, p. 165.

42. Document 149, *Memoria . . . por . . . Lerdo*; and document 19 in *Informe presentado al congreso de la unión el 16 de setiembre de 1873, en cumplimiento del precepto constitucional por el C. Francisco Mejía, Secretario de Estado y del despacho de Hacienda y Crédito Público de los Estados-Unidos Mexicanos* (Mexico, 1873). Cited hereafter as *Informe de Hacienda, 1872–1873*.

as "unalterable opposition," since the terms hardly reveal or do justice to the immense problems, the confusion, the complications, and the internal conflicts and individual anguish that the law and the prelates' stand against it created for the corporations and clergy. The impact of the Lerdo law on ecclesiastical corporations and individual clergy paralleled the effects on laymen: on the faithful and the not-so-faithful, the lordly and the lowly, high government officials and poor tenement tenants. Furthermore, an examination of specific matters reveals inconsistent and contradictory actions on the part of both government and Church authorities. The following pages will treat various effects of the law—the inconsistencies, the evasions and obstructions, the hardships, the complexity of disamortization in general.

1. Conventional sales

The law took effect only after official publication in each locality, thereby providing an opportunity for the Church to transfer real estate to friendly hands in advance. In Morelia, Michoacán, for example, newspapers printed notification of the law on 2 July, but official publication occurred on 5 July. In the interval, ecclesiastical corporations initiated various contracts that the authorities believed evaded the intent of the law and prejudiced the rights of tenants. The state, therefore, ordered an inspection of notarial registers for such sales and prohibited the transfer of title deeds. The government's attitude was not consistent, however. In another decision Minister Lerdo approved the sale of an hacienda by the Augustinian Order of Michoacán because the buyer was the tenant.[43] Actually, the government approved many conventional sales, at times because the sale contract had been concluded prior to the law and on other, more frequent, occasions because tenants did not wish to take advantage of the law either because of lack of funds or because of clerical prohibitions. In order to avoid denunciations detrimental to property values, the government allowed corporations to sell. Inasmuch as the principal object of the law was the disentailment of corporate prop-

43. Resolutions of 16 and 28 August 1856, Labastida, pp. 100–102.

erty, sales to other individuals, even those designated by the corporations, served that purpose. Sometimes the authorities granted corporations permission to alienate property simply to obtain funds to make repairs on other properties or to cover other expenses.[44] Generally, the government acted in these questions under the 30 July regulatory law, which authorized conventional sales if the tenants renounced their adjudication rights.

2. Simulated sales

Simulated sales were another way to avoid compliance with the law. The corporation sold its property to a "dummy" purchaser or to a trusted person, thereby retaining effective ownership and control. The twentieth-century Jesuit historian Mariano Cuevas claimed that among published lists of adjudicators there were some persons who "only appeared as owners"; the bishop permitted, even ordered, this practice in order to preserve certain properties for the Church. During the Intervention in 1865, General Bazaine, Commander-in-Chief of the French expeditionary force, received a report that the Oaxaca clergy held much real estate, partly because persons simply "lent their names" in transactions while the Church retained ownership.[45] In Guadalajara simulated sales were sufficiently frequent to cause temporary suspension of all transactions there on 26 July 1856. And they were common enough for Lerdo to remind state governors that any-

44. See "El provincial de Carmelitas pide licencia para vender la hacienda de Chapulco," AGN, Justicia eclesiástico, vol. 173, fols. 371–81; "Licencia concedida al procurador de Sto. Domingo de Méjico para vender la casa no. 1 de la calle de la Misericordia," ibid., fols. 422–24. See also fols. 432–33 and vol. 174; and "El Guardián de Franciscanos de Jalapa pide se le permita enagenar una parte del terreno del atrio de aquel convento," ibid., vol. 174, fols. 199–202.

45. Luis Pérez Verdía, *Historia particular del estado de Jalisco, desde los primeros tiempos de que hay noticia hasta nuestros días* (Guadalajara: Tip. de la Escuela de Artes y Oficios del Estado, 1910–11), 2:412–13; 18 December 1856, Labastida, p. 71; Circular of 9 October, 1856, Payno, *Leyes*, 1:114–15; Cuevas, *Historia de la nación*, 3:51; and "Informe político," 110, 15 March 1865, Intervención francesa. Documentos misceláneos, 1862–1867, Latin American Collection, University of Texas, Austin.

one acquiring corporate property in order to return it later had renounced his rights to that property, leaving it open to denunciation or auction. It is, however, difficult to know how extensive the practice was since the intent was to conceal evasion of the law.

There were two other methods to evade the law, though the government disallowed the first and the Church the second. One was for a corporation to sell property on condition that the pope validate the sale; if he did not, the property would return to the corporation. Under the circumstances, papal approval was unlikely. The second possibility was for priests to adjudicate the houses they rented if they believed they might be denounced by others, thus keeping the property "safe" in the hands of the clergy.[46]

3. Clerical inconsistency

Church policy and attitudes toward conventional sales, simulated sales, and other evasions of the law were inconsistent. Specific and oft-repeated episcopal statements prohibited taking advantage of the Lerdo law; others ordered clergy and administrators of clerical property not to recognize or cooperate in the execution of the law in any way. Those who disobeyed faced severe ecclesiastical penalties. By those standards, conventional and simulated sales and other evasions should have been, and at times were, prohibited, since they implied recognition of the law. The clergy frequently protested the loss of freedom of action, even though the regulatory law seemed to restore considerable freedom to the Church in the case of conventional sales. Bishop Munguía of Michoacán insisted that permitting conventional sales did not alter the objection to the Lerdo law nor did it restore to the Church full authority over its property. He, therefore, refused to consent to any property alienations, conventional or otherwise, and he ordered all corporations and persons in his diocese to do the same. Firm though the Bishop was himself, many conventional sales did

46. *Siglo,* 8 March 1857, p. 3 and 10 March 1857, p. 2; and "El Gobernador de Zàcatecas comunica que el Provincial de Agustinos de Michoacán ha autorizado las enagenaciones de las fincas de su provincia bajo la condición de que sean nulas las ventas sin la aprobación de Papa," AGN, Justicia eclesiástico, vol. 174, fols. 171–80.

take place, if not in Munguía's diocese. The insistence on complete freedom to dispose of property is curious. The evidence indicates that many years prior to the Lerdo law and during the civil war as well, when the law had been abrogated by the conservatives, alienation of property by a corporation required the permission not only of ecclesiastical authorities but of the conservative government as well.[47]

The following examples provide further evidence of the uncompromising attitude of the hierarchy. A priest adjudicated a house he rented from a Mexico City convent with the sincere idea of keeping it "in apparent ownership" as long as current conditions existed; he intended later to return the house to the corporation. The Archbishop censured the priest for his action and deprived him of his office and benefits. To be returned to good graces, the Archbishop required the priest to rescind the contract of adjudication and seek rehabilitation from Rome. Indeed, the Archbishop caused some "surprise" by his unexpected punishment of clergy who used "straw men" or members of their family to acquire property.[48] In another case, a layman who denounced an ecclesiastical property later wished to restore it to the Church because he was "very religious." He asked as conditions for the return reimbursement for expenses of $600, perpetual secrecy concerning the transaction, and future rent to be determined by agreement with the Church. The Church refused this clear opportunity to reacquire some of its property. In order for the denouncer to "satisfy his conscience," he had to appear before the

47. Circular of 10 September 1856, Munguía, 1:66–67; "Luz de los Reyes, pide se le vende un terreno perteneciente a la cofradía de S. Nicolás, establecida en la parroquia de Capulhuac," AGN, Bienes nacionales, Negocios eclesiásticos, leg. 418, exp. 24; and AGN, Justicia eclesiástico, vol. 173, fols. 53ff. and 245ff., vol. 165, fols. 276–85, 296–302, 398, and 400. A law of 3 February, 1843 and others had prohibited alienation of property of religious establishments without government approval.

48. *Resolución de la Sagrada Congregación acerca de la solicitud que le dirigió un eclesiástico que de buena fe denunció la casa en que vivía con arreglo a la ley de 25 de junio de 1856* (Guadalajara, 1858). See also Bishop Espinosa's letter prohibiting a priest from concluding simulated sales; Pedro, Bishop of Guadalajara, to the Cura of Tlaltenango, December 1856 in Jesús González Ortega, Correspondencia, 1851–1881, vol. 1, Latin American Collection, University of Texas, Austin (cited hereafter as Ortega Correspondencia); José Ignacio Victor Eyzaguirre, *Los intereses católicos en América* (Paris, 1859), 2:345–47; and 12 and 17 October 1856, Díaz López, 1:346–48.

same public official who concluded the transaction, renounce the adjudication, and request cancellation of the title deed issued to him. In addition, he had to declare his "true and constant" desire to leave the property in the same state in which it was prior to adjudication.[49] As part of their nonrecognition policy and because deeds represented the true evidence of ownership, the corporations often refused to transfer the title deeds to the new owners.

The episcopacy's adamant condemnation of the law of disamortization, the refusal to recognize or cooperate with the law, and the punishment of clergy and faithful who did, obscure important contrary evidence. The attitude in some cases was curiously mild, almost indifferent. It is a certainty that clergy, with the Archbishop's acquiescence, did traffic in property and evade the law. At the very least, evasion involved predating contracts concluded after the issuance of the law to get properties into "safe" hands. More than evasion, such practices represented recognition of the law and opposition to it. The prelates constantly forbade the former and condemned the latter. For example, the Puebla government discovered that a Dominican, Ignacio María Feria, had evaded the law by concluding rent contracts with trustworthy individuals for properties belonging to the monastery. The contracts were drawn up after the issuance of the Lerdo law on 25 June 1856 but carried dates prior to the law. Feria concluded these false contracts with at least two different persons for two different monastery properties and for at least two reasons: to get properties into reliable hands, those of his godchildren; and to avoid the financial loss that would occur if the properties were auctioned, since the prelates had prohibited corporations and tenants from cooperating in the execution of the law on pain of excommunication. By his actions, the friar not only recognized the law, but also engaged in actively opposing it. In this case, then, consistency required episcopal censure. Yet, when Feria was jailed, the Archbishop's attitude was that the government was charging Feria with two things, disobedience to the Lerdo law and feigning anterior contracts. For the former, his conduct conformed with that of the prelates; for the latter, his actions did not impede the law's operation, for if the properties did not pass

49. 29 December 1856, AGN, Bienes nacionales, Negocios eclesiásticos, leg. 1873, exp. 1.

to current tenants, they were the ones defrauded, not the government.[50]

Intercorporation transactions represent another species of inconsistency; clerical participation in the operation of the Lerdo law took place when it suited their needs. Thus, the Ecclesiastical Province of Michoacán owed $4,000 to the Archicofradía de Nuestra Señora del Rosario de Santo Domingo of Mexico City. This sum had been lent at interest to the Province for five years in 1796, and the loan had been extended since that time. The attorney for the Archicofradía requested the repayment of the loan (redemption of the capital), but, since the Province lacked the funds to pay the debt, an agreement was reached whereby the $4,000 was to be paid over a two-year period, out of income arising from the adjudication of an hacienda that the Province had owned. The agreement was contingent on papal approval for the Archicofradía to receive the interest payments from the adjudicated hacienda rather than from the Province. Nevertheless, the very fact of the transaction ought to have been contrary to the official and public clerical position on the Lerdo law.[51]

4. Effects and ramifications

The official Church position caused unrest, slowed transactions, and confronted many people with practical and moral dilemmas. Commonly, tenants of ecclesiastical property lacked the funds for outright purchase, so the corporations assumed mortgages on the farms and houses, receiving interest payments in place of rents. Thus, when corporations refused to turn over property deeds, purchasers reacted by refusing to pay interest on the mortgages. The results were profound for laymen and clergy alike. Even though the government

50. See "El religioso domínico de Oajaca Fr. Ignacio María Feria acusado de haber querido adjudicarse unas fincas de su orden," AGN, Justicia eclesiástico, vol. 173, fols. 338–57; and "Expediente promovido por Dn. Mariano Guzmán sobre que se le venda un corral," AGN, Bienes nacionales, leg. 1047, exp. 14, for another example of clerical inconsistency.

51. Vicente Contreras to Benigno Bustamante, 18 January, 1857, in Documentos relativos a la Reforma y a la Intervención, 1850–1867, Latin American Collection, University of Texas, Austin.

issued titles, a purchaser's ownership was never quite as secure as it should have been. Moreover, defective rural titling resulted: lacking the original deed, surveys and demarcations of adjudicated lands tended to be unreliable and a source of future dispute. Corporations suffered because, having sold their real estate and reduced or eliminated their income from mortgages, they lacked resources to carry on corporate functions.

The plight of the regular orders was perhaps typical. Santa Teresa la Nueva Nunnery in Mexico City disposed of nearly all its property under the law, but since the purchasers refused to pay interest, there were not enough funds to cover even one-half of the nuns' food costs. The San Bernardo Nunnery, which prior to the Lerdo law enjoyed a weekly income from rents and invested capital of $400 to $500—a sum sufficient to defray ordinary expenses—had, since the issuance of the law, experienced more than a two-thirds decline in income. The decline was due to two factors: the resistance of purchasers to paying interest on their mortgages; and the sale at auction of the remaining property for far less than the true value because only part of the nunnery's holdings had been adjudicated to tenants. An added financial factor for corporations was denunciations. The effects of opposition to the law and intimidation of the faithful left many properties open to denunciation. The denouncer, as a reward, received a one-eighth reduction in price, a loss absorbed by the ecclesiastical body. The religious could not even turn to the courts because legal action implied recognition of the offensive law.[52]

In addition to these hardships, the Church's attitude raised other problems, including intricate internal legal disputes. One notable case reveals some of the ramifications.[53] The basic issue in the controversy

52. "El presbítero D. Manuel Carlos Armeller consulta si puede exigir de un adjudicatario el pago de los réditos de una capellanía," AGN, Bienes nacionales, Negocios eclesiásticos, leg. 1827, exp. 1; "Adjunto a V. Vicaria Foránea de Almoloya," ibid., leg. 1873, exp. 1; "Relativo al Presbítero D. Cleto Millan sobre la capellanía que disfruta," ibid., leg. 1711, exp. 1; "La M.R.M. abadesa del convento de S. Bernardo, sobre tomar, para alimentos de las Señoras Religiosas, la cantidad que se destinó para una obra en la calle de Mesones," ibid., leg. 74, exp. 51; *Siglo*, 7 September 1856, p. 3; and Lucio Mendieta y Núñez, *El problema agrario de México. Historia. Legislación agraria vigente. Formularios*, 2d ed. (Mexico: n.p., 1926), p. 71.

53. *Testimonio de los autos seguidos por el tesorero de la Muy Ilustre Archicofradía*

that developed between the Archicofradía del Santísimo Sacramento y Soledad de Nuestra Señora in the parish of Santa Cruz in Mexico City and the parish priest, supported by the Archbishop, centered on the terms of foundation of the sodality. Specifically at issue were the corporation's clerical ties. The executive board of the Archicofradía ordered the sale of several of its houses in compliance with the law. The priest denounced this decision, and the Archbishop forbade the sale because of the prohibitions against alienations of ecclesiastical property. The executive board denied that its property was ecclesiastical and under episcopal jurisdiction, citing the royal decree of 1804 that authorized the sodality. That decree stipulated that the executive board be almost entirely composed of laymen, that diocesan intervention be limited exclusively to spiritual matters, and that the corporation's property never be spiritualized. The protests of priest and Archbishop continued despite these provisions and evidence that the property was secular, that is, that it had never been used for parish expenses but only for the pious objects of the foundation.

Early in 1857 the Supreme Court heard the case. Understandably, the decision favored the Archicofradía. With the removal of the "legal" obstacles, other difficulties arose that reveal the operation of the Lerdo law. The adjudication of the houses to the tenants as prescribed by law proved impossible; the tenants were either financially unable or morally unwilling to purchase. The only recourse, therefore, to avoid loss of the one-eighth of the value through denunciations, was public auction. The governor appointed a civil judge, Mariano Navarro, to conduct the auction. Of the seven houses auctioned for a total of $47,300, Navarro himself purchased two.

This detail in the history of a single case adds another dimension to the execution of the law. Officials used their positions not simply to acquire property but to acquire it through dubious or positively illegal practices. Local officials, their relatives, and friends denounced properties specifically exempt from the law, and judges, by previous agreement perhaps, accepted auction bids far below the required two-thirds appraisal value.[54]

---

del Santísimo y Soledad de Nuestra Señora, fundada en la parroquia de Santa Cruz de esta ciudad, en el recurso de fuerza en conocer y proceder interpuesto por el mismo, contra el Illmo. Señor Arzobispo de México (Mexico, 1856).

54. "El sr. cura D. Hermenegildo Mejía sobre que por la autoridad judicial

Needless to say, the use of influence was not limited to the local level; petitioners did not hesitate to justify their requests by citing service, need, or justice. Thus, a member of the Constituent Congress wrote Governor Manuel Doblado of Guanajuato:

> I know that there are several haciendas belonging to convents which, according to the decree of disamortization, should be sold at auction; will I be able to count on your support and influence to make a bid on some one of them in your state? You know that the majority of my fellow Deputies, when they leave here, are going to take up their professions and that I cannot depend on any job nor do I have a knack for asking favors. The President holds me in some esteem and I am certain that he would give me whatever appointment I might ask for; but I don't want it said that I support the government out of self-interest, or even less to lose my independence as a Deputy. I want, then, to return as I came; but now that the sale of those properties is taking place, I would certainly like to acquire one where I could go and live to help defray living expenses and the cost of educating my children, which is my only ambition.[55]

The French Minister, Alexis de Gabriac, though prone to exaggerate, reported in disgust that "provincial governors are confiscating and selling property of the clergy. . . . Everywhere there is shameless pillage. The last resource of the country is being used to enrich some bandits clothed in authority, without really benefiting anyone." Government admonitions against unethical practices or using one's position to acquire property doubtless did not deter the officials.[56]

Opportunism, evasion, and problems notwithstanding, implementation of the law proceeded. Adjudications, auctions, and denunciations took place in the face of prohibitions or with episcopal acquiescence. Transactions occurred with and without the corporations' agreement, with and without the transfer of the original property

---

ha sido adjudicada la huerta de su parroquia y parte del edificio contiguo a la misma," AGN, Bienes nacionales, Negocios eclesiásticos, leg. 1827, exp. 1.

55. Antonio Aguado (Mexico City) to Doblado, 30 July 1856, in García, 31:257. See also the comments of the cleric Eyzaguirre, traveling in Mexico at the time, p. 345.

56. 19 September 1856, Díaz López, 1:326–27; and Bazant, "La desamortización," p. 206.

deeds. Corporations did accept mortgage payments in place of the old rent payments, and intercorporation transactions settled outstanding debts.

Throughout 1856 and 1857 relations between Church and State deteriorated; the gulf between them rapidly became unbridgeable. The government accused prelates and lesser clergy of sedition and fomenting civil war; individual clerics were expelled from some states for their open opposition to the laws. The prelates replied that their duty obliged them to resist passively civil laws that contradicted and attacked divine and ecclesiastical laws. Prelates did not openly incite disobedience to the government; on the contrary, the Archbishop ordered the clergy to refrain from mixing in politics and to do everything possible to maintain peace and respect for legitimate authorities. But excommunication and denial of absolution awaited the faithful who complied with the Lerdo law. These penalties contributed little to tranquillity and respect for civil authority.[57]

Amid increasing tension and conflict, the Reform moved forward. One decree reduced the permanent army to less than 10,000 men and reaffirmed the restriction of military *fueros*. Another, though not secularizing vital statistics, did establish civil intervention to prevent abuses. Finally, the authorities prescribed hygienic burial methods and prohibited interment in churches. These reforms further antagonized both military and clergy, drawing those two powerful interests still closer together.

In this crisis-laden atmosphere, on 5 February 1857 a new, moderately liberal Constitution was promulgated. The Constituent Congress that labored nearly a year consisted for the most part of lawyers, plus some military men, journalists, and bureaucrats. The clergy had been barred, and the working classes were not represented. The presence of a liberal majority did not preclude heated debates, however. Despite the ongoing Church-State conflict, there apparently was general

57. Governor Doblado of Guanajuato expelled various clergy from the state for disobedience. See 6 September and 25 December 1856, 7 and 27 January and 6 February 1857, Munguía, 1:98–105. For Munguía's response, see 2 April and 24 October 1857, 1:107ff., 137–38, and 2:2–3, 46–47; AGN, Bienes nacionales, leg. 456, exp. 5 and 6; and AGN, Justicia eclesiástico, vol. 181, fols. 87–88, 127, and vol. 183, fols. 413–15.

agreement on the reduction or elimination of the political and economic powers of the Church. The Church-State issue, however, was part of larger concerns for stability and order in Mexican society and politics. Major controversies dealt, therefore, with issues of law and order, the powers of Congress and of the president, and centralism versus federalism.[58]

Before the constitution finally emerged, conservatives and moderate liberals, including the Comonfort cabinet, had to defeat radical attempts to secure religious toleration and a better distribution of rural property. These proposals, publicized in the preliminary draft, aroused fears and opposition among large landowners and the clergy. Moreover, this radicalism confirmed the popular belief, fostered by conservatives, that the Congress was the seat of religious impiety and violent demagoguery. The Comonfort administration strenuously and successfully fought against the radicalism in the constitutional draft which it believed opinion would not accept nor the sorely-pressed government be able to sustain.[59]

The finished Constitution, nevertheless, embodied the substance of Mexican liberal principles. In contrast to earlier ones, it did not proclaim Catholicism the religion of the State. Other Church-related articles: prohibited any contract involving the loss of individual liberty, whether by reason of work, education, or religious vow; guaranteed freedom of speech and press; and constitutionalized the Juárez and Lerdo laws. The Constitution, while allowing clergy to vote, barred them from the office of president and from election to Congress, and it empowered the government to intervene in matters of religious worship and external ecclesiastical forms such as processions, bell-ringing, and clerical garb. Finally, all public officials were required to take an oath to support the Constitution or forfeit their positions.[60]

58. Richard N. Sinkin, "The Mexican Constitutional Congress, 1856–1857: A Statistical Analysis," *Hispanic American Historical Review* 53 (February 1973): 1–13. On the Congress itself, see Francisco Zarco, *Crónica del congreso extraordinario constituyente (1856–1857)* (Mexico: El Colegio de México, 1957) and his *Historia del congreso.*

59. A. Portilla, pp. 72–73, 76ff. See also letter of 18 March 1857 from Ezequiel Montes to Joaquín Moreno in Documentos, 1850–1867.

60. *Constitución federal de los Estados-Unidos Mexicanos sancionada y jurada por el congreso general constituyente el día 5 de febrero de 1857* (Mexico, 1861).

The clergy opposed all of the Church-related articles: freedom of press and speech because it implied freedom to attack religion; the bar to election because it deprived them of a right granted other Mexicans; government intervention in worship and the Juárez and Lerdo laws, because they infringed the independence and rights of the Church. The constitutionalizing of those two laws, in fact, extended their application. In including the Juárez law, the Constitution definitively abolished all special courts except military ones in highly selective and restricted circumstances. In the case of the Lerdo law, the formerly exempt village lands known as *ejidos* were subjected to breakup and sale. The extension of the principle of private individual ownership to these areas hurt the communities, as did earlier provisions of the Lerdo law, through alienation of the lands and their acquisition by nonresidents, which ultimately left the communities with insufficient property to support the inhabitants.[61] The provisions on individual liberty worked against monastic vows but did not aid the peons bound by debts to the haciendas.

The Constitution added fuel to the fires of discontent already sweeping the country. Some clergy incited the faithful to defend their religion. Indians revolted to preserve their communal lands intact. The military objected to loss of *fueros* and reduction in the army's size. There was no hacienda, village, or city unthreatened by guerrillas, highwaymen, pronouncements, or Indians in revolt. Taxgatherers and adjudicators of property complained to the government, homes and families were divided, work was unavailable. In the capital, some clergy and army officers plotted the overthrow of the administration. Opponents of the reforms rallied behind "Religión y Fueros"; supporters followed the banner "Constitución y Reforma."[62]

61. See footnote 33, *supra*.
62. Sierra, *Evolución política*, pp. 280–81; letter of Victoriano Zamora to Ortega, 14 April 1857, Ortega Correspondencia, vol. 1; A. Portilla, pp. 85ff; Juan Amador, *Acontecimientos en la Villa de Cós del estado de Zacatecas. El juramento de la Constitución* (Zacatecas, 1857), p. 13; *La política del General Comonfort, y la situación actual de México* (Mexico, 1857); 21 and 2 April 1857, *Colección de documentos inéditos o muy raros relativos a la reforma en México* (Mexico: Instituto Nacional de Antropología e Historia, 1957–58), 1:81, 33–34; *La Nacionalidad*, editorial of Sabino Flores, 17 and 20 July 1856, vol. 1, pp. 4, 2; and 28 November 1857, Díaz López, 1:440.

The government had successfully suppressed uprisings in 1856 and early 1857, but the required oath to the Constitution increased its difficulties. Still, President Comonfort was optimistic. He termed the oath "the most victorious reply to the litany of absurdities by which the conservative party has tried to undermine the confidence of the liberals." As in the past, he hoped to continue his moderate but firm policy. He wished to avoid bloodshed, but revolutionaries had to be punished. He would continue to seek, through conciliation, peace for the chaotic country.[63]

Because of the objectionable articles, the bishops, collectively and individually, threatened to excommunicate any who took the oath to the Constitution, denying them the sacraments of the Church. "Neither ecclesiastics nor the faithful can for any pretext or reason lawfully take an oath to this Constitution," thundered Bishop Munguía. Penalties for those who freely and without reservation took the oath included denial of the sacraments of penance and extreme unction. They were refused burial in sacred ground; alms for the repose of their souls would not be accepted nor church services or prayers offered. In short, the attitude toward the oath and the penalties corresponded to the episcopacy's stand on the Lerdo and other laws. To return to favor the penitent had to retract the oath before witnesses and/or agree to restore ecclesiastical property to the original owner. These requirements meant, in the case of the oath, loss of government employment and, in the case of real estate, loss of the property. With regard to the oath, at least, there was some flexibility. Employees who had nothing to do with the Reform laws or their implementation, such as secretaries and file clerks, could take the oath. The individual might, if it were unavoidable, take the oath, declaring that he was doing so without prejudicing his faith. That qualified oath, however, could only signify that he would not support the Constitution, and thus it would be unacceptable to the government. But punishment would surely befall any who freely and without reservations took the oath.[64]

63. Comonfort to Joaquín Moreno in Mazatlán, 18 February 1857, and to José María Arteaga, 9 July 1857, in Ignacio Comonfort, Correspondencia, Latin American Collection, University of Texas, Austin.

64. "Resoluciones dadas a los que han consultado sobre la protesta de guardar y hacer guardar la Constitución y leyes de Reforma," in Documentos,

The hierarchy's position on the oath increased the tensions and divisions in the country, but the reception of the oath varied widely throughout the Republic, ranging from ready acceptance to violent opposition. In Tabasco the vicar asked the clergy to respect the Constitution, and all state capitals, except San Luis Potosí, accepted the oath without difficulty. Apparently, the oath to the Constitution was sworn peacefully in the majority of places; opposition occurred principally in unimportant towns, those entirely subject to clerical influence. However, in Oaxaca City, although all officials took the oath and a *Te Deum* solemnized the promulgation of the Constitution, the ceremony took place under protest; Bishop José Agustín Domínguez acted under pressure from the liberal governor, Benito Juárez. Furthermore, something of a scandal developed in Mexico City when Cathedral clergy refused to receive public officials as was customary during Holy Week ceremonies. In various localities in a number of states, the publication of the Constitution and the oath occasioned protest—sometimes peaceful, at times violent. Disorders occurred in Jalisco, Puebla, México, Michoacán, San Luis Potosí, Aguascalientes, Zacatecas, Guanajuato, Veracruz, and Tlaxcala.[65]

The genuinely devout who were also good citizens were in a quandary. Some took the oath, retracted in order to receive absolution, then took it again. Others sought priests who would absolve them even though they had taken the oath. Some forfeited their jobs rather than oppose the Church. Those priests who granted absolution without obtaining a previous renunciation of the oath incurred suspension from office, and newspapers announced the invalidity of such absolution. Large numbers of government employees refused to take the oath; in the Mexico City Customs House alone some forty officials lost their jobs as a result of refusal. Reportedly among those refusing to take the oath were twenty-seven generals and high officials, including the prominent Generals Florencio Villareal, Pedro Ampudia, and

---

1850–1867; Clemente de Jesús Munguía, Bishop of Michoacán, 18 March 1857, in Fortino H. Vera, comp., *Colección de documentos eclesiásticos de México, o sea antigua y moderna legislación de la Iglesia Mexicana* (Amecameca, 1887), 2:422; circular of 13 November 1857, in ibid., 1:21; and 28 November 1857, in Munguía, 2:114–16.

65. Toro, p. 330; Vigil, p. 232; Berry, "The Reform in . . . Oaxaca," pp. 85–86; and *Colección de documentos*, 1:18–87. See also Amador.

Martín Carrera.[66] Presumably, the refusals did not disturb the Comonfort government because it could economize on salaries thereby.

Priests refused to hear confessions, perform marriages, or grant
burial to those who had taken the oath or bought Church property.
This clerical posture seemed callous and cruel when the Father Ad-
ministrator of the Hospital of San Juan de Dios in Morelia demanded
that soldiers there for treatment retract their oath and when Father
Buenaventura Merlin of Toluca refused burial to General Plutarco
González because the General had not retracted nor repented his
oath. The Archbishop specifically approved this latter action and reminded the clergy of the requirements for administration of the sacraments to the erring faithful.[67]

A typical retraction was this:

> . . . I swore the oath to the Constitution of the Republic.
> The greatest self-esteem, frivolity of spirit and the force of
> novelty, prompted me to [perform] such a deed, without
> considering with suitable prudence, the duty that my Catholic
> origins impose on me and without keeping in mind the protests
> against the aforementioned political code that have been made
> by ecclesiastical prelates and their circulars about the oath, and
> the common judgment of these eminently learned and impartial
> men; now that, through a gift from heaven, I am aware again
> of my duties . . . my mistake . . . I say that I repent and
> retract the oath. . . .[68]

Reforms continued in the face of opposition and disorders and the
President's own growing uncertainty about the Constitution and his
desire to follow a moderate, conciliatory policy. Among the new

66. A. Portilla, p. 196; AGN, Justicia eclesiástico, vol. 180, fols. 331–33; and
Forsyth to Cass, 10 April 1857, document 4304 in William R. Manning, ed.,
Diplomatic Correspondence of the United States: Inter-American Affairs, 1831–1860,
vol. 9, *Mexico, 1848 (mid-year) to 1860* (Washington: Carnegie Endowment for
International Peace, 1937), p. 911.

67. 20 and 26 March 1857, Díaz López, 1:406–7; and AGN, Justicia
eclesiástico, vols. 179, 180, 181; 11 May 1857, vol. 180, fol. 372; and vol. 174,
fols. 403–16.

68. Monico Prado of Piedragorda, 13 October 1857, in Carlos E. Castañeda, ed., *Nuevos documentos inéditos o muy raros para la historia de México*, vol.
3, *La Guerra del Reforma según el archivo del General D. Manuel Doblado, 1857–
1860* (San Antonio, Texas: Casa Editorial Lozano, 1930), pp. 11–12.

measures was the Iglesias law of 11 April 1857, named for the Minister of Justice, José María Iglesias, which sought to prevent arbitrary parish fees. The law simply reaffirmed earlier ecclesiastical charges for the performance of baptisms, marriages, and burials for the poor classes.[69] The Archbishop ordered strict compliance, even though he knew that many priests would suffer by the imposition of this schedule of fees. The Bishop of Oaxaca, too, supported the law. This Bishop, who was silent on the Lerdo law and strenuously opposed the Constitution, favored this act because it corresponded to the reformist sentiments he espoused to strengthen the clergy. But in some bishoprics, notably in Puebla and Michoacán, where the prelates believed the government had no right to interfere in matters of parish fees, opposition and protests followed. In various localities the authorities used force to secure the required posting of the law and imposed fines for failure to post and for removal of the law once posted. The parish priest of Celaya, for example, was fined $25 on four different occasions because the law was not posted as ordered, though he complained that someone else was apparently removing the document during the night.[70] Another law on 14 September 1857 suppressed the University of Mexico, thus ending clerical direction of education there.

Amid growing trouble in the country, highly placed officials considered abrogating the Constitution. Allegedly, the government was not disturbed by refusals to take the oath to the Constitution because it increased opposition to the charter that the government wanted to abrogate. Comonfort had long been concerned over what he believed to be serious weakening of the executive power in the Constitution. As early as March 1857 the moderate Minister of Development, Manuel Siliceo, contacted various leaders to gain support for a petition to annul the Constitution as being contrary to the national will. Comonfort would be vested with ample powers to govern pending the drafting of a new charter. In October a pamphlet circulated critical of a

69. "Ley sobre derechos, y obvenciones parroquiales," Bassols, pp. 23ff. "Poor" was defined as anyone who earned no more than the minimum necessary for subsistence; personal service in any form as a way to satisfy the fees was prohibited.

70. Berry, "The Reform in . . . Oaxaca," p. 93; A. Portilla, p. 215; Zamacois, 14:547–51; and Munguía, 1:413–15.

Constitution that might be suitable for normal conditions but not for the unusual times the country was passing through. The extreme political turmoil resulted not from the liberal reforms, not from the government's moderation, but from the Constitution. A dictatorship under Comonfort would remedy the situation. Shortly after this pamphlet appeared, Comonfort met secretly with advisors at the home of Manuel Payno in the Mexico City suburb of Tacubaya. Presumably, Payno and General Félix Zuloaga told the President that the Constitution granted the executive too little power and that he could not govern under it. Comonfort expressed a desire to determine national opinion; if influential citizens supported the Constitution, he would maintain it; otherwise he would not force it on them.[71]

Rumors circulated in the capital of an impending coup by the President, but when it happened on 17 December, General Zuloaga led it. The Plan of Tacubaya suspended the Constitution and invested Comonfort with supreme power. Comonfort accepted the Plan in the belief that the majority opposed the Constitution and that it was unworkable because of an imbalance in power between legislative and executive branches of government. Clerical opposition contributed to the decision, too. According to Alexis de Gabriac, the French Minister, two days before the coup the President had confided:

> Today I am convinced of the errors that we have committed and of the outrage my government has practiced against the customs of the masses through the laws against the Church and sternness against the clergy. For a time I had the hope of triumphing, on account of the continuing opposition of the people. I confess that I was wrong. . . .[72]

A mixed response initially greeted the coup. In the capital indifference prevailed. People shrugged their shoulders saying, "new game with the same old cards." In the country the change inspired little confidence. It disgusted radicals and did not satisfy conservatives. Moderates presumably were content and believed Comonfort

71. *La política del General Comonfort*; Manuel Payno, *Memoria sobre la revolución de diciembre de 1857 y enero de 1858* (Mexico, 1860), pp. 22–34; and Siliceo to Riva Palacio, Governor of the State of Mexico, 13 March 1857, in Mariano Riva Palacio, Correspondencia, 1830–1880, Latin American Collection, University of Texas, Austin.

72. 18 December 1857, Díaz López, 1:443.

was the only man capable of preventing anarchy and of dominating the other groups.[73] In a revolutionary situation, however, moderation seldom can contain antagonistic extremist elements. After a brief attempt to govern, Comonfort lost the support of all factions; a thoroughgoing reaction, temporarily under Zuloaga's leadership, set in. Thus, the moderate leader of the Plan of Ayutla, the exponent of reforms and progress through a middle road and reconciliation of all factions, ended by being repudiated by all of them. His elimination from power inaugurated a devastating civil war between adherents of "Religión y Fueros" and "Constitución y Reforma."

The civil war capped a series of reforms that began in 1855 after the overthrow of Santa Anna. The attacks on corporate strictures and privilege, on inequality and injustice, and the strong response of the affected interests plus the alleged defects in the Constitution led to the coup on 17 December 1857. This coup in turn opened the floodgates to full-scale civil war.

The Lerdo law, an important contributor to the chaos that engulfed the reforming efforts, was, at the time and since, much maligned and praised: it was the devil's work or the harbinger of a bright tomorrow. It was, in fact, neither. The law's failure to usher in a new age of prosperity, progress, and democracy was the fault of both the Mexican Church and the law itself. The law did not deprive corporations of their wealth; it did convert landed wealth into cash and mortgages, thus freeing corporations from the burdens of repairs, improvements, and problems of vacancy. The law placed real estate in circulation and increased the number of proprietors. Defects in the law and clerical opposition, however, fostered acquisition of the former ecclesiastical property by the relatively well-to-do, rather than broadly distributing it among the mass of the propertyless. The law did not insist on the division of rural estates, a major mistake. Perhaps 300 of 6,000 ecclesiastical estates were fractioned. Thus, disamortization eliminated ecclesiastical latifundists but created a new group of lay latifundists that represented as much a stagnation or entailment of

73. Forsyth to Cass, 17 December 1857, *Despatches from Ministers*, roll 22, vol. 21; and Edmundo Stephenson in Guanajuato to Madrid in Mexico City, 21 December 1857, in Manuel I. Madrid, Correspondencia, 1840–1859, Latin American Collection, University of Texas, Austin.

property as the old had. In fact, the inclusion of village communal
lands in the law led to the communities' loss of lands and, eventually at
least, to even greater property concentration than before the Reform.
Finally, the failure to create rural credit banks and the imposition of
the *alcabala* helped defeat the liberals' goals. The defects might have
been corrected, as some were by the 9 October 1856 circular and the
nationalization law, if an era of peace had followed the initial reforms.
This was not the case, however.

A great tragedy for Mexico surely was the Church's refusal to accept a law that did it no material harm. The fruits of this opposition
were a disaster for the Church as for the country in general—a civil
war and more radical anticlericalism. Church leaders may well have
believed that they could prevent any assault on their privileges and
power, indeed, that they must prevent it, viewing the early reforms as
only the beginning of a well-planned, all-encompassing attack on the
Church's position that would come whether the measures were accepted or opposed. There was already, in fact, in September 1857,
talk of nationalization of all Church wealth. The Church claimed, too,
that the Lerdo law did not benefit the clergy as the government maintained. Indeed, the basis for property valuation and adjudication was
much lower than the clergy customarily received for their properties,
and a one-eighth reduction in the price was granted to denouncers.
Perhaps, as the prelates claimed, the Church simply could not accept
the Lerdo law because it could not permit any infringement, without
its consent, on its right of ownership. The hierarchy insisted that all
changes had to be made by agreement with the pope. Pope Pius IX, in
December 1856, condemned and declared null and void all decrees
and projected laws against the Catholic religion, the Church, its social
rights, its ministers, and the authority of the Holy See. The Pontiff,
therefore, approved the Mexican bishops' stand. But in July 1857 he
seemed willing to accept the Juárez law, the suppression of most
monasteries, and the government's acquisition of monastic property
on condition that the clergy's political rights and capacity to acquire
real estate again be acknowledged. At this time Ezequiel Montes,
Minister of Justice, went to Rome to negotiate with the papacy.[74]

74. González Navarro, *Vallarta*, pp. 85–86, 145; 27 September 1856, Díaz
López, 1:328; *Manifestación que hace el gobierno eclesiástico de Guadalajara, contra*

The events of December 1857 prevented any possibility of an understanding. If the attitude of the Mexican clergy is open to criticism for reflecting ideas long on the defensive, if not long since outmoded, still their position conformed throughout "with the spirit emanating from the Holy See whose occupant, Pius IX, viewed the advancing wave of liberalism with profound distrust—a movement which must be opposed strenuously."[75]

---

las disposiciones dictadas en Veracruz (Guadalajara, 1859), 30 August 1859, p. 13; and Francisco Santiago Cruz, *La piqueta de la reforma* (Mexico: Editorial Jus, S.A., 1958), p. 11 (information taken from Carlos Alvear Acevedo, *Elementos de historia de México*).

75. Knowlton, "Clerical Response," p. 528.

Chapter 3
Civil War, 1858–1860: From Disamortization to Nationalization

For two weeks or more after the December 1857 coup, Comonfort vacillated, seeking to stabilize his position and win support by appealing to all shades of political opinion. During these weeks the capital remained peaceful, although opposition developed elsewhere, especially in the north, to the changed political situation in Mexico City. By 10 January 1858, fighting had broken out in the city in a three-way struggle for power among Comonfort's supporters, the radicals, and the conservatives. It took ten days to resolve the issue. By 21 January, Comonfort had been overthrown, the radicals defeated, and the conservatives, led by General Zuloaga, installed in power.[1]

The Three Years' War, or War of the Reform, may be divided into two approximately equal parts: from the establishment of conservative power in Mexico City in January 1858 to the nationalization law issued by the Veracruz-based liberals in July 1859; and from July 1859 to the liberal triumph in December 1860. At the time of the December coup, Comonfort jailed Benito Juárez, leader of the liberals and President of the Supreme Court, an office that made him constitutionally next in line for the presidency of Mexico. Shortly before fleeing the capital, Comonfort released Juárez from prison. Because of the unconstitutional coup and Comonfort's support of it, Juárez claimed the presidency. Traveling a circuitous route by land and water, he finally reached Veracruz in May 1858. He established his government there and directed the liberal efforts against the conservatives in Mexico City.

In the capital, clergy and women, especially, greeted the conservative victory with joy. Sermons and pastoral letters expressed the clergy's sentiments. A *Te Deum* was sung in the Cathedral, and Archbishop Lázaro de la Garza could not contain his satisfaction over the

1. 5 and 11 January 1858, Díaz López, 1:451, 455; and Walker Fearn, Secretary of Legation, to Cass, 2 January 1858, and Forsyth to Cass, 14 and 29 January 1858, *Despatches from Ministers*, roll 22, vol. 21.

change in regimes. Providence had undoubtedly taken a hand, and Heaven was still being merciful to the Mexicans, but the Archbishop somberly reminded the faithful of their offenses against God because of the liberal laws. The Puebla clergy, too, were grateful for God's infinite mercy in pardoning the profanation of His Name and the sacrilege under the liberals, who were now being defeated, giving a "ray of Hope" for the future.[2]

The Zuloaga government lost no time in charting its course. On 28 January, it annulled the Juárez, Lerdo, and Iglesias laws and reemployed all who had lost their jobs through refusal to take the oath to the Constitution. Thus, the conservatives undid with a single stroke the major reform measures by restoring military and ecclesiastical *fueros*, voiding all alienations of ecclesiastical property, and abrogating the law on parish fees. The enthusiasm of the faithful overflowed. Decorations bedecked houses and streets in honor of the event—except houses of purchasers of Church property![3]

A lengthy regulatory law on 1 March established procedures for the return of ecclesiastical properties alienated under the Lerdo law which the 28 January decree had abrogated. Notaries and judges were to note in their registers the nullification of all adjudications and sales; local political authorities were to confirm that the nullification had been marked in the records. Adjudicators and purchasers were to return title deeds to the corporations or suffer fine or imprisonment. Apparently, some returned titles but retained the property itself. The conservative government required the return of titles and property

2. *Carta pastoral que el Illmo. Señor Arzobispo de México Dr. D. Lázaro de la Garza y Ballesteros dirige a sus diocesanos* (Mexico, 1858), 12 February 1858; Forsyth to Cass, 29 January 1858. *Despatches from Ministers*, roll 2, vol. 21; and "Sermón que en la solemne función que la Santa Iglesia de Puebla dedica anualmente a Nuestra Señora de Guadalupe en su insigne y nacional colegiata predicó el pbro. Lic. D. Ismael Jiménez el día 12 de febrero de 1858," in *Sermonario mexicano o colección de sermones panegíricos, dogmáticos y morales escritos por los oradores mexicanos más notables, ordenados por un eclesiástico de la Mitra de Puebla, coleccionados y publicados por Narciso Bassols* (Mexico, 1890), 3:196.

3. On 30 March 1858, the 27 January 1857 law on civil registry was also annulled. Munguía, 2:182–85; Forsyth to Cass, 29 January 1858. *Despatches from Ministers*, roll 22, vol. 21; and 2 February 1858, from Josefina in Mexico City to Riva Palacio, her father, M. Riva Palacio Correspondencia.

but agreed to reimburse individuals for the cost of the property; amounts paid in bonds or credits were repaid at once, but because of the shortage of funds, specie payments had to be covered in "paper." However, tenants had to pay the corporations the amount they would have paid in rent for the time they held the property under the Lerdo law. The law permitted tenants who had adjudicated property to remain as tenants under the terms of the prereform contracts; corporations were free to negotiate new leases with tenants or anyone else if the current tenants were not the adjudicators and the properties had been auctioned.[4]

The Archbishop established his own requirements, which, with some refinements, followed governmental provisions. The Church agreed to conclude new rent contracts with tenants regardless of the origin of their tenancy, except that preference would be given to those who could prove prior tenancy of a particular property and eviction for failure to adjudicate under the Lerdo law. The Archbishop also agreed to deduct from the rent owed, for the duration of the Lerdo law, whatever sums had been spent for legitimate repairs and to pay occupants an indemnity for improvements that increased the value of the property. The corporation bound itself not to increase the rent until the indemnity was paid.[5]

The liberals quickly responded to the conservative victory in Mexico City. Claiming to be the legitimate constitutional government, the liberals in Veracruz voided all contracts, appointments, and concessions of the conservatives since the coup, 17 December 1857. Although the Juárez government reserved the right to approve individual acts warranted by circumstances, in general, those persons dealing with the usurpers could anticipate punishment in the event of a

4. Payno, *Leyes*, 2:1–3, 4–18; "El Sr. Cura, con relación a las obras pías de su parroquia [Tacuba]," AGN, Bienes nacionales, Negocios eclesiásticos, leg. 1911, exp. 1.

5. "El señor Cura con relación a la casa número 2 del Puente de los Gallos propia de su parroquia," AGN, Bienes nacionales, Negocios eclesiásticos, leg. 1873, exp. 1. See also *Quinta carta pastoral del Illmo. Sr. Arzobispo de Méjico, Dr. D. Lázaro de la Garza y Ballesteros, dirigida al V. clero y fieles de este arzobispado con motivo de los proyectos contra la iglesia, publicados en Verzcruz por D. Benito Juárez antiguo presidente del Supremo Tribunal de la nación* (Mexico, 1859), document 1, pp. 19–20.

liberal victory. Although the government's caveat was all-encompassing, decrees, circulars, resolutions, and instructions frequently concerned clerical property. These included prohibitions against the voluntary return of property to corporations, nullification of transfers, sales, or modifications in the properties, and the invalidity of mortgage redemptions.[6]

By repudiating the Lerdo law, the conservatives faced potential external difficulties. Foreign nationals who acquired Church property were threatened with its loss and sought the protection of their governments. In March 1858, a group of French subjects asked their Minister, de Gabriac, for help in retaining their property. The Minister was not overly sympathetic, noting that as early as July 1856 he had warned his compatriots that they would have to consider themselves as Mexicans under the law; if litigation with the Church developed, the legation would intervene only in cases of flagrant injustice by the judges. In these speculative affairs the risk was theirs. American citizens who complained to their Minister, John Forsyth, received a more sympathetic hearing. Forsyth counselled submission to authority as the only practical course, but international law certainly entitled them to indemnification: the conservative law was retroactive and arbitrarily destroyed vested rights, an action which no foreign government would tolerate.[7]

Foreign nationals did not object simply, or even primarily, to the annulment of the disamortization law; they recognized the new government's right to do that. The injustice was what really provoked their anguished pleas for help: they objected to their financial loss. They stood to forfeit the 5 percent *alcabala*, or tax, paid to the liberal authorities in cash but returnable in certificates by the conservative government. They were to lose the judicial and notarial fees paid to conclude transactions. These sums were considerable: for a $10,000 house, $500 in tax and $237 in fees. Furthermore, they were subject

6. 28 and 29 January 1858, Ocampo, 2:206, 207; 20 August 1858, Labastida, p. 116; and 3 November 1858, Pallares, p. 122. See Bazant, *Alienation*, pp. 135–75 for the impact of the civil war on ecclesiastical property in various localities in Mexico under both liberal and conservative control.

7. *Siglo*, 8 April 1858, pp. 1–2; 1 July 1856, and 25 July 1859, Díaz López, 1:304 and 2:103; and Forsyth to Cass, 1 and 10 March 1858, *Despatches from Ministers*, roll 22, vol. 21.

to an increasing fine if they failed to return the title deeds unconditionally within ten days after the 1 March regulatory law; they might also lose all or part of the costs of any repairs or improvements made on the properties.[8] In seeking justice, these men sought total repayment of the sums expended in acquiring property.

It is noteworthy that a number of the American residents in Mexico at the time were apparently naturalized citizens, many with only first papers. The United States consul estimated the number as more than one-half out of about 100. Presumably, Mexicans went through the naturalization process so that if they had difficulty because of various activities, such as transactions with Church property, they could claim the protection of the United States government. It is impossible to determine how common the practice was without a careful examination of relevant documents, but at least some American citizens seeking diplomatic aid in defense of their acquisitions bore "foreign" names, such as Manuel G. Lara.[9]

The regime's need for resources was of deep concern to government, Church, foreign nationals, and Mexicans alike. On 15 May 1858 the government levied a tax (*contribución*) on merchants and capitalists. There was great resistance; in fact, most foreigners refused to pay except under threat of force. In three months the government had obtained only about $500,000, one-third of the amount expected. The government also sought to obtain cash from local capitalists, using Church property as security. These entrepreneurs, however, hesitated. They feared nationalization of the property posted as security in the event of a liberal victory in the war; so they were unwilling to offer more than 50 percent of the value of the property. The patriotism of the wealthy had its limits, and the government, failing to stir patriotic sentiments, turned then to coercion; it demanded cash equal to the value of the guaranteed security. The government granted three days for payment, after which it imposed a fine of

8. Charles Whitehead to John Forsyth, 9 March 1858, enclosed in Forsyth to Cass, 10 March 1858. *Despatches from Ministers*, roll 22, vol. 21.

9. Forsyth to Cass, 1 and 10 March 1858, ibid; and Marcus Otterbourg to Seward, 18 September 1862, in *Despatches from United States Consuls in Mexico City, Mexico, 1822–1906* (Washington, D.C.: National Archives, Microcopy File no. 296), roll 6, vol. 11. Cited hereafter as *Despatches from Consuls, Mexico City.*

$1,000 a day. The maximum demanded was $30,000 from the wealthiest individuals—Manuel Escandón, Francisco Iturbe, Ignacio Cortina Chávez, Faustino Goribar, José Pacheco, Félix Béistegui, Joaquín Rocas, Miguel Bringas, and Ignacio Loperena. These gentlemen responded in various ways; some fled and others hid.[10]

If wealthy laymen were not generous, the Church was; it offered the resources at its command to the government, which protected its rights and property. Church wealth, in fact, sustained the conservative regime. The first installment of $500,000 due on an initial $1,500,000 loan was promptly paid in August 1858. In the fall another $1,000,000 was forthcoming. In order to make these payments, ecclesiastical corporations sold their real estate; the purchasers in many cases reacquired properties they originally adjudicated under the Lerdo law. Church property also guaranteed government contracts with foreign bankers; ecclesiastical property deeds covered loans of $700,000 from Nathaniel Davidson, agent of Rothschild and Co., and of $120,000 and $200,000 from Barron, Forbes & Co.[11]

In different phraseology, two diplomats made similar observations concerning these activities.[12] In John Forsyth's words, the Church was "between two fires, in danger first, of being ruined at a blow from the *Puros* [through nationalization], and equally sure of being ruined by degrees by its friends, the present Government."

Alexis de Gabriac commented that the clergy

... understands that the moment has arrived to dispose of its property amicably on advantageous terms, if it does not wish to see itself totally despoiled of it upon the return of the *Puros*. Nevertheless, this system of loans to the government offers the clergy no kind of guarantee, for it will never be reimbursed for the debt.

Willing as the Church might be to support the conservatives' war effort, it was by no means a cornucopia of endless riches. As early as 1

10. 10 July, 1 and 12 August 1858, Díaz López, 2:28, 32, 38; and Forsyth to Cass, 13 February 1858, *Despatches from Ministers*, roll 22, vol. 21.

11. 22 August and 12 October 1858, Díaz López, 2:40, 46; del Castillo Negrete, p. 245; and López Gallo, pp. 206–7.

12. Forsyth to Cass, 13 February 1858, *Despatches from Ministers*, roll 22, vol. 21; and 22 August 1858, Díaz López, 2:40.

August 1858 John Forsyth was reporting that the Church lacked the money to comply with an urgent request to lend the government another $1,000,000, that it was making "extraordinary efforts" to meet the obligation assumed by the first loan, the first payment of which fell due in August, but that it would give a guarantee for another $1,000,000.[13] The capitalists were unwilling, however, to advance the government money on the basis of that guarantee, as noted above. The longer the war lasted and the demands continued, the harder it was to squeeze funds out of the corporations. The Archbishop allocated the loans and exactions among various corporations; these reacted with complaints about the difficulty of raising their quota of the loans and sometimes about the injustice of the exactions as well. The lament of the Prior of the Province of Discalced Carmelites, in a communication to the individual convents on 30 March 1859 reflects the dilemma facing the religious bodies:

> Last year it was my unpleasant duty to inform you of the $1,500,000 loan imposed on the Church in the Archbishopric by virtue of an agreement between the Miter and the government, of which $75,000 was the quota of our Province; with similar regret I now inform you that by virtue of the $700,000 Davidson loan, our portion is $15,000, plus $2,000 more for the loan imposed at the request of President Miramón. . . . For five months I have been evading as far as possible complying because of the distressing state of the Province, but finally potent considerations have led me to consent in giving the announced property of $15,000 in deeds and $2,000 asked by the President, distributing the $17,000 as equitably as possible among the convents. . . . We must support this, paying the amounts, because of the danger that threatens the religion of our fathers, the jeopardy in which the Mexican Church finds itself. . . . The voices of religion and the State clamor urgently for us . . . [to] contribute the amount of the loan.[14]

13. Forsyth to Cass, 1 August 1858, *Despatches from Ministers*, roll 23. vol. 22.

14. del Castillo Negrete, pp. 244–46. See AGN, Justicia eclesiástico, vol. 165, fol. 341 for a similar lament from the Provincial of the Dominican convents.

The Prior's hint of irritation and concern becomes more emphatic in another case. The rector of the congregation of Our Lady of Guadalupe in Querétaro complained about the special tax of 1 percent on all capital over $1,000. This meant the corporation would have to pay $2,668 on its real estate. Ecclesiastical real estate, however, should not have been subject to this new tax because the government had earlier exempted ecclesiastical real estate from any new taxes until the Church loan of $1,500,000 had been repaid. Meeting this demand, the rector noted, meant a payment by the corporation of $444 within fifteen days, a like amount in fifteen more days, and the same during each of the following four months, while the body's total monthly income was only about $500. Lacking any other income, this tax would make it necessary either to suspend all pious works (*obras pías*) that were sustained by the income or to sell some property, which would be difficult because of the strained times.[15]

The plight of the congregation raises the general question of the financial condition of ecclesiastical corporations. There is no doubt that the Mexican Church was extremely wealthy in real estate and mortgages, but this was by no means true of all individual corporations that comprised that entity, "the Church." Individual churches, convents, *cofradías*, and charitable and educational establishments might be quite poor. The size of the capital alone was not a sufficient indication of a body's financial state; the actual income, expenses, and debts also had to be considered. Specific cases illustrate the point.

In 1858 the Archicofradía del Santísimo Sacramento in Santa Catarina Mártir parish owned property worth $23,814: three houses worth $20,900 and readily collectable credits of $2,914. But it owed $37,409 in lawyers' and architects' fees, regular expenses, and interest on loans. The Cofradía de Animas in the San Juan del Río parish held two mortgages with a combined value of $1,250, but no interest had been paid on one for fifty years and on the other for fifty-five. Other confraternities too could not meet expenses with the income from their capital. These deficits were covered through the collection of

15. "El rector de la congregación de N.S. de Guadalupe de Querétaro, sobre si no obstante lo estipulado por el Supremo Gobierno está obligada aquella corporación a escribir la que corresponde de la contribución nuevamente decretada," AGN, Bienes nacionales, Negocios eclesiásticos, leg. 1711, exp. 1.

The Law of Disamortization returns so altered after a three-year trip in the interior that its author cannot recognize it.

Source: *La Orquesta*, 1 March 1861, opposite p. 2

alms.[16] Not only sodalities bordered on insolvency. The Franciscan monastery of Acámbaro, Michoacán, protested a prewar liberal property tax on the ground that it possessed capital of only $680, which yielded interest of $33.25; however, since the monastery itself was valued at $20,000, the tax would be $83.03, or more than twice the yearly income.[17] There is no question that the financial support given the conservatives by the Church, while bearable for some corporations, was a real hardship, if not a disaster, for others. Forsyth had indeed put it well that the Church was "equally sure of being ruined by degrees by its friends, the present Government."

Clerical financial support notwithstanding, the government could not nearly meet its expenses. Paying only one-fourth of administrative salaries cost $900,000 a month, and the army alone absorbed that amount. The army came first, of course, yet the troops of Mexico City, in one twenty-two day period in the spring of 1858, received only seven and one-half days' pay.[18] The government's financial condition was continuously a precarious one: it existed from day to day, trying expedient after expedient—forced loans, taxes, bonds—but the situation continued to deteriorate.

Those living in conservative-held territory faced, on the one hand, conservative annulment of the Lerdo law and, on the other hand, nullification of all conservative acts. A frightful dilemma confronted those involved in property transactions: if they returned the property

16. *Exposición dirigida al Supremo Gobierno por el ciudadano Plácido de Ferriz, con motivo del concurso formado a los bienes de la Archicofradía del Santísimo Sacramento, fundada en la parroquia de Santa Catarina Mártir de esta capital* (Mexico, 1858); "El sr. cura D. Pedro L. de Guevara, sobre unos capitales de la cofradía de Animas de su parroquia," AGN, Bienes nacionales, Negocios eclesiásticos, leg. 1828, exp. 1; and "La municipalidad sobre que de las obras pías se coste la reposición de la Iglesia Parroquial y Capilla del Calvario," ibid., leg. 1711, exp. 1.

17. "El provincial de Franciscanos de Michoacán pide se exceptúe a los conventos de su orden de la contribución impuesta por la ley de 26 de mayo del corriente año," AGN, Justicia eclesiástico, vol. 174, fols. 330–36. A publication of the Ministry of Justice in 1844 showed that the Monastery in question possessed active capital of $10,312 at that time. *Memoria del Secretario de Estado y del despacho de Justicia e Instrucción Pública, leída a las cámaras del congreso nacional de la República Mexicana en 12 enero de 1844* (Mexico, 1844), chart 6.

18. 22 August 1858, Díaz López, 2:40; and Forsyth to Cass, 2 May 1858, *Despatches from Ministers,* roll 23, vol. 22.

to the Church, they would face retribution if the liberals won; if they refused to comply with the decrees of government and Church, anticipating a liberal victory, they would be punished. A possible solution was to return the property, but not voluntarily; then a liberal victory might restore the property to them. Many did just that, accurately guessing the liberal policy.

Not everyone had sufficient foresight to return property unwillingly or involuntarily. Indeed, by no means were all reluctant to do so. Many did so gladly, declaring, whether sincerely or not, that it had been their intention from the beginning to keep the property safe for the Church and prevent the "unscrupulous" from acquiring it.[19] Whatever the real intent or sincerity, the document of cancellation usually indicated the degree of willingness in restoring the property. Possibly a typical cancellation showing voluntary return was:

Francisco Miguel Calapiz, national public scribe.

I certify: that in the margin of the instrument of adjudication granted in my presence with the date of 31 July 1856, in favor of Don José Félix Rodríguez, there has been made a statement of the following nature: "Mexico, 23 February 1808 [*sic*] = on this day there appeared Señora Doña Gertrudis Escudero and she said: that as executrix and heiress of Don Félix Rodríguez, which she has proven to me, she declares: that on behalf of the deceased, as well as the deponent, they never had the intention of taking property belonging to the Church and that if the house was adjudicated to the deceased it was with the intention of returning it to its legitimate owner: that now that the law is revoked and the opportunity of cancelling this instrument having presented itself, she verifies it, indicating that on their behalf this instrument is cancelled, void, and of no value or effect; this writing being put in this margin, concerning which no affidavit is given. In such judgment, that this instrument is cancelled, void, and of no value or effect, I hereby certify. María Gertrudis Escudero = Francisco Calapiz. . . ."

And at the request of the party in interest, I deliver this instrument.

Mexico, February 23, 1858. [rubric][20]

19. See Victoriano Salado Alvarez, *Episodios nacionales*, vol. 5, *La Reforma* (Mexico: Colección Málaga, S. A., 1945), p. 128.

20. "Documentos pertenecientes al convento antiguo del Señor de Santa Teresa," AGN, Bienes nacionales, leg. 125, exp. 5.

A seemingly endless stream of disputes, conflicts, and problems attended reestablishment of normality in ecclesiastical property. Frequent irregularity and complexity characterized operations. Understandably, simulated sales were a source of controversy and litigation. Administrators of corporation property were in an excellent position to take personal advantage of the Lerdo law while seeming to evade it. Colonel Mariano P. Tagle, treasurer of the Archicofradía de la Preciosa Sangre, obtained various properties of the corporation by illegally predating sales contracts when in fact the transactions were concluded only after the disamortization law. Such dealings violated not only civil laws and ecclesiastical orders, but rules of the foundation as well; these often held invalid any alienations of corporate property. Abrogation of the Lerdo law brought many of these transactions to light. When a tenant refused to pay his rent because Tagle was not the legitimate owner, Tagle, perhaps foolishly, took him to court. The case reached the Supreme Court, which decided against Tagle in May 1859.[21]

One of the most common issues that clogged court dockets after the annulment of the liberal laws concerned the rights of tenants. Political changes alone promised confusion. Legal technicalities and interpretations complicated seemingly simple questions. One Ignacio D. rented an outbuilding, part of a larger house complex, through all the political and legal changes. Prior to the Lerdo law, he had paid rent to the owning convent, then he paid the adjudicator of the property, and finally with the reaction, he once again became the tenant of the corporation. Suddenly he was evicted. The corporation concluded a rent contract with a new tenant because Ignacio D. had not come forward to arrange a new agreement with the convent as conservative decrees required. Ignacio D. argued successfully that the conservatives ordered the restoration of property to pre-Lerdo law conditions insofar as possible. Since he was the long-standing, continuing tenant through the various political upheavals, there was no need for him to conclude a new rent contract. The court agreed, returning him to tenancy.[22] Without doubt, this was a particularly rich era for lawyers to ply their trade.

21. 25 May 1859, M. Riva Palacio Correspondencia.

22. *Gaceta de los tribunales de la República Mexicana, dirigida por el Licenciado Luis Méndez* (Mexico), 11 August 1860, 1:507–10.

The Church, so vigorous an opponent of disamortization even to the point of threatening those who acquired clerical property with eternal damnation, might understandably assume a very firm, uncompromising attitude when restored to its full rights and authority. In fact, however, evidence indicates a lack of rancor toward adjudicators. The Church displayed a willingness to be fair to the disobedient faithful as well as a natural interest in the financial aspect of the property question. Permitting adjudicators to remain as tenants served both these ends; allowing some reimbursement for improvements made on properties by adjudicators exemplified the Church's fairness. The amount, however, was usually less than the actual value of improvements, and it was not in cash but with a noninterest bearing note remaining as long as the tenant remained in the house and the corporation did not alienate the property. If either condition changed, the note was to be redeemed by the corporation.[23]

Under the circumstances, of course, corporations would not have profited by evicting all adjudicators. It would have been unrealistic to do so and probably impossible to find new tenants. In the matter of improvements, it was merely politic to make some concessions since they enhanced the value of the real estate and cost the corporation nothing. Certainly the foreigners who complained to their ministers did not think that either the government or the Church was doing them any favors. Nevertheless, the attitude of the prelates in these matters seems more conciliatory than was necessary.

The Church's solicitude was naturally greater when a dispute involved a former tenant who had suffered for refusing to adjudicate a property. The Rayón case illustrates this concern which was complicated by financial considerations. Josefa Rayón, loath to adjudicate the portion of a house she rented, vacated it, and someone else purchased it by adjudication. With the conservative reaction, the Archbishop heeded her petition and restored Señora Rayón to tenancy, but the adjudicator resisted eviction. The failure to resolve the conflict between Rayón and the adjudicator prejudiced the interests of the religious corporation, which could conclude a new, more favorable

23. "Documentos pertenecientes al convento antiguo del Señor de Santa Teresa, Expediente relativo a las mejoras y arrendamiento de la casa no. 3 de la calle de Santa Teresa la antigua, perteneciente al convento del mismo nombre," AGN, Bienes nacionales, leg. 125, exp. 5.

rent contract with the adjudicator. Señora Rayón's rent was $25 a month; the entire property earned $37 a month for the corporation. So the Archbishop resolved the impasse by granting Rayón $25 a month for life with which to pay for other living quarters; in return, she renounced her rights to tenancy of the house in question. This was an equitable solution because Rayón was poor and because the rent on the whole house could easily be doubled, thus offsetting the annuity to her.

The claims of the wife of the adjudicator, General Agustín Alcérreca, complicated the financial question. She maintained that at the time of adjudication the house was abandoned and in disrepair. If the Archbishop had returned the house to Rayón, then the General ought to have been reimbursed for improvements made on the property. With the Rayón claim settled, the new agreement concluded with General Alcérreca stipulated that he would pay $65 a month rent for the whole house, or $28 more than the original rent. The corporation would use $25 of the rent to pay Señora Rayón and $3 to pay monthly interest on a $600 mortgage encumbering the house. Thus, its net income would be the same as before. The corporation also obligated itself for Alcérreca's improvements, without interest and with no fixed time limit unless a change in ownership or tenancy should occur, at which time it agreed to pay the General 5 percent interest and to redeem the amount within three years.[24]

Three years of war. Glowing optimism about the durability of a hard-pressed regime without access to ports and customs revenues. Reversion of property. New contracts. Evasion. Denunciations. Abrogation of "evil laws." *Te Deums.* A "ray of hope." "Providence taking a hand." The Archbishop might well have pondered that point. Were his Church's rights worth the human and material cost being exacted? And were these stoutly defended rights being observed in the territory under liberal control—the greater part of the Republic? No, indeed!

24. "Documentos pertenecientes al convento antiguo del Señor de Santa Teresa, El Señor mayordomo del convento de Santa Teresa la antigua, consulta sobre la casa no. 7 de la calle de este nombre, de que eran inquilinos las Señoras Rayones," AGN, Bienes nacionales, leg. 125, exp. 5.

The civil war raged across the country, devastating the land and exhausting resources: agriculture, mining, industry, commerce—all suffered. Production was inadequate to satisfy the needs of the people, the internal movement of goods increasingly slowed and became more localized, not only from lack of production but because of the insecurity of the roads. The United States consul in Veracruz reported:

> Haciendas are abandoned, ranchos deserted, and even whole villages pillaged and sacked, leaving nothing but desolation wherever the armies of the contending parties have made their tracks. Many of the most valuable and productive Sugar, Coffee, and grain plantations have gone to waste for the want of labor to cultivate them, the operarios [workers] having been forced into the ranks of the army.[25]

The Juárez government in Veracruz of necessity granted broad powers and independence of action to liberal governors and military commanders. At the same time, it was deluged with denunciations of clerical properties returned to the former owners in conservative-held territory. Santos Degollado, commander-in-chief of the forces in the field, was vested with full power in matters of war, finance, and other branches of government in the areas under his control. No sooner had the government installed itself than the Ministry of Finance received from would-be denouncers long lists of properties allegedly returned spontaneously to religious bodies by adjudicators in conservative-held territory. Speculators did not hesitate to turn conditions to their advantage; if the price was right, risks were worth taking. In Mexico City agents of liberals and conservatives combined to make compromises and perpetrate "incalculable abuses" in dealing with the two governments. Allegedly, the liberal Minister of Finance, Melchor

25. Consul R. B. J. Twyman to Cass, 30 September 1859, *Despatches from United States Consuls in Veracruz, 1882–1906* (Washington, D.C.: National Archives, Microcopy File no. 183), roll 7, vol. 7. See also Bulmaro García Solorzano, *Problemas monetarios y del desarrollo económico de México* (Mexico: Taller de Avelar Hnos. Impresores, 1963), p. 73; Justo Sierra, vol. 13, *Juárez, su obra y su tiempo* (Mexico: Imp. Universitaria, 1948), pp. 152–53; Manuel Valdés, *Memorias de la guerra de reforma* (Mexico: Imp. y Fototipia de la Secretaría de Fomento, 1913); and Planchet, pp. 159ff.

Ocampo, consistently and illegally accepted promissory notes for 80 percent of the payment for Church property.[26]

While speculators had a field day in Veracruz with denunciations, governors and commanders in the field indiscriminately took ecclesiastical property to sustain the liberal cause. In August and September 1858 the constitutionalist governors of Nuevo León, Coahuila, and Zacatecas, charging that pious funds were being used to arm and support the enemy, appropriated clerical capital for their war effort. They demanded redemption of mortgages, sold estates, and collected interest payments. The Governor of Jalisco, Pedro Ogazón, proposed to Degollado the nationalization of all clerical property in order to prevent its use by the enemy and to relieve the liberals' acute need for resources. Degollado, not able to go so far on his own authority, met with Ogazón. The resultant decree on 8 August authorized the Governor to use, as a loan, clerical capital supporting public instruction. In addition, certain types of debtors of the Church had to lend, at 25 percent discount, the equivalent of one year's interest on the amount owed. Others pursued a similar policy, although they might pick out different property or religious bodies to assault. Most extreme was the nationalization of ecclesiastical wealth decreed during the first half of 1859 by General Jesús González Ortega, Governor of Zacatecas, and by Santiago Vidaurri in the northern states under his control.[27]

The exigencies of war generally resulted in disposal of clerical property on almost any terms. Financial need led liberal officials in some cases to conduct a careful search to discover clerical wealth to appropriate; then shocking contracts were concluded with debtors. General Epitacio Huerta, Governor of Michoacán, claimed that he never permitted redemptions of mortgages for less than 10 percent in cash, the rest in bonds, cheaply purchased. But elsewhere, in Veracruz, Guanajuato, and Zacatecas, mortgages could be redeemed or acquired for 5 or 7 percent of the amount in specie.[28] Specific terms

26. Ocampo, 2:165ff.; and Guillermo Prieto, *Lecciones de historia patria escritas para los alumnos del Colegio Militar*, 4th ed. (Mexico, 1893), p. 408.

27. Manuel Cambre, *La guerra de tres años, apuntes para la historia de la Reforma* (Guadalajara (?): Biblioteca de Autores Jaliscienses, 1949), pp. 125–26; and Zamacois, 15:151–53.

28. *Memoria en que el C. General Epitacio Huerta dió cuenta al congreso del estado del uso que hizo de las facultades con que estuvo investido durante su administración*

of transactions aside, the constitutionalist government unquestionably concluded agreements of doubtful legality, dealings that became long-standing sources of litigation and dispute over the validity of denunciations and preference of rights.

The passions and necessities of war drove liberal generals to persecute and despoil the Church. General and Governor Jesús González Ortega of Zacatecas was perhaps an extreme example. In a 16 June 1859 decree he prescribed death for any cleric who in any way fostered disobedience to the federal laws; death for any who asked for or accepted the retraction of the oath to the Constitution; death for any who refused the sacraments to those who had taken the oath or acquired Church property. Later in June he suppressed religious communities and expelled all clergy from the state. He nationalized ecclesiastical property, prohibited religious processions, and on 14 July 1859, promulgated a civil marriage law. Although the death penalties prescribed in the June decree were not carried out, the later decrees were implemented.[29]

Thus, in the second year of the war the states were clearly outdistancing the central authorities in the issuance of anticlerical measures in general and in the appropriation of Church wealth in particular, but apparently President Juárez hesitated to issue federal reform laws, believing the time inopportune. Generals Degollado and González Ortega sent Manuel Romero Rubio to Veracruz where he and Miguel Lerdo tried to convince the President to act.[30]

Radical national anticlerical measures were issued midway through the Three Years' War; the most important of these affecting Church property was the Law of Nationalization of 12 July 1859. A number of considerations prompted the liberal government to take this and other drastic steps at that time. Liberals disagreed primarily on the question of the timing of extreme measures against the Church. Even though the government controlled the coasts, the customhouses, and the bulk of the national territory, it was in desperate need of financial

---

dictatorial, que comenzó en 15 de marzo de 1858 y terminó en 1° de mayo de 1861 (Morelia, 1861), pp. 40–42.

29. Ivie E. Cadenhead, Jr., Jesús González Ortega and Mexican National Politics (Fort Worth: Texas Christian University Press, 1972), pp. 24–25; and Planchet, pp. 137–38.

30. Planchet, p. 138; and Prieto, p. 403 and footnote to p. 403, p. 498.

resources. Traditionally, customs receipts constituted the prime source of government revenue. The daily income at the major port, Veracruz, was $2,500 or $3,000. Obligations to British and French bondholders absorbed one-half of this, and other charges and costs left the government only 30 percent of the gross receipts.[31] Miguel Lerdo wished to obtain needed funds by nationalizing Church wealth and using it as collateral to guarantee a loan from the United States. This move would obviate the need to cede Baja California to the northern neighbor—an unpalatable last resort to acquire funds. President Juárez and Melchor Ocampo, on the other hand, although very concerned with realizing the Reform that would deprive the Church of its wealth and moral guardianship over the State, wanted to accomplish this goal without fundamentally injuring the religious sentiments of the country. They believed the appropriate time to issue the laws was when military victory was won or assured, because the Church was trying to turn the civil conflict into a religious war. The populace might support such a war and thus lengthen the conflict if the laws were issued prematurely.

Juárez' decision depended on various factors. The states were already acting, and uniformity demanded federal laws. Firm leadership in the war, the desire to deprive the clergy of the resources with which it sustained the conservative cause, and the matter of a loan were all important considerations. Nationalization was not, however, precipitously or capriciously decreed; it had for some time been discussed and contemplated.[32]

Circumstances of the civil war thus justified nationalization in dif-

31. McLane to Cass, 21 December 1859, *Despatches from Ministers*, roll 25, vol. 24.

32. On the question of motives, aims, and expectations, see Jesús Romero Flores, *Comentarios a la historia de México (1821–1861)* (Mexico: Talleres de Imprenta de la Editoria B. Costa-Amie, 1958), pp. 311–12; José C. Caladés, *Don Melchor Ocampo, reformador de México* (Mexico: Editorial Patria, S.A., 1954), p. 353; Sierra, *Juárez*, pp. 155, 157, 159–60; McLane to Cass, 7 May 1859, *Despatches from Ministers*, roll 24, vol. 23; Prieto, p. 403 and footnote to p. 403 on p. 498; Planchet, p. 138; Rafael de Zayas Enríquez, *Benito Juárez su vida—su obra* (Mexico: Tipografía de la Viuda de Francisco Díaz de León, 1906), p. 88; and William M. Churchwell, United States Special Agent to Mexico, to President James Buchanan, 22 February 1859, in Manning, vol 9, document 4366, p. 1034.

ferent ways. The act may also be viewed as a part of liberal ideology, necessary to achieve long-standing goals, a precondition for which was the elimination of the political and economic power of the Church.

On 7 July 1859 the liberal government issued a sweeping proclamation that prepared the way for the specific measures that followed. The manifesto to the nation charged clerical elements with promoting the bloody war with the sole aim of preserving their interests and prerogatives. Order and liberty were impossible as long as these and other despotic, hypocritical, and immoral elements existed. The manifesto projected various Church-related reforms to cope with the situation, as well as other measures to regenerate the country.[33]

In the days and weeks that followed, the liberals made a beginning—on paper at least. Justifying nationalization of ecclesiastical property on 12 July 1859, the government again accused the clergy of being the primary stimulus to the war, of having done everything possible to evade laws issued to benefit the Church, and of constantly obstructing public order. Since the Church used its wealth to support a ruinous civil war, the only way to end the war was to deprive it of resources.[34]

The scope of the 12 July decree was broad. Provisions included nationalization of all property administered by the secular and regular clergy and separation of Church and State. As a result of separation, the government definitely renounced claims to patronage, which had been a source of dispute since Independence. Thereafter, the Church was free to appoint its clergy, create new dioceses, reorganize the ecclesiastical divisions of the country, and receive papal communications without civil interference. Presumably, separation signified that the State would not interfere in the spiritual realm. The law suppressed all male religious orders and other ecclesiastical corporations, although certain of the monastery churches remained open for worship. The female orders continued to exist, but any nun who wished to leave could do so. The law nationalized all capital of the

33. *El gobierno constitucional a la nación* (No publishing information; signed by Juárez, Ocampo, Manuel Ruiz, and Miguel Lerdo in Veracruz).
34. *Leyes de Reforma*, pp. 109–16.

nunneries in excess of that actually needed for maintenance. But, at the same time, the government set aside funds to return to the excloistered nuns the money or dowry paid upon entering; the former male regulars, reduced by the law to the status of secular clergy, received a "severance" gratuity. All novitiates were closed, and novices were prohibited from taking final vows. These actions meant, of course, eventual extinction of the orders.

A regulatory law on nationalization followed the next day, 13 July.[35] It detailed rules for the disposal of relevant real estate and redemption of mortgages. Financial, social, and political considerations were basic: deprive the Church of its wealth, secure resources to wage the war, and distribute the property as widely as possible. The law ordered the division of the monastery buildings, the appraisal of each fraction or part, and their sale at auction. A minimum acceptable bid was two-thirds of the value of the property, one-third payable in cash, the remainder in bonds of the public debt. Payment terms were lenient. The buyer was to pay the bonds immediately, but the cash was payable over a period of from five to nine years at 6 percent interest, with preference given to offers of immediate payment.

Equally easy terms prevailed for the redemption of clerical mortgages. Mortgagors (*censatarios*) liquidated their debts by paying three-fifths in public bonds and two-fifths in cash over a forty-month period. The lack of internal bonds led to acceptance of bonds of the external debt as well. For a time during the war, the government extended to eighty months the time allowed for the cash payments. A further concession granted discounts to those wishing to pay the cash amounts at once rather than in installments or promissory notes (*pagarés*). Debtors had thirty days to declare their intention to take advantage of the law; for ten days thereafter anyone else could ask to redeem the mortgage. After the time limits expired two things happened. Mortgages not spoken for were auctioned; also, mortgages and real estate that the government was unaware of, so-called occult property, were open to denunciation. Because of the "hidden" nature of this property, denouncers needed to pay only 30 percent of the amount in specie, 70 percent in bonds. As a further inducement to execute nationalization, the states received 20 percent of the sums

35. Payno, *Leyes*, 2:75–94.

obtained in cash for public works, and officials implementing the law kept 5 percent of the specie. In other notable provisions of the law, the government ordered the auction of clerical property not yet disentailed; rural estates that had been adjudicated but returned to the clergy were ordered subdivided and sold. Thus, nationalization attempted in some measure to correct apparent defects in disamortization through the division of monasteries into lots and by fractioning some large rural properties. The government later authorized all proprietors to subdivide their property, distributing any mortgages proportionately among the parts, and it abolished the transfer of ownership tax on those properties.[36]

At the time the liberals in Veracruz proclaimed a program for victory and for Mexico's future well-being, coincidentally the conservatives in Mexico City did the same. General Miguel Miramón, then head of the government, issued a manifesto to the nation on 12 July embodying his ideas for the "social reorganization" of the country.[37] According to the General, Mexico required a dictatorship as the only means to reorganize society and prepare for a durable constitution. The country was in all respects in an unsatisfactory state—in finance, agriculture, industry, commerce, education, justice, individual security. Miramón proposed to correct these deficiencies. He would reduce the size of the army and federal bureaucracy, reorganize and simplify judicial machinery, foster public works and foreign immigration. He acknowledged the nullification of disamortization and promised to respect and protect the Church and its interests, prerogatives, and independence. Determined to "annihilate the germ of discord that always [promoted] civil war," the General promised to act vigorously, "to march forward."

The conservative and liberal programs provide an interesting contrast. They agreed on many points: the need to reorganize the ad-

36. 3 August 1859, *Código de la Reforma, o colección de leyes, decretos, y supremas órdenes, expedidas desde 1856 hasta 1861* (Mexico, 1861), p. 122; 28 January and 6 February 1861, Labastida, pp. 192, 68–69; and Blas José Gutiérrez and Flores Alatorre, eds., *Leyes de Reforma, colección de las disposiciones que se conocen con este nombre publicadas desde el año de 1855 al 1870* (Mexico, 1870), vol. 2, pt. 2, p. 114.

37. *Miguel Miramón, general de división en gefe del ejército y presidente sustituto de la República Mexicana, a la nación*, 12 July 1859 (Mexico, n.d.).

ministration of justice, reduce the size of the army, promote colonization, and generally improve the economy. But they quite obviously
differed on the causes of the country's condition and on the remedies,
particularly with regard to the Church. Miramón did indeed march as
he had promised, but only on the battlefield and not always forward;
the Veracruz government, as promised, continued with reforms.

Enactment of a series of notable anticlerical measures followed
nationalization within the short space of a month. On 23 July 1859 a
civil marriage law required the performance of all marriage ceremonies by civil authorities, but religious rites were also permitted. On
28 July a civil registry law eliminated clerical control of vital statistics;
recording of births, marriages, and deaths became the responsibility
of civil judges. Other measures secularized cemeteries and reduced
the number of religious holidays. Later, on the eve of the liberal
victory in December 1860, a final act established religious liberty. The
law guaranteed equal protection to all faiths, but the government
warned, while promising noninterference in purely religious matters,
that any failure to observe the civil laws would be punished. This law,
further, ended the right of asylum in churches, restricted the ringing
of church bells, and prohibited religious acts and solicitation of alms
outside churches without prior written authorization of the government.[38]

In large measure the civil war determined the implementation of
the nationalization laws. The first alienations took place in fifteen
states and territories in which the Church had the least property, San
Luis Potosí, Michoacán, and Zacatecas being the richest. The liberals
encouraged transactions in conservative territory even though official
publication of the law, and thus legal implementation, could not be
carried out there. However, many denunciations of property located
in conservative-controlled areas were made to the liberal government
in Veracruz. The transactions would then be consummated when the
liberals regained control. At the same time, the government sought
financial resources and punishment of those who willingly returned
property to the Church. It affirmed denouncers' rights to property if

38. *Leyes de Reforma*, pp. 123–50, 31 July 1859, pp. 151–57, and "Libertad
de Cultos," 4 December 1860, pp. 207–15; and 11 August 1859, *La Reforma.*
*Leyes y circulares espedidas por el Supremo Gobierno Constitucional de la República,
desde su manifiesto de 7 de julio de 1859* (Mexico, 1861), p. 141.

they paid the transfer-of-property tax and conceded to them the advantage of paying for 65 percent of the property in bonds, rather than 60 percent, if they paid at once. The extent of these operations depended on speculators' perceptions of prospects for the liberal cause; there is some indication that operations were not as great as the Veracruz government hoped.[39]

The scope of nationalization was broad; its provisions were virtually all-inclusive. Secularization of schools and hospitals, educational and charitable establishments in general, followed. The property remained to support the institutions but under secular control. Nationalization applied even when clerical owners retained rights to use property, as was the case with episcopal and parish houses, some other buildings attached to churches and destined solely for the Faith, and hereditary chaplaincies (*capellanías de sangre*). Despite clarification of what nationalization covered, as with the Lerdo law, specific cases required special orders. Chaplaincies were somewhat unique. Though included in nationalization, the chaplains rather than the government were especially to benefit. Thus, owners of property encumbered to sustain a chaplaincy were to redeem the mortgage and pay the chaplain the principal or capital. The government's attitude toward chaplaincies related to the nature of the foundation and the fact that they did, in a sense, already represent individual property.[40]

As has been seen, trafficking in former ecclesiastical property took place in Veracruz before and after nationalization; in the field, liberal governors and military commanders were largely a law unto themselves, disposing of property as they saw fit. Military commanders unquestionably disposed of considerable ecclesiastical property for sums far below the real value. General Pedro Ogazón in Jalisco was

39. Payno, *Leyes*, 2:97–100; Ocampo, 2:165ff; 12 October 1859, Díaz López, 2:116; and Manuel Rivera Cambas, *Los gobernantes de México* (Mexico, 1873), 2:598.

40. Labastida, p. 500; 12 August 1859, *Código de la Reforma*, pp. 123–24; 7 September 1860, "Leyes civiles vigentes que se relacionan con la iglesia, y sentencias pronunciadas con arreglo a ellas por los tribunales de la República," in Fortino Hipólito Vera, *Apuntamientos históricos de los concilios provinciales mexicanos y privilegios de América, estudios previos al primer concilio provincial de Antequera* (Mexico, 1893), p. 76; Order of 6 January 1861, Pallares, p. 156; and Robert J. Knowlton, "Chaplaincies and the Mexican Reform," *Hispanic American Historical Review* 48 (August 1968): 421–37.

"And how are things going, dear?"
"As you can see, child; the government, which never ceases to lavish its favors on the poor, is granting us a definite benefit. What more could one ask than to assure the sale of our credits at 5 percent?"

Source: *La Orquesta*, 13 March 1861, opposite p. 14.

perhaps typical. Practically every hacendado or proprietor in the rich districts of Ameca, Sayula, Autlan, and Zapotlan owed clerical corporations $5,000, $10,000, or $20,000. Ogazón harshly demanded redemption of most of the debts within a short time, fifteen to forty-five days. Because of the precarious financial situation, however, terms were lenient: 30 percent in cash and 60 percent in bonds obtainable at 3 or 4 percent of their value; the remaining 10 percent the General remitted altogether. Thus, one could redeem a $10,000 mortgage for about one-third of that amount. Generals Jesús González Ortega, Ignacio Zaragoza, and Pedro Ampudia acted similarly, though varying the precise formula. Ampudia appointed Francisco Mejía, a future Minister of Finance, divisional paymaster and Chief of Finance for the state of Mexico. In that capacity, Mejía's primary concern was procurement of resources for the army. To this end he obtained court and notarial registers and noted the mortgages held by the Church. Mejía then made appointments to meet with all of the debtors and ordered them to pay all or part of what they owed. When one hacendado, in debt for $60,000, failed to keep his appointment, Mejía, with General Ampudia and an armed escort, proceeded to the hacienda and simply stripped it of as much grain and goods as possible as compensation for the funds not obtained. Apparently, Ampudia liked the looks of the estate, worth about $300,000, so he decided to denounce it. Such were the extralegal methods used to procure necessities for a campaign.[41]

It is impossible to determine exactly how much Church wealth supported military operations or served other purposes. The government did earmark large amounts of capital for various worthy ends. Some amounts indemnified those injured during the bombardment of Veracruz during the war, and income from the sale of the remaining monasteries in the Federal District paid for the seizure of the

41. Pérez Verdía, *Historia particular*, 3:94–95; *Memoria . . . por . . . Lerdo*, p. 32; Genaro García, ed., vol. 11, *Don Santos Degollado, sus manifiestos, campañas, destitución militar, enjuiciamiento, rehabilitación, muerte, funerales y honores póstumos* (Mexico: Librería de la Viuda de Ch. Bouret, 1907), pp. 113–14; 25 August and 18 December 1860, Ortega Correspondencia, vol. 2; and Francisco Mejía, *Memorias* (Mexico: Ediciones del Boletín Bibliográfico de la Secretaría de Hacienda y Crédito Público, 1958), pp. 33–35. These *Memorias* are a duplication of the manuscript "Epocas, hechos y acontecimientos de mi vida, y de los que fuí testigo" in the Latin American Collection, University of Texas.

Laguna Seca convoy by the constitutionalists in September 1860.[42] One important result of the liberals' actions was to make it difficult for the Church to fulfill its normal functions and meet its customary obligations. The now voluntary tithes were one source of income. Bishop Pedro Barajas of San Luis Potosí told the faithful that failure to tithe was contrary to God and to commandments of the Church and constituted a grave sin. He would arrange with people payment of part of the back tithes they owed and remit the remainder.[43]

The laws issued from Veracruz were essential to maintain leadership of the liberal movement in the hands of the federal government and to provide a basis for some coherence in Reform. They were indispensable to the establishment of civil supremacy, and nationalization of Church wealth did to some extent disarm the enemy that had used its resources to support rebellions against liberal authorities. However, the laws provoked further clerical protests and stiffened conservative resistance as much as they heartened the liberals.

Bishops' pastorals claimed that the Church was innocent of the charges leveled against it. As on other occasions, the bishops insisted that their political conduct was irreproachable and that the clergy had not promoted the war. As was customary, the Church had simply placed its resources at the disposal of the legitimate government, in this case the conservatives. Consistent with earlier protests, the prelates affirmed the infallibility and divine nature of the Church; they contended that the economic provisions of the laws constituted robbery, while the moral aspects were a combination of pompous verbiage of demagogues and an accumulation of errors, imputations, and calumnies. Others joined in a chorus of dissent: the women of Mexico City and Morelia; the Toluca Superior Court of Justice; authorities and inhabitants of other towns; and, of course, the conservative press and government in Mexico City.[44]

42. Decrees of 11 February and 24 October 1860, Labastida, pp. 294, 343.

43. 4 March 1860, *Carta pastoral del Illmo. Sr. Dr. D. Pedro Barajas, Obispo de San Luis Potosí, dirigida a sus diocesanos* (San Luis Potosí, 1860).

44. 29 July, 1859, *Carta pastoral del Illmo. Sr. Arzobispo de México, Dr. D. Lázaro de la Garza y Ballesteros, dirigida al V. clero y fieles de este arzobispado con motivo de los proyectos contra la Iglesia, publicados en Veracruz por D. Benito Juárez, antiguo presidente del Supremo Tribunal de la nación* (Mexico, 1859). See, for example, 7 September 1859, *Quinta carta pastoral* . . . ; 30 August 1859, *Manifestación que*

The sanguinary struggle continued for nearly a year and a half after the issuance of the Reform laws. During that time, the clergy, believing the conflict to be just, legal, and necessary to eliminate the enemies of God, rarely spoke of peace or urged the opposing factions to end the bloodshed. In 1860, however, some efforts were made to end the war. The British proposed a four point program: an armistice, a national assembly impartially elected to determine the future government of Mexico, a general amnesty, and religious toleration and civil equality. The plan failed. Conservatives and liberals alike refused to accept the last point, and Juárez would not even admit discussion of reform of the Constitution for which liberals were fighting.[45]

In the capital, clergy continued to use their dwindling wealth to support the conservative cause. Increasingly, the only difference between liberal and conservative use of Church property, albeit an important one, was that of consent. This had to a degree always been true, but in the midst of the civil war the similarity was especially striking. Both factions appropriated clerical wealth for various purposes. In the fall of 1859, Alexis de Gabriac perceptively summarized the current situation and foresaw a future source of conflict:

> . . . little by little the property of the Church is passing into the hands of the conservative party in order to escape those of the demagogues. The only difference is in the manner, but these sales of property made in a friendly way, with the consent of the Church in support of the government of Mexico, would provoke innumerable disputes [the day the Juárez government returned in triumph]. There are a great many foreigners, above all Frenchmen, who have hastened to denounce in Veracruz properties of the Church, thus preempting the purchasers who had the intention of doing the same here. . . .[46]

---

hace el gobierno eclesiástico de Guadalajara . . . ; Manifestación que hacen al venerable clero y fieles de sus respectivas diócesis y a todo el mundo Católico los Illmos. Sres. Arzobispo de México y obispos de Michoacán, Linares, Guadalajara y El Potosí, y el Sr. Dr. D. Francisco Serrano como representante de la mitra de Puebla (Mexico, 1859); and Zamacois, 15:266–70.

45. Vigil, pp. 425–26; and McLane to Cass, 5 July 1860, *Despatches from Ministers*, roll 27, vol. 26.

46. 12 October 1859, Díaz López, 2:116. See also John Black, U.S. Consul in

"*Well, then, the government disamortizes its debt for overdue payments by disposing of the property that, according to the Law of Nationalization, belongs to it.*"
"*So, won't that disposal make it impossible later for the government to meet its future obligations?*"
"*Now that is a theological question, my dear friend.*"

Source: *La Orquesta*, 13 March 1861, opposite p. 14.

By mid-1860 the conservatives had exhausted their resources—taxes, forced loans, bonds—every means had been used. The Church had generously given of its temporal possessions; now at last it surrendered worked silver, jewels, and other precious objects from the churches themselves. In August the government requested and ecclesiastical authorities agreed to raise $300,000 to cover expenses for a fortnight. By the end of the month, reportedly, the silver had yielded only $53,000, and in September the churches in the Puebla area provided $10,000 worth of worked silver.[47]

Even late in the war an occasional hardy speculator risked punishment by the liberals, whose victory was by then quite certain, and concluded advantageous agreements with the conservatives. The contract concluded by Pío Bermejillo, a Spaniard, in September 1860, is revealing. For one-half million pesos worth of ecclesiastical property deeds, Pío Bermejillo gave $100,000 cash, $50,000 in Peza bonds, and twenty-five carts valued at $2,000 each. Peza bonds issued by the conservatives in 1858 had quickly depreciated to 5, 4, 1½, and even ½ percent of their face value. The carts at auction brought only $700 each, half in cash and half in clothing.[48]

Perhaps this agreement represents an extreme because of its late

Mexico City, to McLane in Veracruz, 1 May 1859, *Despatches from Ministers,* roll 24, vol. 23; and 5 September 1859, Díaz López, 2:107.

47. Miguel Galindo y Galindo, *La gran década nacional, o relación histórica de la guerra de reforma, intervención extranjera y gobierno del Archiduque Maximiliano, 1857–1867* (Mexico: Imprenta y Fototipia de la Secretaría de Fomento, 1904–1906), 1:306–7; A. de la Londe to French Minister of Foreign Affairs, 28 August 1860, Díaz, 2:185; and Augusto Rendón to Amado Julián (Jacdet) from Mexico City, 28 August 1860, and Enrique A. Melleville to Ortega from Mexico City, September 1860, in Ortega Correspondencia, vol. 2.

48. Luciana A. de Baz de Degollado from Mexico City, 30 September 1860, in Ortega Correspondencia, vol. 2. Another report stated that Bermejillo offered $25,000 in cash, $85,000 worth of carts with mules, $150,000 in Peza bonds, and $40,000 for freight and back debts. Augusto Rendón to Benito Quijano, 23 September 1860, in Ortega Correspondencia, vol. 2. See also 16 July 1858, *Correspondencia de Juárez y Montluc, antiguo cónsul general de México,* trans. Alberto G. Bianchi (Mexico: A. Pola, 1905), p. 33. These and other specifics dealing with problems of nationalization may be found in Robert J. Knowlton, "Some Practical Effects of Clerical Opposition to the Mexican Reform, 1856–1860," *Hispanic American Historical Review* 45 (May 1965): 246–56.

date. Nevertheless, the transaction is characteristic of the way speculators built fortunes from the war, taking advantage of the desperate government and even greater advantage of the Church. The government, with its forced loans and threatened imprisonment for failure to lend money, and the Church, hurling excommunication at the liberals, scarcely merited much sympathy for the treatment received at the hands of speculators. The latter, too, had to measure the risk involved, and they were cautious in the terms they accepted.

Whether speculating in ecclesiastical property with the conservative government or the liberal, those men advanced their personal interests if not the interests of the causes they supported. Years later, the small coterie of influential advisers surrounding dictator-President Porfirio Díaz—the *científicos*—counted among its group men whose fortunes derived from Church property acquired at bargain prices. Of the largest capitalists at the beginning of the Porfirian regime, a number either built their fortunes through speculation in clerical real estate or at least were prominent in property transactions during the Reform.[49]

Whatever the frantic last-minute expedients, time had run out. The clerical-conservative cause was lost, or at least a round in the struggle had been lost. In late December 1860 General Jesús González Ortega entered Mexico City at the head of a liberal army. The civil war ended, but the problems involving former ecclesiastical property did not.

49. Wilfrid Hardy Callcott, *Liberalism in Mexico, 1857–1929* (Stanford, Calif.: Stanford University Press, 1931), p. 142; and José C. Valadés, *El porfirismo, historia de un régimen*, vol. 1, *El nacimiento, 1876–1884* (Mexico: Antigua Librería Robredo de José Porrúa e Hijos, 1941), p. 71.

Of the capitalists listed: Antonio Mier y Celis, Faustino Goribar, Felipe Iturbe, Nicanor Béistegui, Pedro del Valle, Juan Bringas, Pío Bermejillo, José de Teresa, Isidoro de la Torre, Francisco and Miguel Bush, Manuel Escandón, José I. Limantour, Sebastián Camacho, Ramón Guzmán, and Carlos Heghembeck, Valadés cites only the Heghembeck and Limantour fortunes as having been built through speculation in ecclesiastical real estate. However, other names on the list were prominent in dealings during the Reform period, e.g., Béistegui, Bringas, Escandón, and Bermejillo.

Chapter 4
Interlude: Nationalization between Wars, 1861–1863

Among the noise of the bells ringing at the time of the angelus and of the frenzy of the people, I entered this great city which, adorned—full of arches, drapings, flowers, and very gay streamers— was crowning González Ortega and the troops he commanded whose number reached, in my judgment, about 25,000 men. The noise of the carts, transformed into a hymn of the masses, formulated the rejoicing, and order and concord embellished a day that outdid in greatness the reception of the trigarantine army.[1]

When the constitutionalist army entered Mexico City on 27 December 1860, the joycul citizenry greeted it with garland-adorned streets and houses—a heroes' welcome for the victors. President Juárez entered the city on 11 January, another occasion for great rejoicing. The scenes were perhaps reminiscent of that other January three years earlier when flower-bedecked houses greeted conservative eyes. There was at least one notable difference in 1861, however: the clergy did not welcome this occasion as representing a new hope for Mexico; thanks for Divine intervention were not heard; the Cathedral did not reverberate with a *Te Deum* as in 1858.[2]

If the new French Minister, Alphonse Dubois de Saligny, was right in saying that "The whole country, tired of the civil war, especially having a thirst for order and tranquility, was resolved to recognize and sustain the new government,"[3] the respite and the harmony were short-lived. The liberal government faced a colossal task and, as it turned out, insuperable problems. It was necessary to reorganize ad-

1. Guillermo Prieto to Doblado, 2 January 1861, in Castañeda, p. 269.
2. W. F. Cloud, *Church and State or Mexican Politics from Cortez to Díaz* (Kansas City, Mo., 1896), p. 165.
3. Saligny to French Minister of Foreign Affairs, 28 January 1861, Díaz López, 2:207.

ministration, justice, and the army. Confidence and order had to be restored; the Reform laws must be fully implemented. Resources had to be found for a multitude of tasks. Here were the great obstacles to stability and progress: chaotic finances and an empty treasury. There were no funds to meet military and administrative expenses: the majority of public income was committed. No possibility existed for foreign or domestic loans on acceptable terms.[4]

The indomitable Juárez faced the mountain of problems with firmness and decision. The Reform laws were officially published in the capital. The Congress granted the President full authority to act and authorized him to raise $1,000,000 at once. Rating high priority were punishing notable opponents of the regime, ending irregular property transactions, restraining governors and military leaders, and dealing with the issue of property returned to the Church.

Several measures and decisions served these ends in the space of a few weeks. One expelled leading opponents including the Spanish Ambassador and high-ranking churchmen.[5] Another, repeating wartime edicts, annulled all contracts, appointments, and concessions made by the conservatives. On the same day, 3 January, reasserting its claim that the Church was responsible for the Three Years' War, the government levied a fine upon the Church of one-third of the tithes and one-fifth of parish emoluments. Parishes that had not damaged the liberal cause were exempt from this burden, however. A further financial expedient, particularly related to nationalization, restricted the powers of state finance offices. The restraints included temporary suspension of wartime payments authorized by military commanders and a prohibition against disposal of promissory notes (*pagarés*), acceptance of credits, and interpretation of the law. The government sought at the same time to obtain information on the status of nationalization in regard to such matters as redemptions, adjudications, and pending operations.[6]

4. García Solorzano, p. 73; and Galindo y Galindo, 2:19–20.
5. These included the Archbishop, Lázaro de la Garza y Ballesteros; the Bishop of Tenagra, Joaquín Madrid; the Bishop of Michoacán, Clemente de Jesús Munguía; the Bishop of San Luis Potosí, Pedro Barajas; and the Bishop of Guadalajara, Pedro Espinosa. Order of 17 January 1861, Bassols, pp. 156–57.
6. "Daños y perjuicios ocasionados por la guerra," 3 January 1861, *Leyes de*

In accord with general liberal goals, early in February 1861 the government secularized all hospitals and charities administered by ecclesiastical corporations. This was the sole change intended; secular authorities, eventually the municipalities, replaced clerical direction of the institutions. Existing property and income remained as before; mortgagors even needed special approval to liquidate their debts.[7]

Not the least of the President's problems was the multitude of property transactions that governors concluded during the war, many highly irregular if not illegal. The approval of these dealings apparently resulted from Minister of War González Ortega's energetic defense of the idea to the other ministers. History repeated itself nearly four years later when President Juárez confirmed, for a fee, extralegal alienations of nationalized property in the state of Chihuahua. In the midst of a desperate struggle against the French-supported empire of Maximilian, Juárez perhaps yielded to state pressure, or hoped to gain some support or resources, or simply accepted a *fait accompli*.[8]

While it is not possible to identify the most important task facing the reestablished liberal government, the handling of nationalized clerical property must rank as a major one. The worst possible conditions accompanied promulgation of the relevant measures, and uniform rules had to be established for adjudications, purchases, denunciations, and redemptions. Property transactions during the war lacked uniformity; many were irregular or illegal. The cavalier disposal of ecclesiastical wealth by military commanders and governors was treated in the most expeditious and politic way by simply approving the actions. However, a mass of property transfers occurred in conservative-held territory. The liberal government dealt with these illegal transactions by accepting denunciations and concluding contracts for that property. The disamortization law, the nationalization law, even the Constitution caused disputes among adjudicators, tenants, and denouncers over preference of rights and ownership titles.

Reforma, pp. 126–28; Bassols, pp. 150–51; and 31 January 1861, Ortega Correspondencia, vol. 4.

7. "Secularización de hospitales y establecimientos de beneficencia," *Leyes de Reforma*, pp. 227–28; and Labastida, pp. 361, 371.

8. E. Huerta to Ortega, 15 February 1861, Ortega Correspondencia, vol. 4; and decree of 12 November 1864, Labastida, pp. 485–86.

Disputes, in turn, led to many administrative and judicial actions and resolutions.[9]

It is difficult to imagine greater confusion. Disputes arose at once. The civil war and the official publication of the law caused controversies over rents and problems for tenants. During the war, individuals residing in liberal areas bought properties located in the conservative-held Federal District, but they obviously could not take possession or receive title. After the liberal victory these purchasers tried to collect rent from tenants from the date of their transaction. The government considered these attempts unjustified and further maintained that, since these purchasers had not received titles nor redeemed mortgages, the government legally deserved the rents due since the official publication of the nationalization law in the capital on 28 December 1860. Fortified by this belief, the government issued decrees benefiting tenants pending the issue of general, standard rules. One such decree excused the January rent for tenants paying less than $25 a month and for those paying rent to hospitals and charitable establishments. Those whose rent exceeded $25 a month who came forward voluntarily needed to pay only two-thirds of their rent. More significant was the decree exempting all tenants of clerical property paying less than $25 a month from all rents due up to 31 December 1860.[10]

Mortgagors, too, experienced problems. The government set a time within which those who had property mortgaged to the Church, all of which was now nationalized, could make arrangements for the liquidation of the debt; "redemption of the capital or mortgage" was the term used. After expiration of the time limit, the property could be denounced by anyone willing to make the mortgage redemption. The short time allowed following the official publication of the law, coupled with the shortage of government officials to handle operations, caused hardships. The organization of the Special Office to handle property transactions followed by many days the publication of the law. Worse yet, there was only one office for the Federal Dis-

9. Payno, *Leyes*, 2:123. See Bazant, *Alienation*, pp. 176–255, for government efforts in the 1860–1863 period to regularize and conclude the nationalization process in the capital and selected states.

10. 16 January 1861, *El Archivo Mexicano. Colección de leyes, decretos, circulares y otros documentos* (Mexico, 1856–1862), 5:57–58, 112.

trict, and it lacked sufficient, as well as expert, personnel to expedite operations and resolve difficulties. Francisco Mejía himself, the head of the Special Office, did not have the extensive knowledge necessary to handle the complex juridical, fiscal, and economic questions. Even if he had, he could not possibly have handled those matters and still have had time for the pure mechanics of the office. Such at least were the complaints.[11]

Not only did difficulties arise from bureaucratic organization and time limits; there was confusion over the procedure to follow in redemptions. Circulars issued in Veracruz had altered some provisions of the 13 July law on nationalization; these included articles on hereditary chaplaincies, property of nunneries, and the time allotted for the payment of bonds and specie to the treasury. Not all of these circulars had been published in newspapers, nor was newspaper publication considered official. Thus, some people believed they had no obligation to comply with the laws until official publication. Others thought an obligation did exist. This confusion and uncertainty created obstacles to the fulfillment of nationalization, raising questions and lawsuits which could ruin those the laws intended to favor, the legitimate possessors of the property.

Of far greater importance than these "irritants" was a broad range of property transactions that took place during the civil war under both the conservative and liberal regimes. There were several aspects to this question.[12] A great many people returned property acquired under the Lerdo law to the ecclesiastical corporations. Some did so for reasons of conscience even before the conservatives annulled the law. Others acted only as "dummy" purchasers or with the intention of returning property when conditions permitted. Still others, however, did so only after the conservatives decreed on 28 January 1858 the return of the property and threatened those who did not comply with fines or imprisonment. Some, despite threats and laws, refused to restore the property to the Church.

Considering the diverse circumstances, it would have been unjust for the victorious liberals to treat all cases in the same way; distinctions had to be made. The "degree of willingness" in returning property

11. Article by Sabino Flores in *Siglo*, 20 January 1861.

12. Unless otherwise noted, the following is based on articles by Sabino Flores in *Siglo*, 24, 27, 29 January and 6 February 1861.

provided the logical basis for distinctions. Notations made on the deeds (*escrituras*) at the time of transfer facilitated the determination of "willingness." Obviously, those individuals who maintained possession either because they were fortunate enough to be in liberal territory or because they refused to comply with conservative orders should continue in secure ownership. Those who returned the titles without a notation that they did so voluntarily or simply stating that they were submitting to the law of 28 January presumably acted "unwillingly," complied with force. Therefore, they should be considered the true owners and be restored to ownership. Those who indicated voluntary return of property to the Church, however, lost all rights to it. The liberals did in fact incorporate distinctions in the important law of 5 February 1861, but notations on the titles were not an infallible guide. The agents of the corporations, in order to insure the "voluntary" return of properties, refused to accept titles without a notation showing consent.

Speculators added another dimension to the tangled property question. Naturally, those who dealt in ecclesiastical property during the war wanted to minimize their risks. One way to do so was to buy property as cheaply as possible. Other possibilities existed as well. A major fear for purchasers of Church real estate was that the original adjudicators would later claim the property. Simply concluding a contract with a corporation was insufficient guarantee of secure ownership. The new purchasers, therefore, sought out the adjudicators who returned the property to the Church and had them cede their rights. Another danger for speculators was claims against them if original adjudicators tried to recover property from third parties to whom the speculator had sold. To avoid this danger, contracts stated explicitly that the seller was not liable for evictions or any guarantees. The opposite might happen, too, since buyers were equally interested in security. Transactions of Mariano P. Tagle are an example. Tagle, as noted in Chapter 3, was an officer of an *archicofradía*. Under the Lerdo law, he purchased several of the corporation's houses, probably through simulated contracts. When the conservatives took over, he sold some of them. In the sales contract Tagle agreed to the

> . . . eviction, security, and guarantee in such a way that always and forever the aforementioned properties will be safe and

secure for the buyer; nor will a third party who represents a
better right appear against them or anything that belongs to
them, nor will any suit, attachment or opposition be put against
them, or if a suit be occasioned, as soon as the grantor is
informed and summoned according to law, he will appear in
defense and follow and conclude it at his expense until the
buyer is left in quiet and peaceful possession; and if he is unable
to give security, he will return [to the buyer] the price, the
increase in value that the properties have acquired with time
[and expenses, injuries, interest, and damages].[13]

Another aspect of the problem of property transactions, implied
above, was that conventional sales by ecclesiastical corporations took
place under the protection of the conservative regime. There were a
multitude of sales either of real estate reacquired under the conservative laws of 1858 or of property not yet alienated under the Lerdo law
of 1856. The liberals automatically viewed all of these sales as illegal
because the Lerdo law and the Constitution of 1857 prohibited
ecclesiastical corporations from owning or administering real estate.
The fact that the property was voluntarily returned to a corporation
did not mean that it had the right to reacquire and then sell it. Legality was simple enough to determine in this area; practicality was quite
a different matter, and the two did not always coincide. Illegal or not,
these transactions were not always annulled.

One of the technical points facing liberal authorites involved denunciations of property voluntarily returned to the clergy in conservative areas. The liberal government sold this property to the denouncers. However, the nationalization laws did not take effect until
promulgated in each locality; therefore, the disamortization law remained in force in all parts of the country until the official publication
of the nationalization measures. Anyone voluntarily returning property to the clergy was thus subject to the stipulation in the 1856 law
that if adjudication had not taken place within three months, the

13. "Escritura de venta de una casa marcada con el no. 2 y sus acesorias
anexas, ubicada en la 1ª calle de Sta. Catarina Mártir; otorgada por el Sr. Dn.
Mariano Tagle a favor del Sr. Dn. José Gárnica; y reconocimiento que este
último otorgó por $12,000 a favor de la Archicofradía de la Preciosa Sangre
de Cristo, en los términos que dentro se espresan," AGN, Bienes nacionales,
leg. 1600, exp. 30.

tenant forfeited his rights to the subtenant or, lacking one, to a denouncer during a fifteen-day period. Failing all this, the property was to be auctioned. Under this provision the government could legally resell or auction those properties. The significance of this provision was that many people did not willingly return their properties to the Church and hence, in justice, should not have lost their rights to denouncers. As it turned out they did not, but the wartime policy complicated the entire property question when issues arose over preference of rights.

It might seem a reasonable conclusion that the motives prompting all property transactions during the war were the liberal or conservative laws or support of the war effort; this was not the case, however. There were also sales that would have been concluded even in the absence of the extraordinary conditions. One *cofradía*, for example, sought and received the Archbishop's permission to sell two of its houses to the tenants. The houses were old; the income from them, after maintenance, was insufficient to pay for the pious works supported by the income from them.[14]

The end of the civil war brought a clear and pressing need for legislation. A comprehensive law was necessary to bring together all valid decrees, orders, and directives, a measure that would, as Minister of Finance Guillermo Prieto explained, "resolve the diverse doubts and overcome the grave difficulties" that had appeared in carrying out the nationalization of ecclesiastical property. The Minister of Foreign Relations, Francisco Zarco, agreed that:

> It is necessary to harmonize the laws of reform and their
> explanatory circulars on the point of disamortization of
> mortmain property, to reconcile their observance for legitimate
> interests, to obtain resources for the treasury, and to avoid all
> kind of abuses. The work of the reform, besides its social
> importance, to be useful and beneficial must be a work of
> strict justice and high morality.[15]

14. "D. Rafael Meana, Síndico de la mesa del Sr. de la Sta. Veracruz en Toluca, sobre que se le permita vender las fincas que le pertenecen," AGN, Bienes nacionales, leg. 418, exp. 27.

15. Circular of Zarco to state governors, 20 January 1861, p. 11, enclosed in dispatch 2 of John B. Weller to J. S. Black, Secretary of State, 18 February

The law of 5 February 1861 was designed to meet these needs. In its sixteen sections, the law ranged from rights of adjudicators, tenants, and denouncers, to redemption of mortgages. It dealt with chaplaincies, educational and charitable property, and many other difficult problems.[16]

Part I established categories of legitimate adjudicators, making an effort to be fair and just to those who had returned property to the Church during the war. Willingness to return property was the general criterion used to validate or annul rights, but this criterion was suspended in the case of spinsters, widows, orphans, minors, and those who returned property on their deathbed.

Part II annulled, without exception, all sales made by the clergy without the express authorization of the liberal government. However, those who had bought Church property prior to the 1857 coup and later returned it could recover their original rights, as long as there was no injury to a third party, by payment of an additional 20 percent of the purchase price.

Part III regulated denunciations. The law broadly defined valid denunciations as those made in conformity with the Lerdo law and related circulars, those made to the federal government, or those revalidated by it. The government designated two periods for valid denunciations. In the first period, from the Lerdo law, 25 June 1856 to nationalization, 13 July 1859, a valid denunciation required a certificate of denunciation and receipt for the *alcabala*. In the second period, from 13 July 1859 to 5 February 1861, requirements included the certificate of denunciation and the record showing proper payment. Denouncers of property voluntarily returned to the clergy, excluding those who met the conditions designated in Part I of the law, were considered legal substitutes for the original purchasers. This section of the law provided, in addition, that disputes over preference of rights should be decided in the courts and that adjudicators who lost their rights could reacquire the property if it had not been denounced under the same terms as applied to denunciations.

Parts V, VI, and VII treated redemptions, stipulating the accept-

1861, in *Despatches from Ministers*, roll 28, vol. 27; and Circular dated 21 February 1861, from the Minister of Finance to the governors accompanying the law of 5 February, in Payno, *Leyes*, 2:165.

16. Payno, *Leyes*, 2:127–63.

able amounts and conditions of payment of specie, bonds, and promissory notes and establishing monetary penalties, even loss of the property, for those who failed to conform to the provisions of the nationalization law.

Part VIII ordered the public auction of all real estate to which no adjudicator, bidder, conventional buyer, or denouncer had a right, including specifically the monastic buildings.

Part IX established rules and procedures for the disentailment of chaplaincies and the redemption of the capital supporting them. The terms varied; percentages due in cash and bonds and time limits depended on the type of chaplaincy.

Part X exempted capital of charitable and educational establishments from the redemption provisions of the nationalization laws. Public authorities would regulate all matters pertaining to the institutions' direction, administration, and funds.

Part XI ordered the redemption by debtors of all mortgages held by nunneries that were not set aside by the government for dowries and nunnery expenses. Upon the extinction of a nunnery, these mortgages, too, would be redeemed. Even as the 1859 nationalization law had required the return of the amount of their dowry to nuns who left the cloister, so too, under the new law, legal heirs received the settlement in case of a nun's death, and novices received what they had paid upon entering the nunnery.

Part XIV of the law approved definitively the completed contracts and transactions involving nationalized property that had been carried out by state governors and military chiefs during the war. It prohibited governors, however, from retaining more than 20 percent of the amount of any future transaction involving nationalized property, the percentage that the law already granted to the states.

Much of the lengthy and detailed law of 5 February simply repeated earlier decrees or orders. But in so doing, it sought standardization and regularization as well as the establishment of a sound and reasonable basis for future nationalization operations. The law attempted to set just but firm criteria and procedures. It intended, with some concession to political expediency, to regularize transactions that had taken place during the civil war. These intentions are especially evident in the articles dealing with adjudicators and denouncers and in the approval given to the many irregular, if not outright illegal, actions of governors and military men. The federal government quieted fears of possible annulment or revision, which at the very least would have aroused formidable protests. The law by no means answered all questions, and it certainly did not satisfy everyone, but it did represent an important and necessary step toward normalizing the nationalization process.

Although this law presumably answered most questions, resolved areas of conflict, and assured smooth operations, criticism appeared at once. The criticism, of specific points as well as the entire law, came from various quarters—liberals, foreigners, speculators. Less than a week after its promulgation, Manuel María de Zamacona denounced the measure in an editorial in the important liberal paper *El Siglo Diez y Nueve*. The substance of Zamacona's condemnation was that the 5 February law flouted the essence of disamortization and nationalization. Financial considerations replaced social and economic goals. The original acts had emphasized the division of property and its wide distribution among the poor. Now, however, the government established short time limits for mortgage redemptions and severe penalties for overdue monthly payments on the mortgages. These provisions hurt the poor and benefited wealthy speculators.[17] The *Club Reformista* similarly protested the injustice of the law. Reflecting the militancy of the Club and the meager means of most members, the petition asked that all who had cooperated with the conservatives or returned property without protest should forfeit all rights to clerical property and that those possessing the property be forbidden to increase rents for three years. This petition reflected a common complaint that legislation tried to meet, without complete success.[18]

Foreign nationals who trafficked in ecclesiastical property believed the law injured them. The protest of those important interests was swift and portended possible international complications should their governments support them. Nearly five years earlier, following the law of disamortization, foreign nationals had sought assurances of their governments' support of their acquisition of clerical property. Then, as later, foreign residents tended to consider themselves juridi-

---

17. *Siglo*, 11 February 1861; Manuel Rivera Cambas, *Historia de la intervención europea y norte-americana en México y del imperio de Maximiliano de Hapsburgo* (Mexico, 1888–1895), 1:395; and Prieto, p. 411.

18. *Siglo*, 11 February 1861; and Payno, *Leyes*, 2:185–86.

cally as Mexicans only when it was to their advantage. If laws or political upheavals operated to their disadvantage or harmed their interests, then they believed they were immune and deserved special consideration. Their governments were likely to share these views. These protests represented a potentially dangerous situation for the Juárez government, despite a law of February 1856 that subjected foreign nationals who acquired immovable property to Mexican law and courts.[19]

Except for the common theme of injustice, the basis of the foreigners' complaint differed from that of the domestic opposition. There did seem to be a correlation with wealth, however. Foreigners and the wealthy founded their complaints on constitutional guarantees of property ownership and prohibition of retroactive laws. They argued that, prior to disamortization in 1856, clerical corporations were acknowledged as legal proprietors and that purchases under the succeeding conservative regime were legally concluded. To void these transactions constituted confiscation of property and abrogation of constitutional guarantees. The 5 February law did exactly that by annulling all sales by the clergy lacking the express authorization of "constitutional" authorities and by asserting that ecclesiastical property had always belonged to the nation.[20]

Variations on the same theme reflected the multiple possibilities and the complexity of the issue. Some reasoned that since retroactive laws were illegal and since no law was valid until officially published in a locality and since the nationalization law was not published in Mexico City until 28 December 1860, all sales of clerical property prior to that date were valid. Others claimed that when the same property was sold to different individuals—denounced by one in Veracruz and sold to another in Mexico City—then that fundamental law should apply, to wit, if there were several conveyances at the same time, the purchaser in possession of the property should keep it—in these cases, the purchaser in conservative-held Mexico City.[21]

19. See 1 and 10 July 1856, Díaz López, 1:304–8.

20. 18 February 1861, Payno, *Leyes*, 2:377–91. The group of protesters included Barron, Forbes & Co., Pío Bermejillo, Candido Guerra, I. B. Jecker & Co., N. Davidson, I. de la Torre, T. Horncastle, the widow Suárez Ibáñez, I. Bentley, Antonio Escandón, and L. Leuthner & Co.

21. *Exposición que ha presentado al Exmo. Señor Presidente de la República la comisión nombrada por la reunión de compradores de fincas del clero, que tuvo lugar en*

The Juárez government remained unimpressed by these arguments, refuting them with statements sometimes as specious as those
of the petitioners. For instance, the Minister of Finance denied that
the law of 5 February was retroactive. Ecclesiastical property had not
become national property on a specific date; it had always belonged to
the nation. Therefore, the government could not assume any obligations contracted by the clergy, and it owed no indemnity to purchasers
since any claims were properly against the clergy.[22] The Minister, with
his own semantics, cut through the semantics of those who had guessed
wrong in the war; they had contracted with the clergy and were
now vainly trying to defend their threatened interests. Nevertheless,
critics believed they were justified in asserting the illegality, or at least
the injustice, of a retroactive law and in proclaiming the inviolability
of private property. Moreover, confusion was understandable inasmuch as the government, in the 1856 Lerdo law, did acknowledge
clerical ownership of the real estate ordered disentailed. Then, in
nullifying all property transactions carried out by the clergy during
the civil war, the government maintained that it had owned clerical
property even before the 1859 nationalization law. This claim was
true in the sense that after implementation of disamortization in 1856
no property should legally have been in corporate hands to sell, and,
since the liberals won the war, contrary edicts of the conservatives
could be ignored or invalidated. Annulling wartime clerical sales was a
way to punish those who had sought to guarantee their acquisitions by
buying two titles—one from constitutional authorities and the other
from the clergy. What amounted to a fine of 20 percent of the unpaid
balance owed on property was sufficient to revalidate the purchase.

Nullification of all those sales helped to depress property values, an
unanticipated development perhaps. Unanticipated or not, the depreciation of real estate was one unfortunate result of nationalization
and of the unsettled conditions. The availability of large numbers of
properties on the market in itself kept prices depressed, but other

---

*el Teatro Principal, y acordó representar contra las disposiciones del decreto de 5 de
febrero de 1861*, signed 25 February 1861, by Eulalio María Ortega, Ignacio
Baz, and Vicente Gómez Parada, representing various other individuals
(Mexico, 1861). Also in Payno, *Leyes*, 2:393–445.

22. José M. Iglesias and Guillermo Prieto, *El Ministerio de Hacienda del 21 de
enero al 6 de abril de 1861* (Mexico, 1862), pp. 26–36.

factors operated, too. Proprietors feared denunciations, valid or not, that might dispossess them or oblige them to sustain lengthy and costly litigation. Maintenance and improvement of property were often disregarded; real estate could not easily be bought and sold at full value because of the insecurity of titles. Only in 1892, during the Díaz regime, was the insecurity ended.[23] In reality, the government faced a dilemma that prevented earlier action: if it closed the door on denunciations of occult property it stood to lose great sums of money and leave many people unjustly in possession of property; on the other hand, by not acting, it allowed insecurity and the depressed value of real estate to continue for years. In any case, at the time, property suddenly flooded the market; it could be bought with a 40 percent payment in specie and 60 percent in government bonds, which were available at a fraction of their face value. Speculation in both property and bonds resulted.

The liberal victory affected not only speculators but many others who dealt with the clergy or the conservative government. Foreign nationals who forcefully made their cases apparently included the humble as well as the mighty. The United States Minister, John B. Weller, spoke for the "many citizens" of the United States who:

> In some cases, . . . in good faith, invested nearly all their means in purchasing dwelling houses, in which they are now residing with their families. This decree [of 5 February] proposes to eject them without a hearing, without trial, unless they will now purchase from the Government and pay the consideration over again.[24]

Weller maintained that liberal abrogation of all transactions with the conservatives during the war was publicized in such a way that residents were ignorant of the decrees and that Americans had to deal with the conservatives or lose their houses. Mexican authorities, on the other hand, continued to insist on the justice of their position. The

23. Felix F. Palavicini et al., *México: Historia de su evolución constructiva* (Mexico: Talleres Tipográficos Modelo, S. A., 1945), 3:128.

24. Weller to Francisco Zarco, Minister of Foreign Relations, 13 February 1861, enclosure in dispatch 2 from Weller to Black, 18 February 1861, *Despatches from Ministers*, roll 28, vol. 27. See also Saligny to French Minister of Foreign Affairs, 8 March 1861, Díaz López, 2:216–17.

law contained no innovations; purchasers knew the risks they were running; legal action was available to those who believed legitimate rights were infringed.[25]

It is difficult to judge overall how effective diplomatic pressure was, but in specific instances it did yield results. Just as the Juárez government acknowledged various transactions that did not prejudice the rights of third parties by payment of a "fine," so, too, it concluded satisfactory arrangements, particulary with important banking firms. Concessions may have been made to avoid alienating sources of future loans or simply to terminate amicably the disputes arising from diplomatic pressure of governments on behalf of their citizens. At least the latter was the official reason given.[26] Whatever the explanation, the validation of these transactions took place while the government repeated decrees nullifying contracts concluded with the clergy.[27] The settlements in effect levied a fine on lenders to the conservatives while approving their acquisitions of clerical real estate. In this way, the treasury obtained some resources and avoided difficulties with foreign powers. Agreements with Barron, Forbes and Co. and with Nathaniel Davidson involved sizeable sums. Barron, Forbes had received clerical mortgages and real estate in exchange for two loans to the conservative government of $120,000 and $200,000. The Juárez government recognized these property acquisitions in return for $30,000 in cash and $20,000 in vouchers for the Laguna Seca convoy, sequestered by the liberals during the war. The Nathaniel Davidson agreement was similar. In exchange for clerical real estate and mortgages, Davidson had extended a $700,000 credit to the conservatives—$475,000 in specie and the remainder in bonds of the internal debt. He confirmed his acquisitions for $62,000 in cash, $10,000 in bonds, and $54,000 in mortgages, whose income was to be used to support nuns. Both these agreements meant, however, that

25. Francisco Zarco to Weller, 28 February 1861, enclosure in dispatch 3 from Weller to Seward, 18 March 1861, and Weller's reply to Zarco, 5 March 1861, *Despatches from Ministers*, roll 28, vol. 27; and José María Godoy to Riva Palacio, 13 September 1862, M. Riva Palacio Correspondencia.

26. Zarco to Weller, 2 April 1861, *re* G. W. Barnes case, enclosure in dispatch 5 from Weller to Seward, 5 May 1861, *Despatches from Ministers*, roll 28, vol. 27.

27. 24 May 1861, Labastida, p. 220; and 29 August 1861, Bassols, p. 169.

the government had to invalidate the acquisition of the same properties by other legal purchasers—adjudicators and denouncers—and indemnify them with other properties. The Barron, Forbes case involved twenty-five houses and mortgages worth nearly $48,000.[28]

Perhaps not all foreigners were so fortunate. The controversy involving the Spaniard, Pío Bermejillo, is interesting for the not uncommon complexities that could develop. During the war, Bermejillo obtained, among other things, an ecclesiastical mortgage for $64,000 covering three houses. After the war the mortgagor, Genaro Béistegui, denounced the mortgage and agreed to its redemption, but Bermejillo refused to relinquish the deed as ordered by the Ministry of Finance. The courts then instructed him to turn over the deed or present it for cancellation; again Bermejillo refused, insisting that he had legally acquired the property, and, besides, the deed was in the Spanish legation. Finally an embargo, or court restraint, was placed on an hacienda that Bermejillo claimed. The resolution of this dispute is uncertain.[29] Based on his dealings with the enemy, Bermejillo should have been punished. On the other hand, his foreign nationality may have saved him as it did others.

Not only does this case illustrate the activities of speculators and the difficulties they faced, it also foreshadowed an area of future serious conflict. As it continued, the case was appealed from a government ministry to the courts. That procedure led to jurisdictional disputes between administrative and judicial officials in questions concerning nationalized property. Such disputes seemed to obscure the merits of a case in a forest of legalities. The courts were, in any event, deeply involved in the controversies between individuals over ownership of nationalized properties, and the administration of justice suffered criticism for decisions rendered.

Allegedly, judges frequently ordered the dispossession of persons whose rights to properties were in order and who had properly redeemed mortgages. One judge, it was said, even granted possession of

28. López Gallo, pp. 206–7; and 27 March and 6 May 1861, Labastida, pp. 128–29, 225–26.

29. Ygnacio Reyes, *Rectificación de algunas especies vertidas en el cuaderno impreso de Don Joaquín Llaguno sobre el embargo de la hacienda de San Jacinto* (Mexico, 1862).

the same house successively to eight different individuals.[30] Such charges, whether accurate or not, illustrate the continuing state of confusion over preference of rights and the difficulty the courts faced in coping with the complex issue.

The halls of justice were not the only center of confusion and dubious dealings. Despite legal provisions to the contrary, the Ministry of Finance, in order to obtain funds, granted discounts on promissory notes and remitted interest due in exchange for cash redemptions of mortgages. Then, too, friends of officials received preferential treatment, and the government accepted bonds with ruinous allowances in exhange for enormous quantities in promissory notes. This last practice contributed to the monopolization of property. One person obtained over $100,000 worth of overdue promissory notes in return for bonds and a small amount of cash. He thus became, in effect, the owner of a large number of nationalized properties.[31]

The comments of the Chief of the Special Disamortization Office clearly illustrate several facets of the speculation in properties. Francisco Mejía was indignant over the sacrifice of property and the common shady transactions. The government allowed payment of cash and bonds to extend over a period ranging from 30 to 80 months with bonds commanding only 5 to 7 percent of their face value. Furthermore, many denouncers were foreigners, such as L. Bonhome, Davis, Loperena, and Morales Puente. Bonhome, a prominent example, denounced over 100 properties in 1859, valued at $505,800; the estate of La Tenería alone was worth $95,000. The liberals' extreme need for arms and money dictated acceptance of the denunciations in return for a pittance: the 5 percent transfer of property tax; 5,000 to 8,000 rifles valued at $12 each but costing Bonhome only $6 or $7 each; and $6,000 or $7,000 in cash. When the time came after the war to revalidate these transactions, Mejía used his official position to deprive the speculator of 12 or 15 of the houses on the basis that others had previously adjudicated them.

The sacrifice of nationalized wealth extended beyond wartime denunciations to the postwar disposal of promissory notes. These notes derived from agreements between the government and the possessors

30. *La Orquesta* (Mexico), 25 May 1861.
31. *Siglo*, 29 April 1861.

of nationalized property and supplied the means for the liquidation of part of their debt. The law of 13 July 1859 (Article XI) provided that mortgagors were to pay off their debt, 60 percent in bonds of the national debt and 40 percent in cash. The 40 percent was payable in 40 equal monthly installments secured by the promissory notes. As with denunciations, Mejía used his office at the auction block to mitigate the effects of government policy. In the spring of 1861, the Office of Disamortization held nearly $4,000,000 in promissory notes. Each month the Office collected the $180,000 or $200,000 worth of notes that matured and forwarded the sums to the treasury. Large numbers were not redeemed, however, leading the Minister of Finance to order the auction each week of $200,000 worth of these past-due notes. Mejía believed these auctions would only benefit speculators further and be disadvantageous to the treasury. Some people lacked confidence in the permanence of the property operations, while others hoped for the return of the conservatives; therefore, only speculators would bid at the auctions, agreeing among themselves in advance to acquire the notes for only a fraction of their value. The Minister believed the auctions should realize 50 or 60 percent, a sizeable proportion of the value. Events, by Mejía's own account, substantiated his fears. The expected speculators arrived to bid: Morales Puente, Lorenzo Ceballos, Bonhome, and one other. The law required bidders to present a commercial bond (*fianza legal de comercio*). The lack of these documents made it possible for Mejía to adjourn the auction. But the following week the same bidders reappeared with the proper papers. The first two series of promissory notes of $1,000 and $2,000 sold for 13 percent of their value. Mejía then persuaded a friend to join the bidding to boost the price, and the remainder of the notes sold for 50 or 60 percent of their value.[32]

In the circumstances, it was reasonable to expect bribery as a means of securing sympathetic treatment by government officials. In auctions the speculators' offer of a share of the spoils, up to 25 percent of the amount of the transaction, presumably did not sway Mejía. A counterpart of bribery, and an equally understandable and durable

32. Mejía, pp. 48–50, 53–55. Mejía's account throughout is highly favorable to himself, partly no doubt because he later came under heavy criticism for malfeasance as Minister of Finance. However, to show operations that occurred, it is probably reliable.

practice, was the use of influence. Prominent individuals, perhaps unfortunately isolated out in the states away from the center of power, solicited the aid of highly placed friends in Mexico City. The expectations were uniform—to acquire or redeem property on the best possible terms; this generally meant for 10 or 15 percent of the amount payable in cash, which was legally set at 40 percent; the cheaply obtainable bonds were of no concern.[33] The French Minister, Saligny, expressed a common view when he wrote that having decided to take the enormous wealth from the clergy, the government

> . . . thought much less of benefiting the country with it than in destroying, without hope of recovery, this immense fortune, and throwing it as a stipend to its party, above all to some of its personal friends. Thus, it had been calculated that there hardly remains to the treasury 15 percent, according to some, 20 percent according to others, of the value of the property confiscated from the clergy.[34]

The evidence clearly sustains the lenient terms for disposal of property and the irregularities involved; less susceptible of proof is the contention that the government deliberately pursued a policy to enrich "its personal friends."

The extreme conditions under which property transactions took place created a multitude of disputes that came before the courts dealing with preference of rights and the nullification of clerical contracts. Two specific cases reveal some of the complexities of the litigation.

In 1860 an ecclesiastical corporation sold to one Vicente D. a property that had been adjudicated originally under the law of disamortization and then returned to the corporation when the conservatives annulled the law. After the liberals triumphed and nullified such sales, Vicente D. restored the property to the original adjudicator as required. He then went to court to demand that the corporation

33. Trinidad García de la Cadena in Zacatecas to Ortega in Mexico City, 25 March 1861, Ortega Correspondencia, vol. 4. See also 21 September 1870, in Alberto María Carreño, *Archivo del General Porfirio Díaz, memorias y documentos* (Mexico: Editorial "Elede," S.A., 1947–1959), 9:29–31.

34. Saligny to French Minister of Foreign Affairs, 3 April 1861, Díaz López, 2:229.

manager reimburse him for the purchase price and improvements he had made. Since the adjudicator was the rightful owner under the disamortization law, Vicente D. charged that the manager had misrepresented the corporation as the owner and was, therefore, obligated to refund the purchase price.

The manager disclaimed responsibility; he was simply the agent for the corporation. Furthermore, he was unaware of the liberals' nullification decrees at the time of the sale, and these had no effect in Mexico City until published there. On the other hand, Vicente D. was aware at the time of the purchase that it was an illegal transaction under liberal laws; he was liable, therefore, for the consequences. Vicente D. insisted that both parties knew the transaction was illegal from the liberal point of view, and since the money had been paid to the manager, not to the corporation, the manager should return it. The court ruled that the relevant law and decrees had been sufficiently publicized so that those who purchased clerical property under the conservatives did so with the certain knowledge of the illegality of the transactions and the risks involved. Therefore, Vicente D. must return the property to the original adjudicator without reimbursement from the corporation or its manager.[35]

Many cases hinged on technical points such as the dates transactions took place, the fulfillment of contract terms, and legal procedures. Typical was the disputed ownership of a Mexico City house between the well-known liberal general Enrique Ampudia and Señora Manuela del Valle de Escobar. The General based his claim on his denunciation of the property in Veracruz, the government's acceptance of his redemption, and its issuance of the title deed. In rendering Ampudia a favorable judgment, the court found that his title preceded the redemption of Señora del Valle de Escobar in Mexico City and that she forfeited her rights by voluntarily returning the house to the Church, even though as a widow she qualified for special consideration under the 5 February law. On appeal, however, the Supreme Court reversed the lower court's decision, ruling that the lady had proceeded properly, while Ampudia had not proved his case. He failed to prove the voluntary return of the house to the Church, and he had not complied with the redemption requirements until long

35. *Gaceta de los tribunales*, 19 October 1861, 2:814–17.

after Señora del Valle had fulfilled her obligations. The Supreme Court, however, did allow Ampudia to claim from the government the amounts he had already paid.[36] These and similar cases provide insight into the operation of the law and the resolution of disputes arising from property transactions during the civil war.

Different criteria apparently determined the attitude of the judicial and executive branches of government toward disputes over property. The fundamental consideration of the courts, appropriately, was justice; the administration had to consider political implications. The judges were remarkable in their fairness and sense of justice. They displayed a lack of vindictiveness toward corporations and many individuals who had cooperated with the conservatives. The courts seemed little swayed in their decisions by the importance or influence of those involved. Officials in the executive branch, however, had to consider hard political realities. Practical facts of life dictated approval of dubious and illegal transactions of foreign lenders and speculators, military commanders, and governors. However, only a short-sighted and overly cynical critic, and there were those, could assert that the liberal government originally issued the laws on property and subsequently used the ecclesiastical wealth simply to enrich a few supporters.

Nevertheless, there was legitimate concern over the dissipation of the former clerical property and the illegality of some transactions. Congressional interest in these matters was one of several property-related problems that confronted the government. In the late spring of 1861, the Chamber of Deputies directed its attention to these issues with the intention of ending abuses and imposing legislative authority over nationalization matters.[37] The legislators' proposals, however, were of doubtful practicality, although they were theoretically sound.

Deputy Juan Suárez Navarro proposed the creation of a joint executive-legislative commission to review nationalization operations,

36. Ibid., 2 August 1862, 3:601–8. For another preference of rights case, see ibid., 30 August 1862, 3:681–86, in which the courts found against the company of the wealthy speculator, José I. Limantour.

37. Sessions of 30 May, 13, 18, 19, 20 June, and 9 July 1861, in Felipe Buenrostro, *Historia del primero y segundo congresos constitucionales de la República Mexicana* (Mexico, 1874–1882), vol. 1, pt. 2, pp. 83–84, 126, 141, 143–46, 179.

invalidating all those carried out contrary to the law. He further recommended making current procedures more stringent by fixing the
amount payable in cash at auctions, accepting promissory notes only
from reliable persons, and retaining direct government ownership of
real estate as long as the purchase price remained unpaid. In support
of his proposals, Suárez Navarro claimed that nationalized property
was sold for one-third of its value. In addition, payment for even the
reduced amount was such that the government, instead of obtaining
funds, made payments and indemnified purchasers. There was much
occult wealth, and there were many questionable transactions. There
were also the outlandish denunciation and adjudication procedures,
such as denunciations, during the war, of properties returned to the
Church out of fear and under duress. These properties were justifi-
ably restored to adjudicators following the liberal victory, but then the
government indemnified the denouncer, sizeable amounts being involved. Yet another practice was for purchasers, claiming that the
properties were in poor repair, to have successive appraisals made
until the price was far less than the property's legitimate worth—as
much as one-fifth of the true value. All such dealings represented the
nation's loss. Revision was mandatory in the interest of the treasury
and for the reputation of the liberal party, which was compromised by
the rapacity and cynicism of a few who turned to personal advantage
what should have benefited the entire nation. Inaction by the Congress opened deputies to charges of conspiring in the fraud, according to Suárez Navarro.

Critics of the proposed review commission questioned the practicality of reviewing all operations and the authority of Congress to consider specific cases in contrast to its acknowledged right to make general rules. Then there was the question of jurisdiction. The proposed
commission conceivably would infringe on areas of judicial and
executive responsibility. By altering contracts, revision also implied an
attack on the sanctity of property. Indeed, the legislature refused a
government request to limit proprietors' authority to raise rents as an
infringement on the rights of ownership. Supporters of the Suárez
Navarro proposal replied to the critics by pointing out that revision
was not a new policy, that it was already being done by executive
agencies, and that the commission would not be a tribunal; it would
make no decisions on conflicting interests nor infringe on the author-

ity of others. It would merely examine certain acts and submit recommendations to the Congress.

Although a narrow two votes (60 to 58) defeated the Suárez Navarro proposal, the deputies did take some action that reflected their dissatisfaction with the state of nationalization affairs and particularly their concern over the administration's permissiveness toward debtors. One measure required the Ministry of Finance to submit to the legislature all data relative to denunciations, substitutions, property appraisals, compensations, and extensions of time limits granted in nationalization operations. The legislature also denied the government's request to extend the time limit allowed for the payment of bonds in redemptions and to eliminate the extra charge of 50 percent for tardy payments. The deputies were apparently unwilling to make concessions to debtors at the expense of reducing the burden of the public debt. This concern with permissiveness toward debtors was an enduring one; it would reappear after the fall of the Empire in 1867. Greater stringency proved no more practical then, however, than it did on this earlier occasion.

A pamphlet written by Ysidoro Guerrero in 1865, at the time when Emperor Maximilian was considering revision, provides further information, presumably from a disinterested party, on the operation of the laws and on the abuses and irregularities that took place. This lengthy analysis explained the conditions that justified the need for the law of 5 February 1861 and the continuing problems after that law which warranted a general revision process.[38] In so doing, he reiterated and confirmed various of the comments and complaints from different individuals mentioned in preceding pages. In describing abuses, Guerrero juxtaposed those who benefited from the law with those who suffered loss. Among beneficiaries of the unsettled conditions were tenants and dummy purchasers. By promoting litigation, the "feigned grantees" frustrated the laws through legal entanglements, while tenants used civil strife and judges' attitudes to remain for years in houses without paying any rent. Others who acquired clerical property suffered from the great expense of litigation, high taxes, hatred felt for possessors of nationalized property, and the resistance encountered in even obtaining a hearing in the courts.

38. Ysidoro Guerrero, *Unas cuantas palabras a "La Era Nueva" sobre la cuestión de revisión de la ventas de bienes nacionalizados* (Mexico, 1865).

Guerrero, following in general the 5 February 1861 law, described in some detail the circumstances facing different types of purchasers of nationalized property. The emphasis of his commentary bolstered the need for revision.

Adjudicators constituted one group. The Lerdo law forced corporations to dispose of their real estate but allowed them to retain mortgages on the property, earning 6 percent annual interest. The ecclesiastical corporations, however, resisted the receipt of interest. Miguel Lerdo, the Minister of Finance, had foreseen this attitude and stipulated that refusal to accept interest payments freed the new owners of all future responsibility to the corporation; instead, the government would receive these payments and hold them for the corporations. The adjudicators, however, paid neither the clergy, who resisted payment, nor the government. As a result, for more than a year, until the successful conservative coup, adjudicators enjoyed the benefits of proprietorship without paying anything. On the other hand, some lawyers maintained after nationalization that the law excused interest payments in the redemption of mortgages. They persisted in this opinion despite a 27 July 1859 circular that clarified the matter of redemptions because of the impossibility of implementing the law due to the war and despite a January 1861 circular that provided that interest be incorporated into the part of the mortgage payable in cash.

Denouncers and buyers at auction formed a second category. The law of 5 February 1861 validated three types of denunciations. This validation was necessary because of the different laws—disamortization and nationalization—and related circulars and because of conditions imposed by the civil war. Nevertheless, confusion existed over what were valid denunciations. Lawyers, for example, confused wartime denunciations to federal authorities in Veracruz with denunciations under the Lerdo law. These attorneys tried to convince denouncers that their purchases were null for one reason or another, either because they had not made their denunciations before the federal government, had not paid the tax within the required time, had not purchased the property at auction, or had paid more in bonds and less in specie than specified. The confusion could only be resolved by closer study of existing laws.

According to Guerrero, demanding attention especially was the provision of the 5 February law that required property to be sold if three months passed without payment of the promissory notes. Many of these notes existed, paralyzing commerce and discrediting the government. The notes proved that many denouncers and debtors were not paying sums owed for nationalized property. Auctions provided another opportunity for abuses. Earlier legislation had stipulated the auction of properties unredeemed within thirty days, but the Veracruz government prohibited that procedure in order to prevent bidders from acquiring properties at two-thirds of their real value.

Another category of purchasers included clergy. Those who suffered in this group were poor priests living in isolated places who were victimized by the upper clergy. In 1859 when General Miramón planned to attack Veracruz, various firms supplied him with money. In return, a council composed of upper clergy gave these firms deeds to property that had endowed poor priests. The dealings with Nathaniel Davidson and Company were an example of such a case. As for the redemptions of the mortgages encumbering those properties, the prohibitions and threats of their superiors prevented the priests from acting. Other capital or mortgages utilized in these deals during the war passed into the hands of speculators, according to Guerrero. When the injured parties claimed restitution of the property involved in the deals, acquired by others contrary to the Reform laws, the speculators appealed to the Archbishop, accusing the claimants of quoting the hated laws; speculators also used all their influence in the courts to prolong legal proceedings to the detriment of the injured.

Another type of transaction was the use of nationalized property to indemnify foreigners for losses suffered in civil conflicts. Such claims were common since Independence. In this case, revision of the agreements involving nationalized property ought not be contemplated because of possible repercussions.

Finally, there was the group who purchased clerical property during the war and tried to maintain ownership by alleging the retroactivity of the 5 February law. Guerrero agreed with the Juárez government's interpretation that the 1856 Lerdo law made all purchases from the clergy during the war illegal. In addition, circulars on 9 October and 12 November 1856 and 10 February 1857 invalidated all such contracts. The 5 February 1861 law was, therefore, not retroactive in its effects, and revision of such contracts quite rightly could be insisted upon.

While the proponents of revision could readily enough support their case, their practical wisdom in urging such a move, perhaps even their actual motives, are open to question.[39] Ample evidence confirms the irregular transactions and the disposal of ecclesiastical property at a fraction of its value. A few individuals acquired large amounts of the property. Strict legality and a desire for justice, thus, justified the revisionists. However, the results of a comprehensive review and extensive revision were unforeseeable. That would be attempted during the Empire with unsatisfactory results. Then, too, any attempt to review and, on the basis of strict legality, to annul operations carried out during the civil war by military commanders and governors might well precipitate opposition that could be disastrous for a government making valiant efforts to cope with many problems and control the still unstable political situation in the country.

Negotiations with the United States to secure a loan added a further complication to the domestic nationalization scene. The United States had constantly and consistently sought by treaty to purchase Mexican territory, or to extend a loan guaranteed by Church property that would pass to the United States in case of default by the government of Mexico. United States ministers vigorously pursued this project with the government of Comonfort before the Three Years' War, with the conservative government of Zuloaga and the liberal government of Juárez during the war, and with the Juárez government after the liberal triumph. Despite great need and tempting offers, both the Comonfort and Zuloaga governments declined to sign a treaty. The Juárez government did conclude the Ocampo-McLane treaty during the war, but the United States Senate rejected it. Now in the postwar

39. The question of congressional revision at the time coincided with a rivalry between Congress and the executive which was fundamental to every issue. Thus, the motive for revision may have been as much a desire to place a rein on executive authority and to thwart the administration as it was a concern for legality. On the issue, see Frank A. Knapp, Jr., "Parliamentary Government and the Mexican Constitution of 1857: A Forgotten Phase of Mexican Political History," *Hispanic American Historical Review* 33 (February 1953): 65–87.

period, another treaty was signed on 6 April 1862. The intent of the Doblado-Corwin treaty was to advance money to Mexico or to pay interest on the foreign debt to forestall foreign intervention. Although intervention by European powers began in late 1861, the treaty was signed anyway. It provided for a loan of $11,000,000 secured by a lien on all public lands and nationalized property still available, such as promissory notes and mortgages held by the Mexican government. The United States Senate rejected this treaty as well. In fact, the conclusion of the treaty was of doubtful legality. The Senate, with the United States engulfed in civil war, passed a resolution on 25 February 1862 declaring it inadvisable to negotiate a treaty that would require the United States to assume any portion of the interest or principal of Mexico's debt. Thomas Corwin was aware of this resolution, but proceeded nevertheless.[40]

Prior to the treaty's rejection, the Mexican government suspended all alienations of property. The reason was that the anticipated loan from the United States was to be guaranteed by the nationalized property not yet redeemed, adjudicated, or earmarked for some specific purpose. The effect of this order was such that the government issued a clarification; the earlier order meant simply that income from nationalized property was not to be disposed of but should be set aside as a guarantee for the loan. The intention was not to suspend redemption operations.[41] These orders created some difficulty. Federal treasury officials in the states believed that the collection and retention of matured promissory notes could not be accomplished because the money would enter state treasuries and be spent for state needs, thereby prejudicing the United States treaty and compromising the government's credit. Consequently, promissory notes were not diligently collected. Aguascalientes resolved the problem when Ponciano Arriaga ordered the prompt collection of promissory notes and the maintenance of careful accounts. He then permitted the state government to dispose of the money for its urgent needs, with the

40. Corwin to Seward, 29 October and 29 November 1861, *Despatches from Ministers*, roll 29, vol. 28; 16 April and 5 May 1862, ibid., roll 30, vol. 29; and Rivera Cambas, *Historia de la intervención*, 1:660–61.

41. 2 May 1862, Gutiérrez and Alatorre, vol. 2, pt. 2, p. 623; and 21 May 1862, Dublán and Lozano, 9:457–58.

understanding that state revenues would be encumbered expressly for repayment.[42]

The government's policy toward the nunneries, to reduce their number and consolidate them, created an emotional issue which added further to the burdens of the administration. In the Federal District, implementation of the order took place during the night of 13 February 1861. The 542 nuns and 16 novices in 22 nunneries were reduced to 9 establishments. The remaining 13 were closed and the buildings sold. The funds obtained from the sales were divided, one-half to support educational and charitable institutions and the

42. Ponciano Arriaga in Aguascalientes to Terán, Minister of Justice, in Mexico City, 24 July 1862, and Arriaga to Terán, 31 July 1862. Terán Correspondencia, 1:99–100, 102.

"It is easier for a camel to go through the eye of a needle than for an adjudicator to go through revision."

Source: *La Orquesta*, 18 March 1865, opposite p. 2.

other one-half to establish a fund for pensions to widows and orphans. Unfortunate abuses apparently attended the execution of this
operation. The resettlement of the nuns in the middle of the night
was upsetting, and some of the commissioners in charge and their
friends plundered the convents, taking paintings, furniture, jewels,
even tiles from the towers. The flimsy excuse for this theft, that the
goods were "unowned" (*mostrenco*), was without foundation; the property belonged either to the nation or to the nunneries.[43]

Consolidation may have proven traumatic, but the sisters were not
yet at the end of their travail. Shortly before evacuating the capital
city before the French advance at the end of May 1863, the Juárez
administration took a final logical step in its Reform program by
suppressing the nunneries. The suppression of novitiates earlier had
assured the extinction of these institutions, and through nationalization, the government already had at its disposal most nunnery wealth.
Justification for suppression at this time was twofold: the incompatibility of nuns' vows with individual liberty and freedom of worship,
and the need to obtain all possible resources to fight the French.[44]
The law stipulated the division of the convent buildings and the sale at
auction of the individual pieces or units into which they were fractioned. Some of the buildings, however, were reserved intact for use
as hospitals and as lodgings for the indigent and the families of deceased heroes. Certain designated nunnery churches were allowed to
remain open for public worship. The government obligated itself to
return the amount of nuns' dowries and to provide for their subsequent maintenance. If possible, the former nuns were to return to
their parents' homes, but in no case could they reside with or remain
under the influence of clerics. The government actually tried to protect the ex-nuns from persons who might seek to deprive them of
their dowries. Local political authorities appointed commissions com-

43. Circular of 1 February 1861, Dublán and Lozano, 9:32, the 5 February
law incorporated this order; Labastida, pp. 184–87; and Rivera Cambas, *Los
gobernantes*, 2:610. For a description of the removal of the nuns of La Concepción, see Juan de Dios Peza, *Epopeyas de mi patria. Benito Juárez. La Reforma. La
intervención francesa. El imperio. El triunfo de la República* (Mexico: J. Ballescá y
Cía., Sucesores, 1904), pp. 33–37.

44. 26 February 1863, *Leyes de Reforma*, pp. 253–56. The Sisters of Charity
were exempt from the law since they were not considered as devoted to a
communal life, but rather consecrated to the service of suffering humanity.

posed of three women to frequent the residences of former nuns to insure that they were not abused and that they lacked no necessities.[45]

Inasmuch as voluntary excloistration had previously been authorized, it is impossible to say how many nuns welcomed their new freedom and willingly returned to or were welcomed in their former households. Doubtless some had been forced to enter nunneries to deprive them of their inheritances or to rid the family of an unmarriageable daughter. Still, many, perhaps most, were satisfied with the cloistered existence and returned to it when the opportunity presented itself during the French occupation. In fact, some continued for many years to evade the law and to live in religious communities. The Church opposed this law, as it had earlier ones, forbidding the nuns to return to their families, calling it a sin, and urging their continued communal life.[46]

Following the liberal victory in the civil war, President Juárez pursued a policy of moderation toward the defeated, hoping to heal the wounds and overcome the hatreds of war. Nevertheless, during the two and one-half years before the French interventionist army occupied the capital, he insisted on strict compliance with the laws. Extremists frustrated his intentions to some extent: clerico-conservative opposition on the one side; liberals intent on a harsher, more intractable policy toward the vanquished on the other side. The President's course became more difficult, too, when roving conservative guerrilla bands murdered liberal leaders Melchor Ocampo, Santos Degollado, and Leandro Valle. The clergy, for its part, continued to agitate and fulminate against the government, causing Juárez to decree in August and December 1862 the imprisonment or deportation of any priest arousing hatred of the laws or the government. The government prohibited, also, the wearing of clerical garb outside churches and suppressed all ecclesiastical governing boards, or *cabildos*, except that of Guadalajara. This exception thus recognized that *cabildo's* patriotic attitude as the only one that protested the French Intervention and urged opposition to the invader.[47]

45. Decree of 13 March 1863, Bassols, pp. 183–87.
46. *Siglo*, 4 March 1863, p. 4.
47. Laws of 30 August and 8 December 1862, Bassols, pp. 172, 177–78;

Despite these measures, Juárez insisted upon the strict maintenance of the laws and reproached authorities who, in their zeal to punish clerical abuses, interfered "unnecessarily" in religious matters. Officials flouted separation of Church and State by forbidding sacraments of baptism and marriage unless the individuals first presented a civil registry certificate. Some authorities even demanded that priests submit an estimate of their expenses and an accounting of their emoluments. The federal government forbade these intrusions into the spiritual realm and demanded strict compliance with the spirit of the laws.[48]

Extremist officials account for some abuse of the laws, but, unquestionably, the hostile attitude of some clergy prompted the interference against which the government reacted. The regulars caused trouble. Some nuns rejected government financial support and instead begged for alms, hoping to arouse popular sympathy. Monks and friars of the suppressed orders wandered about the countryside, fanning flames of discontent and trying to arouse the religious sentiments of the people. Priests raised difficulties over the administration of sacraments to those who complied with the civil registry laws. This was an important personal problem, but a negligible one officially. The interest of federal officials was in compliance with the law; if, because of the law, there were differences between a priest and a couple who desired a religious as well as a civil marriage ceremony, that was an issue between them—secular authorities ought not interfere. However, separation of Church and State notwithstanding, governmental officials would not allow clerical incitement against the laws nor permit the retraction of the oath to the Constitution to stand as a layman's price for receiving the sacraments.[49]

Prieto, p. 407; and 30 August 1862, Agustín Rivera y Sanromán, *Anales mexicanos: La Reforma y el segundo imperio,* 3d ed. (Guadalajara, 1897), p. 134.

48. Law of 15 August 1862, Bassols, p. 173. This law did not end the problem; as late as 20 December 1868, the government issued an order against such actions.

49. Wyke [C. Lennox Wyke] to Lord J. Russell, 27 May 1861, in *Correspondence Relative to the Present Condition of Mexico, communicated to the House of Representatives by the Department of State* (Washington, D.C., 1862), p. 249; Wyke was British Minister from 1862 to 1864. Cited hereafter as *Present Condition of Mexico, 1862.* Circular of the Minister of Government, 13 March

The most desperate of the problems was the financial one. The possession of Church wealth notwithstanding, the government acknowledged its bankruptcy. On 17 July 1861, it suspended payments on the foreign and domestic debt for a two-year period. This suspension provided the excuse for foreign intervention. The law created a Superior Treasury Board (*Junta Superior de Hacienda*) whose chief function was to liquidate the foreign and internal debt.[50] The Board was to administer and dispose of remaining nationalized property. Its authority encompassed all promissory notes held by the Special Office of Disamortization, the income from all pending redemptions, all unredeemed mortgages of nationalized property, and monastery buildings and land. The law empowered the Board to decide all questions pending on the laws of disamortization and nationalization, as long as the interested parties had agreed to accept the Board's decision, thereby renouncing recourse to the courts. Finally, the Board was to distribute the sums collected among the nation's creditors, which included the Laguna Seca convoy, nunneries, and the foreign conventions. The Board's extensive jurisdiction over nationalized property was limited only by special exceptions of the federal government, such as the states' rights to receive 20 percent of the income from nationalization operations.

The appointment of officials, the transfer of case files and other records, the problems of establishing and organizing a new governmental agency—all caused delay and confusion. Six weeks after the issuance of the law, the Board still was not fully organized.[51] The

---

1861, and 24 November 1862. Bassols, pp. 161, 176; and 31 October 1860, Ortega Correspondencia, vol. 3.

50. Payno, *Leyes*, 2:343–50. A decree of 13 April 1862, suppressed the Superior Treasury Board whose functions were taken over by the Ministry of Finance, a special section of which was to handle matters relative to disamortization and nationalization. Labastida, p. 303.

51. The Board consisted of a president (Mariano Riva Palacio), two principal advisers or "vocales" (Ezequiel Montes and Ignacio de Jáuregui), two substitutes, a secretariat, and three sections. These last were: an accounting section (collection and distribution); public credit section; and a disamortization section. The total budget for the Board was $56,340. Comunicaciones oficiales entre el Gobierno y la Junta suprema de Hacienda creada el 17 de Julio: proyectos de reglamento y presupuestos, 1861, Latin American Collection, University of Texas, Austin.

creation of the Superior Treasury Board aroused fears that its powers were too great and that it would encroach on the jurisdiction of the judiciary. Criticism was particularly strong of its authority to collect all credits arising from disamortization and nationalization and to decide all relevant cases as long as the parties agreed to this procedure in advance. The government, however, saw no alternative to cope with the financial disaster facing it.[52]

The announcement suspending payment on the debt, an admission of the prostrate financial condition of the country, came as a great surprise. Many observers supposed that the immense wealth of the Church would more than cover all commitments. A popular view alleged that Church wealth had been squandered, frittered away, often unnecessarily or deliberately, enriching a few individuals. In the opinion of the British Minister, Sir Charles Wyke:

> Animated by a blind hatred toward the church party, the present government has only thought of destroying and dissipating the immense property formerly belonging to the clergy, without, however, at the same time taking advantage of the wealth thus placed at their disposal to liquidate the many obligations which at present weigh them down and cripple their resources. . . . A considerable amount [of Church property] had, doubtless, been spent in repaying advances at exorbitant interest, made to the liberal party when they were fighting their way to power; but still enough ought to have remained after satisfying their creditors to have left them very well off. . . .[53]

United States Minister Thomas Corwin, the month prior to suspension, prophesied disappointment for those who hoped that Church wealth would suffice to pay off the public debt because that wealth had been virtually exhausted during the war.[54]

Careful analysts and observers could see that the property question was far more complex than Wyke acknowledged. Manuel María de Zamacona, Minister of Foreign Relations, replied to Wyke's criticisms:

52. See *Siglo,* 4 August 1861; and instructions from Manuel María de Zamacona to Juan Antonio de la Fuente, Mexican Minister to France, 29 July 1861, in *Present Condition of Mexico, 1862,* p. 59.

53. Wyke to Russell, 27 May 1861, *Present Condition of Mexico, 1862,* pp. 248–49.

54. Thomas Corwin to Seward, 29 June 1861, ibid., p. 13.

. . . I am sure that if the matter were reduced to figures, and the actual value of the Church property put on paper, with the positive depreciation that value has undergone owing to the civil war; and if, moreover, there be taken into consideration the sums paid from this source toward the extinction of the national debt, the discount at which the government has been compelled to transact their negotiation in order to realize this property and the surplus which still remains, I am sure, . . . that the charge of having squandered many millions will be found exaggerated.[55]

The previous British Minister, George Mathew, shed further light on the disposal of the property and tended to agree more with Zamacona than with his compatriot. Mathew explained that

. . . while forced contributions, plunder, and immense supplies from the Church and its supporters have enabled Generals Zuloaga and Miramón to sustain the civil war for three years, the Constitutional government abstained from such acts. . . . Their resources, during this lengthened period, were drawn from advances by individuals, on bonds for far larger sums, payable at the close of the war, and from the actual sale of a great part of this property at 25, 20, and even 15 percent of its supposed value.

The advantageous disposal of the remainder was most detrimentally affected by the circulation of reports calculated to prevent the restoration of confidence, and the consequent investment of money in the purchase of nationalized property; and the government have consequently been obliged by their necessities, after trying in vain every better mode of sale, to dispose of the property on "pagarés" (or promissory notes) to be paid off by instalments extending over several years.

These "pagarés," again, they are compelled to sell by auction, at a heavy discount, to provide for the daily subsistence of the troops, and the maintenance of the government.[56]

Estimates, allegations, and explanations of what happened could be multiplied, drawing on contemporaries and later writers.[57] Most state-

55. Zamacona to Wyke, 27 July 1861, ibid., p. 297.
56. Mathew to Russell, 12 May 1861, ibid., p. 247. Mathew was Minister from 1859 to 1862.
57. See, for example, Justo Sierra, *Juárez*, p. 241; and Pablo Macedo, *La*

ments, whatever the major emphasis, contain elements of truth. Ecclesiastical wealth sustained the war efforts of both liberals and conservatives; disposal of property took place at a fraction of its value. After the war, redemptions occurred on the easiest of terms. Speculation on a large scale took place. Unjust and illegal or barely legal transactions were common. But the terms "squandered" and "frittered away" are highly relative. Obtaining resources to fight the war was of paramount importance at the time. The liberals wished also to effect quickly a gigantic transfer of property to disarm the clergy and create interests favorable to the liberal cause in order to make the Reform irreversible. In this effort the reformers succeeded. How much wealth was disposed of in the above ways will never be known, but those actions go far toward explaining the disappearance of the wealth.

Moreover, ecclesiastical wealth tended to be exaggerated, and critics failed to consider its availability. These two factors account for the shocked surprise that greeted the government's admission that it could not meet its obligations. No one knew how much wealth the Church possessed. Contemporary estimates ranged from a low of $50,000,000 by a conservative clerical source to $600,000,000 by a French lawyer. Then and since, liberals and conservatives, revolutionaries and reactionaries, politicians, intellectuals, journalists, and scholars have offered estimates covering the entire range between the extremes. Calculations have been based on varying factors or components of clerical property; they have varied with care of analysis. At the time, part of the difficulty arose over uncertainty about what property precisely was available for nationalization that would yield income; part of the surprise derived from the outward splendor and luxury of churches and many clergymen. The actual wealth of the Church available for appropriation based on this writer's own research was probably between $100,000,000 and $150,000,000, but nearly everyone at the time, except the clergy, thought the wealth beyond calculation and at least sufficient to pay for a few wars and to amortize the public debt with millions to spare.[58] One astonished observer believed the fabulous wealth of the Church

evolución mercantil. Comunicaciones y obras públicas. La hacienda pública. Tres monografías que dan idea de una parte de la evolución económica de México (Mexico: J. Ballescá y Cía., Sucesores, Editores, 1905), pp. 420–21.

58. See Appendix 1.

had all entered the national coffers—more than $200,000,000 in real estate, jewels, and worked silver. In the six months since the reestablishment of the government in the capital, $30,000,000 in former clerical wealth had entered the treasury, and yet the treasury was empty.[59] There existed, then, an exaggerated opinion of the ecclesiastical patrimony and the amount of that wealth in 1861.

Furthermore, a simplistic view prevailed concerning the availability of the riches. The government earmarked large sums for specific purposes, thus making real estate and capital unavailable for ordinary transactions. Capital supporting educational and charitable establishments remained destined for those purposes. Repayment of nuns' dowries and their support absorbed some $4,000,000 worth of property.[60] Families of those who died defending the liberal cause received property. Still other real estate was utilized for public purposes, especially for hospitals, schools, and correctional houses.

A few examples reveal the diverse uses of the property. The family of General Miguel Contreras Medellín received a ranch in Colima and some houses in Guadalajara, worth $15,000. The General, political chief of Guadalajara and governor of Colima, died fighting the conservatives. The widow and children of Colonel José María Sánchez Román obtained $15,000 worth of former clerical property. The *ayuntamiento* of Tepeaca got the building of the Colecturía de Animas for a correctional house and trade school. The civil institute of Durango acquired the seminary with its buildings, capital, and library to aid public education. A house belonging to the Bishop of Guadalajara was ceded to the *ayuntamiento* of the village of San Pedro Analco, Jalisco, for use as a school and offices. Conversion of conventual buildings for similar purposes was common. Epitacio Huerta, for example, converted monasteries in Michoacán into a hospice, a hospital, and a trade school. The size and nature of these structures, in fact, made it difficult to dispose of them, and sensibly they were often converted to public uses of one kind or another.[61]

59. J. Lisson to General Ramón Castillo, 15 July 1861, in Ortega Correspondencia, vol. 5.

60. Rivera Cambas, *Los gobernantes*, 2:597.

61. Huerta to Ortega, 25 February 1861, Prieto to Chief of Finance in Jalisco, 30 March 1861, and Mariano Alvarez to Ortega, 22 November 1861, in Ortega Correspondencia, vols. 4 and 5; Resolution of 15 February 1861,

In the context of the amount of disposable property at the government's command, pending litigation, occult property, simulated sales, and the difficulty of collecting the sums owed for nationalized property must be noted. The extensive pending litigation posed a financial problem for the treasury, since litigants were not making redemption payments as long as their cases were in the courts. The government, whose rights to payment were clear and quite independent of the personal rights of disputants, therefore, invalidated all suspensions of monthly payments that had been granted for the period of litigation. As long as one of the parties in a preference of rights case held the property, he was obligated to make payments; failure to do so meant loss of redemption rights, even if the litigation ended in the possessor's favor. If the court judgment was adverse and the successful party wished to redeem the mortgage, he had to pay at once all that the former possessor had paid. Otherwise, he, too, lost his rights.[62] It appears, as mentioned earlier, that while the Church lost much wealth, it saved a large but undeterminable amount through simulated sales. Other property remained unknown to the government, hidden. Canons, bishops, and other clerical supporters sold properties, protecting themselves through trusted, "dummy" purchasers; the fear of nationalization led clergy to conclude many financially disadvantageous real estate contracts. Cash, titles, and mortgage deeds from the simulated sales were hidden. Allegedly, the wealthy Carmelites and Dominicans, when they vacated their monasteries, took with them large amounts of cash and many title deeds. Men who owed debts to the Church were not likely to volunteer that information to the government if they could avoid it.[63]

Gutiérrez and Alatorre, vol. 2, pt. 2, p. 364; Resolutions of 5 and 10 April 1861, Labastida, p. 393. For disposal of the religious buildings in the Federal District, see *Informe presentado al Congreso de la unión el 16 de setiembre de 1874, en cumplimiento del precepto constitucional por el C. Francisco Mejía, Secretario de Estado y del despacho de Hacienda y Crédito Público de los Estados-Unidos Mexicanos* (Mexico, 1874), pt. 2, document 27, pp. 273ff (cited hereafter as *Informe de Hacienda, 1873–1874*); Antonio García Cubas, *El libro de mis recuerdos* (Mexico: Imprenta de Arturo García Cubas, Sucesores, Hermanos, 1905), pp. 22ff.; and Manuel Romero de Terreros, *La iglesia y convento de San Agustín* (Mexico: Instituto de Investigaciones Estéticas, 1951), pp. 25–31.

62. 10 September 1861, *El Archivo Mexicano*, 6:562–63.

63. Hilarión Frías y Soto, *Juárez glorificado y la Intervención y el Imperio ante la*

The existence of occult property and the conclusion of simulated sales explain the continuing importance of denunciations of property. The inadvertent loss and destruction as well as the deliberate concealment of property titles and mortgage deeds also made it difficult to discover ecclesiastical real estate and constituted major reasons why nationalization operations dragged on, uncompleted, until the end of the century, with the result that titling remained insecure and property values depressed.

The government encountered another grave problem in the collection of sums due it from nationalized property. The number and nature of orders issued reveal the difficulty. The law of 5 February 1861 clearly specified rules for the payment of debts in bonds and promissory notes and established penalties for failure to fulfill these obligations. Many paid no attention, however, necessitating new orders and threats. On 25 March 1861 the government extended until 5 April the time limit for adjudicators to present themselves at the Ministry of Finance to acknowledge mortgages. On 5 May the government announced that the Special Office of Disamortization would sell mortgaged property unless mortgagors presented themselves to satisfy the promissory notes and bonds due. In December a circular ordered the Superior Treasury Board to secure compliance with the relevant articles of the law, failing which the property in question was to be sold. Five months later, holders of matured promissory notes were instructed to present them at the Ministry of Finance within one month or forfeit their rights and have the property disposed of by the government. The thirty-day extension granted for compliance the following month indicates the ineffectiveness of this threat.[64]

Further evidence of the government's relative lack of success in coercing debtors was its practice of selling overdue notes to others for collection. Purchasers of the notes then, as creditors, technically became owners of the property. At this point then, and for a long time to come, two significant and serious problems confronted the government: first, to discover all nationalized property and its location

---

verdad histórica, refutando con documentos la obra del señor Francisco Bulnes entitulada "El verdadero Juárez" (Mexico: Editora Nacional Edinal, S. de R.L., 1957), p. 163.

64. Payno, *Leyes*, 2:212, 229; and Circular of 16 December 1861, and 23 May 1862, Labastida, pp. 266, 267.

and to get the possessors, or debtors, to redeem it; second, to insure fulfillment of the conditions of sale, that is, prompt payment of the promissory notes and retirement of the bonds.

The suspension of debt payment on 17 July 1861 in any case signaled foreign intervention, which had been promoted for some time by diverse elements. Foreign observers considered the establishment of a monarchy under a foreign prince the only solution to Mexico's chronic instability and other problems that prevented the full realization of her great potential. In 1856 a Frenchman, A. de Radepont, submitted a report to that effect to French Imperial officials. In 1859 an anonymous pamphlet published in Paris urged foreign, preferably French, intervention as the only salvation for a Mexico that was in danger of losing more territory to the United States and that was rent by disunion and bloody war.[65]

Two years later, an English journalist justified the need for intervention and expressed the typically optimistic opinion of Mexico's wealth and potential. Domestic warfare, dishonesty, and misgovernment had not destroyed commerce or impaired the basic wealth of the country. European control would do wonders for the nation. The British Minister, George Mathew, more somberly judged that "without some foreign interposition, the dismemberment of the republic and a national bankruptcy appear all but inevitable."[66]

As early as the last Santa Anna administration (1853–1855), official agents sent to Europe sounded out governments on the possibility of establishing a foreign prince in Mexico. The efforts of these agents gained favor at the French court for various reasons, and the Juárez action of 17 July, coupled with United States' absorption in its own domestic affairs, provided favorable circumstances for the occupation of the country and the establishment of a monarchy. Britain and Spain agreed in the London Convention of October 1861 to join France in forcing collection of the debts. A joint expeditionary force was sent to Mexico, despite the fact that on 23 November 1861 Juárez rescinded the 17 July decree as it applied to payments on the foreign

65. September 1856, Díaz López, 1:337ff.; and *Algunas indicaciones acerca de la intervención europea en Méjico* (Paris, 1859).

66. *The Morning Post on the Affairs of Mexico*, 26 September 1861, p. 2, Latin American Collection, University of Texas, Austin; and Mathew to Russell, 12 May 1861, *Present Condition of Mexico, 1862*, p. 247.

debt. Britain and Spain withdrew from the country after France's true intentions became clear and after they had reached agreement with Mexico on the loan conventions. The Mexican Church in general favored and had been a moving force behind intervention. The Church was willing to compromise the country's independence, hoping to regain its property and influence under a foreign prince.[67]

The prospect of foreign intervention, like the earlier Reform legislation, divided Mexican society. In December 1861, when the three-power pact became known, the ecclesiastical *cabildo* of Guadalajara and several of the constitutional reform clergy urged the populace to defend the independence of Mexico. The states and the liberal press also rallied to the Juárez government. Liberals, shortly before divided by factionalism, closed ranks to face the threat from abroad. As he had during the war, the President nullified all acts and contracts of the French invader and successor regime.[68] Intervention provoked a spate of pamphlets supporting or denouncing the action. Opponents attacked the motives cited for intervention, such as debt collection and the establishment of order and stability in Mexico. They also denied the justice of the move, especially since Mexico was willing to negotiate on the debt. Defenders in contrast emphasized the chaos, insecurity, and factionalism in the country. Proponents of intervention labeled the liberals as traitors and a minority faction lacking general support. They denounced the Constitution and anticlericalism while hailing the French as saviors, necessary to restore order and prosperity.[69]

67. José María Gutiérrez de Estrada, Juan N. Almonte, and José Manuel Hidalgo were leading promoters of monarchy in Mexico; a prominent clerical promoter was Dr. Francisco J. Miranda. José Manuel Hidalgo, *Proyectos de monarquía en México* (Mexico: Editorial Jus, 1962), written in 1867; and García, vols. 1, 4, and 13, *Correspondencia secreta de los principales Intervencionistas Mexicanos, 1860–1862* (Mexico: Librería de la Vda. de Ch. Bouret, 1905–1907). See also Rivera y Sanromán, p. 100.

68. *Primer calendario de la guerra estranjera con los principales documentos relativos a ella para el año de 1863* (Arreglado al meridiano de México, 1862 [*sic*]), p. 32; and 13 December 1862, Labastida, p. 485.

69. 20 November 1862, José Ramón Pacheco, *Cuestión de Méjico, cartas de D. José Ramón Pacheco al Ministro de Negocios Extranjeros de Napoleón III, M. Drouyn de Lhuys* (Mérida, 1863); Manuel Payno, *Carta que sobre los asuntos de México dirige al señor Gen. Forey* (Mexico, 1862); *Observaciones y comentarios a la carta que*

The crisis of French intervention, as the civil war that preceded it, forced the government to utilize nationalized property. In Puebla General Jesús González Ortega used it to pay for arsenal supplies and fortification of the city, violating orders to use a 1 percent tax then in effect for those purposes. Far more damaging in its effects was the required redemption of mortgages, the income from which sustained schools and charities. The liberal government had made special provisions to benefit these important establishments, including tax exemptions and the designation of certain lands for schools. But the extraordinary demands to meet the invasion defeated the good intentions. Just two days after the much-heralded Mexican victory over the French at Puebla on 5 May 1862, the government ordered mortgagors owing $8,000 or more to public charities to redeem the mortgages immediately, paying one-fourth in cash and three-fourths in bonds or credits. Exactly two months later a similar decree required redemption of mortgages of over $4,000.[70] The schools were next. Actually the September 1862 measure, demanding the immediate redemption of mortgages owed them, included only schools that were not functioning either because they had been suppressed or because they had encountered difficulties in opening.[71] Nevertheless, these actions, necessitated by the war, damaged charities and education, a loss that the country could ill afford.

The demands of war also partially justified the suppression of the nunneries in February 1863, noted above. Nevertheless, the French, though delayed by the Mexican resistance at Puebla, could not be stopped, and late in May 1863, the liberal government evacuated the capital.

On 1 June 1863 the French entered Mexico City; President Juárez from the north led the ensuing four-year struggle for the independence of the country and Reform principles. With the French occupa-

---

D. Manuel Payno ha dirigido al señor Gen. Forey (Veracruz, 1863); E. Masseras, *El programa del imperio* (Mexico, 1864); and *Ligero bosquejo de la actual situación en Méjico. Artículo publicado por "El Veracruzano" en sus números correspondientes a los días 7 y 10 de octubre último* (Madrid, 1862).

70. Rivera Cambas, *Historia de la intervención*, 2:92; 8 August 1862, Comonfort Correspondencia; and Order of 7 May 1862, and Circular of 7 July 1862, Labastida, pp. 369–70.

71. 2 September 1862, Labastida, p. 394.

tion, Mexico City assumed a pre-Reform air. Clergy went about clothed in their vestments. Nuns returned to their cloisters. Churches, closed by the liberals, reopened. The Holy Eucharist was publicly carried in a procession on 4 June.[72] Old centralists, "Santanistas," the wealthy, and clerics staffed the administration. José María Gutiérrez de Estrada, one of the principal promoters of intervention, wrote:

> As far as the spirit that animates the French, the significant
> phrase in General Forey's proclamation to his troops should
> not be forgotten, "Honorer la religion et ses ministres." A
> world of hope opened for me upon reading these words. . . .[73]

The Church hierarchy welcomed the French as saviors. This attitude soon changed, however, when it became clear that neither the Emperor Napoleon III nor the Archduke Maximilian intended to abrogate the Reform legislation or to restore their property to them.

72. Zamacois, 16:513.
73. Gutiérrez de Estrada to Dr. Francisco J. Miranda, 30 October 1862. García, 4:206.

Chapter 5
The French and the Property Question, 1862–1864

Emperor Napoleon III on 3 July 1862 instructed General Elié Frèderic Forey, Commander-in-Chief of the French Army in Mexico, not to ally himself with any party while in the country. He should show great deference for religion, but at the same time give security to all those who had acquired nationalized property. [1] Nine months later, Napoleon again impressed upon Forey the necessity of giving guarantees, particularly to legitimate purchasers of nationalized property. Furthermore, although the provisional government ought to protect the Catholic faith, it should establish the principle of freedom of worship.[2]

After the occupation of the capital in June 1863, General Forey issued a manifesto in accord with these instructions. The French, he declared, were in Mexico to help establish a freely elected government marked by order, justice, and respect for religion, property, and family. Owners of national property acquired in conformity with the laws had nothing to fear, for only fraudulent sales would be revised. The new order would protect the Catholic faith and would restore the bishops to their dioceses, but Forey indicated that Napoleon would view with pleasure the proclamation of freedom of worship.[3]

This statement of French intent had a disquieting effect on supporters of the Intervention, who had hoped for the complete restoration of the Church's privileges and position. This public manifesto, however, was not the first indication that intervention would not fulfill the expectations of its Mexican promoters. Earlier, General Forey had unsuccessfully asked Dr. Francisco J. Miranda, a leading clerical pro-

1. Elié Frèderic Forey, "Correspondencia de Julio 3, 1862–Abril 23, 1864," Napoleon to Forey, 3 July 1862, in Intervención francesa. Miscelánea, 1867–1869, Latin American Collection, University of Texas, Austin.
2. Napoleon to Forey, 4 April 1863, ibid.
3. Elié Frèderic Forey, *Manifiesto a la nación mexicana* (Mexico, 12 June 1863).

ponent of intervention, to work for a union of parties in the country and to accept accomplished facts.[4]

One of the pressing tasks for the French upon occupation of Mexico City was the establishment of a provisional government. General Forey appointed a thirty-five man Superior Governing Board (*Junta Superior*) on 18 June. This body in turn chose three of its members plus two alternates as the Executive Power. Then the Board expanded its membership by choosing 213 citizens to form an Assembly of Notables. Ministries and ministers, a full-fledged bureaucracy, were appointed. This Assembly voted on 11 July to establish an imperial form of government and designated the Archduke Ferdinand Maximilian, brother of the Austrian Emperor, as the ruler. A committee proceeded to Europe to offer the Mexican crown to Maximilian. In the meantime, the provisional executive became a Regency of three eminent conservatives: Generals Juan N. Almonte and Mariano Salas and the Archbishop of Mexico, Pelagio Antonio Labastida. It was this Regency, or the clerical component, that initially obstructed French policy. In this transitional period, French authorities controlled military affairs and some foreign affairs. Otherwise, they restricted themselves to making recommendations to the Regency. That this was an unsatisfactory arrangement soon became evident.

For a time, the French intention notwithstanding, operations in nationalized property were paralyzed. On 10 July 1863 the Regency ordered suspension of remodeling work on the former convents because they were going to be returned to the nuns. More important, on 24 July the Regency directed that no action be taken by authorities with respect to ecclesiastical property pending a definitive settlement. Pursuant to this order the Minister of Justice suspended adjudications and payments of promissory notes; courts were not to hear any disputes concerning adjudications. The judges reportedly would resign en masse if Forey commanded the courts to hear cases dealing with nationalized property. Besides the interim government's action, the clergy compounded General Forey's problems by visiting occupants of former ecclesiastical property and making the tenants promise not to pay rent to the current proprietors. Clergy alleged that the sales

4. Francisco J. Miranda in Orizaba to R. Rafael, 12 May 1863, in García, 13:40.

were to be annulled and that tenants who did pay rent would have to do so twice because the Church was the only true proprietor. On the other hand, as early as 11 August a rumor circulated that a decree was being prepared to validate all nationalization transactions that had been effected in conformity with the laws.[5]

Archbishop Labastida, who did not assume his place on the Regency until 18 October, took advantage of tenants' resistance to paying rent and of the courts' refusal to hear cases dealing with rents and promissory notes. He convened the Regents on 20 October to protest the rumored ratification of the Reform laws. The Archbishop had already expressed his ideas on the correct way to handle the property question to the new commander of the French expeditionary force, General Achille François Bazaine, who replaced Forey in August 1863. The gist of the prelate's proposal was that the property be returned to the Church. Bazaine could not agree to this; his instructions, identical to those of his predecessor Forey, directed him to fulfill the nationalization law and to revise fraudulent acquisitions in favor of the State rather than the clergy.[6]

In this uncertain period, two significant documents shed light on the process and status of nationalization. One was a report to the Archduke Maximilian by one of the Mexican delegates sent to offer him the throne; the second was a dispatch by General Bazaine. Maximilian received the report on 6 October 1863 at Miramar, his palace on the Adriatic.[7] The purpose of the document was to obtain annulment of part or all of the property transactions under liberal

5. 10 and 24 July 1863, José Sebastián Segura, ed., *Boletín de las leyes del imperio mexicano, o sea código de la restauración. Colección completa de las leyes y demás disposiciones dictadas por la intervención francesa, por el supremo poder ejecutivo provisional, y por el imperio mexicano, con un apéndice de los documentos oficiales más notables y curiosos de la época* (Mexico, 1863–1865), 1:149; Francisco de Paula de Arrangoiz, *Méjico desde 1808 hasta 1867. Relación de los principales acontecimientos políticos que han tenido lugar desde la prisión del virrey Iturrigaray hasta la caída del segundo imperio* (Madrid, 1871–1872), 3:135; Manuel Siliceo in Mexico City to Comonfort, 2 and 11 August 1863, in Comonfort Correspondencia; and Pablo Gaulot, *Sueño de imperio*, trans. Enrique Martínez Sobral (Mexico: A. Pola, editor, 1905), pp. 196–97.

6. 26 October 1863, Díaz López, 3:284–85; and Arrangoiz, *Méjico*, 3:135, 137, 161.

7. Arrangoiz, *Méjico*, Appendix 4, 3:23–27; and Zamacois, 16:779–84.

laws. To achieve this goal, the writer used two techniques: he cited proof of the illegality of the operations and aroused sympathy for those injured by the laws.

The Miramar report contained an historical summary of the property question. It acknowledged that the clergy sold property during the civil war to pay taxes imposed by the conservative government, the legal government of Mexico. Juárez annulled those transactions without reimbursing purchasers and then resold the property. At the same time, he reimbursed foreign purchasers because their ambassadors complained. These injustices aside, the Miramar report insisted that most liberal sales during the war were illegal. Juárez, recognized only by the United States, was not legally president. Even had he been, only Congress could authorize such despoilment as took place. Furthermore, the sale of clerical wealth was scandalous: ridiculously low prices and up to eighty months to pay; secret agreements confirming sales; disregard of the law requiring that national property be appraised and publicly auctioned.

In a different vein, the Miramar report lamented the suffering of the poor because of damage to charities and schools. Ecclesiastical capital supporting these establishments had been taken and the buildings sold. It was unjust to respect those property sales which represented the interests of only two or three thousand people, most of them foreigners, while the interests of the great mass of the population suffered. At the very least, seminary buildings, episcopal palaces, parish houses, hospices, and schools should be restored to the clergy. Nuns were another deprived group. Their property belonged to them personally and consisted largely of dowries; it ought not be classified as Church property. In conclusion, the report advised the Archduke that purchasers of nationalized property, especially French and German, though convinced of the illegality of the sales, were working assiduously to have the French government approve the acts of the Juárez government.

The bias in the Miramar document is understandable, considering the sympathies and affiliations of the delegates to Maximilian. But from the liberal viewpoint it contained half-truths and falsehoods. Thus, under the 1857 Constitution, Juárez, as President of the Supreme Court, was the legal president of Mexico following the 1857 coup, even though most foreign powers recognized the conservative

government in Mexico City, the capital of the country. He did have
the authority to issue the Reform laws because Congress invested him
with extraordinary powers. It was true that the liberal government
annulled many conservative contracts and upheld some transactions
made by foreigners, but according to the liberals, Juárez was within
his legal rights to annul the former, and circumstances dictated the
latter. It was true that charities and schools suffered, but largely because the government needed funds to combat the Intervention. Despoilment of the nuns, at least financially, did not occur; their dowries
were to be returned. Finally, it was true that certain interests were
striving to have the Reform laws upheld, but others were working
with equal determination in the opposite direction, as shown by the
Archbishop's actions and this very report.

While the Miramar analysis concentrated on past events, General
Bazaine, in his dispatch, focused on the current situation. He noted
the uneasiness among the people and the uncertainty that shrouded
property dealings because proprietors could not sell for fear of
threatened revision. As a result, transactions in real estate were even
more static than when the clergy held the property in mortmain. The
French commander promised to improve the situation, and he soon
did act. Apparently, Maximilian and Napoleon agreed that a definitive decision on Church property should await the new ruler's arrival
in Mexico and an agreement with the Pope. In the meantime,
Bazaine's orders were to insure that promissory notes circulated and
that the courts accepted cases of refusal to pay rents.[8]

In late October and early November the breach widened between
the intervention authorities supported by Regents Almonte and Salas
and the Archbishop and his supporters. The *Periódico Oficial* noted on
23 October that courts were refraining from hearing cases involving
the refusal of debtors to pay their promissory notes and tenants of
former clerical properties their rents, contrary to the will of the Empire. On 7 November 1863 Bazaine instructed the Regents to direct
the courts to handle such cases. Two days later, without Labastida's
approval, the Regency complied.[9]

8. Gaulot, p. 204; and Francisco de Paula de Arrangoiz, *Apuntes para la
historia del segundo imperio mejicano* (Madrid, 1869), p. 151.
   9. 9 and 11 November 1863, Segura, 1:419–21.

Archbishop Labastida opposed this directive. He believed, and tried to convince the other Regents and General Bazaine, that questions dealing with promissory notes and rents ought to remain suspended until the arrival of Maximilian. The prelate termed the 9 November directive anti-Catholic, immoral, and scandalous, as well as antieconomic and impolitic. The order, whose intent was to approve Juarist acts, affronted the Pope and assigned to Napoleon a role diametrically opposed to his generous intentions, according to Labastida. It deprived Maximilian of resources and would multiply his difficulties. Conveying his sentiments to Teodosio Lares, President of the provisional Superior Governing Board, the Archbishop warned that such acts would dissuade the great majority of Mexicans from support of the Empire, while concessions would simply hearten dissidents. As a Regent, he disavowed his support of the 9 November order and directed Lares to consider it null.[10]

The 9 November order deepened the controversy between interventionist and Mexican governmental authorities. The various governmental sections or departments accepted the Archbishop's view. On 12 and 13 November, they uniformly refused to accept the Regents' directive. The officials justified their refusal on various technical grounds, for example, that the subsecretary of Justice, not the Regency, had issued the order.[11] Labastida's obstruction did not deter the real wielders of power, however, and his continued opposition led to his removal from the Regency on 17 November.[12] The Archbishop's protests to the French Minister of Foreign Affairs yielded no more than a polite reply; the Minister lamented that the prelate's conscience required him to protest Bazaine's actions and separate himself from affairs, but he approved the General's policies.[13]

10. Pelagio Antonio, Archbishop of Mexico, to the president of the Junta Superior de Gobierno, 10 November 1863, in Teodosio Lares, Correspondencia y otros documentos, 1833–1867, Latin American Collection, University of Texas, Austin.

11. J. Y. Pavón to Lares, 12 November 1863, and Antonio Fernández Monjardín to the president of Junta Superior de Gobierno, 12 November 1863, in Lares Correspondencia.

12. Díaz López, 3:295; and Labastida to Lares, 17 November 1863, in Lares Correspondencia.

13. 13 January 1864, Díaz López, 3:313–14. José Manuel Hidalgo, a leading interventionist, explained the division in the Regency on the property

The ecclesiastical hierarchy's patience ended with the issuance of a governmental directive on 15 December that served to confirm the despoilment of Church wealth. This order was apparently prompted by General Bazaine's intervention with governmental authorities on behalf of a French subject, Pascual Lavaig, who claimed that a Mexico City court refused to hear his suit to collect on a mortgage. As a result, the Secretary of Justice and Ecclesiastical Affairs in December amplified the 9 November directive, declaring that there were no obstacles to legal action with respect to clerical property.[14]

On 26 December leading prelates strenuously objected to the 15 December and earlier orders.[15] Their protest reflected their frustration and exasperation. Before, one enemy persecuted the Church; now there were two: the attacks from the liberal government continued, while a so-called friendly authority in Mexico City joined the old enemy in destroying the Church. The churchmen could no longer keep silent "now that the palliatives and reservations with which the first arrangements were clothed are cast aside. . . ." To do so would be inexcusable and would make them accomplices in those acts. They protested the 24 October (the reference was apparently to the 23 October notice in the *Periódico Oficial*), 9 November and 15 December orders. They condemned approval of the laws of nationalization. They decried the Regents' disregard of Church interests in cer-

---

question and the 9 November directive. For the sake of order and tranquility, Regents Almonte and Salas favored continued circulation of promissory notes. To do otherwise would overturn completed and accepted acts and cause disturbances by the many concerned foreigners and Mexicans. The Archbishop, on the other hand, believed the action consecrated the sale of Church property, something only the pope had the authority to do. Hidalgo, p. 138.

14. 21 December 1863, Segura, 1:474.

15. The Archbishops of Mexico, Michoacán, and Guadalajara and the Bishops of San Luis Potosí and Oaxaca signed the protest. Corwin to Seward, 27 January 1864, dispatch 51, enclosure B, *Despatches from Ministers*, roll 31, vol. 30; Protest of the Episcopate to the Regents, 26 December 1863, Documentos, 1850–1867, pp. 2–22; and *Protesta de los Obispos Católicos contra la intervención francesa* (Mexico, 26 December 1863). It may be that this circular (15 December) was not publicized until 21 December; if so, that helps account for the ten-day time lag between the date of the circular and the bishops' protest. Time needed to prepare the protest would also be a factor.

tain measures concerning charitable property and the refusal to restore the nuns to the parts of their nunneries not yet sold.

The bishops' disappointment at the turn of events is understandable. Napoleon's orders lacked consistency, or at least his private instructions differed from the public pronouncements. Privately, he vowed never to permit a blind reaction in Mexico.[16] Public manifestos, on the other hand, though urging religious freedom, spoke of the will of the people and implied abrogation of fraudulent acquisitions of nationalized property. The Regency went beyond this partial endorsement of nationalization in apparently confirming all transactions. The bishops found it difficult to conceive of a government established in opposition to the Juárez government implementing the laws that were the essential and only cause of the division of Mexicans and of the civil war. The prelates urged the revocation of the objectionable orders, a suspension of the proceedings in property matters, and the search for a canonical and civil solution that would harmonize legitimate interests and conscience. They warned that if the offensive orders were not withdrawn, the earlier penalties established for the disamortization and nationalization laws remained in effect. Thus, anyone participating in any way in the despoilment of the Church faced excommunication and would therefore be denied absolution, even at the point of death, unless the requirements established by the Church were met.

The Supreme Court quickly aligned itself with the prelates and the bureaucracy against the Regents. On 30 December the Court denied the Regents' competence to issue such decrees because laws were to be prepared by the Superior Governing Board, not the Regency. In a lengthy exposition, applauded by the bishops and several other judges, the Court agreed completely with the prelates' 26 December protest.[17] The judges grounded their position on more than three centuries of law and tradition. From the Conquest to the 1857 Con-

16. Napoleon to Almonte, 16 December 1863, in Galindo y Galindo, 2:665.
17. [30] and 31 December 1863, and 7 January 1864, in Lares Correspondencia; "Oficio dirigido por el Supremo Tribunal a la Regencia del Imperio, en que se opuso al cumplimiento de las circulares de 9 de noviembre y 15 de diciembre de 1863, relativos a la enagenación de los bienes del clero," in García, 13:193–203; and "MS en poder de Sr. Lic. D. Mariano Lara," Intervención francesa, 1862–1867, pp. 8–18.

stitution, canon law and national constitutions consistently guaranteed the Church's right to property. The Reform laws were an aberra-
tion issued by a government in name only. The laws were unjust and
based on force and therefore invalid. In the event that appeal to
ancient laws and traditions was insufficient, the judges placed themselves on the side of right and justice, defending the masses against
the interests of a few speculators. With emotion the jurists described
how monopolistic possessors of properties and promissory notes,
armed with the illegal laws, would descend on helpless debtors, ruin-
ing them because most lacked the means to meet their obligations.
Disaster, too, would befall agriculture, commerce, and other productive elements. The Regency's orders thus signified misery for the
majority and benefits for only a few despoilers of the Church. A
caveat ended the Court's brief: failure to examine and revise the
Reform laws as solemnly promised and as justice demanded augured
intensification of the warfare being waged against the Intervention;
the antimonarchist, anti-Catholic element would be joined by those
whose religious principles and material interests were injured. The
Court's stand in opposition to General Bazaine and the Regency
earned its dissolution on 2 January 1864 and the replacement of the
judges with new appointees.

The Supreme Court judges were neither the first nor the last to
allude to the monopolization of ecclesiastical property, but a contemporary breakdown of acquirers of Church property provides an interesting complement to the Court's observations. The newspaper
La Sombra reported that three groups of people acquired the
$100,000,000 of Church property that had "entered the treasury."
The largest block, $65,000,000, went to the foreign colony. Far be-
hind, with $23,000,000 worth of property, was the upper class, a
group that mostly opposed nationalization—a party of "Order" composed of clergy, managers of convents, wealthy merchants, and
capitalists. Finally, obtaining about $12,000,000 in property was the
middle class of lawyers, doctors, artists, merchants, military men, and
pensioners.[18]

Despite the legal and religious arguments, historical and contemporary, and despite the dire warnings of bishops, officials, and magis-

18. *La Sombra* (Mexico), 20 January 1865, pp. 1–2.

trates, the Regents held to their course, prodded by Bazaine and backed by Napoleon's instructions. But neither the French nor the Regents maintained their policy without continued obstructions. In Mexico City incendiary writings circulated secretly against the French army, portraying the clergy as dispossessed and persecuted. In Puebla Labastida's threatened excommunication made it difficult to retain Mexicans in administrative posts. Although in June 1863 some clergy in Aguascalientes had protested the French Intervention, in both Aguascalientes and Morelia, clergy denied the last sacraments and refused burial to persons who declined to return to the Church property they had adjudicated. Bazaine, in retaliation, directed officials to prevent such abuses, promising otherwise to withdraw the French army from those areas. The General's position on the property question was clear-cut, although his overall policy was conciliatory. For example, clergy might continue to use buildings for educational, charitable, and religious purposes, but these structures belonged to the State, and the Church could never regain ownership.[19]

Toward the end of 1863, while General Bazaine campaigned in the north, an incident in the capital revealed the tense relationship between the French military authorities and the Mexican clergy. It was customary for French Catholic soldiers to attend Sunday mass in the Cathedral, entering by the front middle door. One Sunday when the soldiers appeared about eight o'clock in the morning, the door was found closed to them. When informed, the commandant, General Neigre, ordered the door blown open by cannon. This threat induced the clergy to open the door, and mass was celebrated as usual.[20]

Although General Bazaine promised vigorous action upon his return to Mexico in February 1864, conditions remained unsettled: the clergy continued their opposition; the property issue was still con-

19. 16 January 1864, and Marquis de Montholon, French Minister to Mexico, 20 January 1864. Díaz López, 3:314–16; *Diario del Gobierno de la República Mejicana* (San Luis Potosí), 27 June 1863, p. 4; and Bazaine to Almonte, 14 March 1864, and Bazaine to General Douay in Guadalajara, 20 March 1864, in García, vols. 18, 20, 22, and 27: *La intervención francesa en México según el archivo del Mariscal Bazaine* (Mexico: Librería de la Viuda de Ch. Bouret, 1908–1909), 18:72–75, 105–7.

20. Corwin to Seward, n.d. (received in Washington in December; internal evidence indicates it was probably written late in November 1863), *Despatches from Ministers*, roll 31, vol. 30.

fused. In February there was some cause for optimism; the prelates seemed divided in sentiment. Bazaine believed that the Archbishop of Guadalajara and the Bishops of San Luis and Puebla understood the French policy of conciliation and wished to support the government rather than follow Labastida in his opposition, an attitude to which the mass of people remained indifferent. Within a few months, however, it was clear to Bazaine that little had changed. The clergy continued to raise difficulties for the authorities; they were seditious and intolerant. Clerical intrigues created uneasiness of spirit and conscience. Clergy continued to deny the last rites to those who refused to return nationalized property or to abjure the oath to the Constitution. General Douay, commandant in Guadalajara, reported that, despite repeated requests, certain judges maintained their resistance to considering questions concerning nationalized property.[21]

With conditions in the country unsettled and the clergy disenchanted with the French Intervention, the youthful royal pair, Maximilian and Carlotta, arrived in Mexico City on 12 June 1864 to assume their imperial duties. Certainly the most important matter demanding resolution was the Church question. Although Maximilian and Carlotta had an audience with Pope Pius IX in Rome while en route to Mexico, they made no serious attempt to reach an accord. Moreover, the Emperor failed to study the ecclesiastical question thoroughly before coming to Mexico. These were grievous blunders. He probably should have achieved an accommodation with the Vatican prior to coming to Mexico or, better still, before irrevocably committing himself to the imperial crown.

The Mexican bishops greeted Maximilian's arrival in the capital with a pastoral letter in which they noted that they had always remained aloof from political considerations and deplored party strife. It would be a work of Divine Providence if Maximilian would calm the nation's conscience with respect to the grave ecclesiastical question. Since Napoleon, and Maximilian as well, had decided to settle the religious question in a liberal sense, this pastoral could only be construed as a warning that the existence of the Imperial government depended on a solution of the Church problem favorable to the

21. Gaulot, p. 268; 25 February 1864, Díaz López, 3:331 28 July 1864, García, 20:200; Bazaine to the subsecretary of Justice of Maximilian, 30 May 1864, García, 20:87–88; and García, 22:81–82.

Church. The French Minister to Mexico found two things evident in the pastoral: "a very pronounced sentiment of distrust, scarcely veiled beneath a phraseology of double meaning, and the very clear intention of not making concessions on the question of secularization of clerical property."[22]

Hopes and expectations, fears and anxiety surrounded the new Emperor. His failure to settle the Church question quickly prolonged and increased the uneasiness. An atmosphere of uncertainty prevailed, stimulating rumors: disamortization would be gradually modified; the Colegio de Niñas, owned by a Spaniard, would be returned to the Church; a request would be made to validate clerical sales during the Zuloaga and Miramón regimes. As a result of these rumors, alarm and intrigues increased daily, while indecision continued.[23]

Whatever the expectations, fears, and rumors, Maximilian had no intention of fulfilling clerical hopes. He had moderate leanings and hoped to win the liberals to the Empire. His was to be a regime above parties and special interests; he was the ruler of all Mexicans. Maximilian staffed his ministry with moderates, and he succeeded in winning the adherence of some prominent liberals such as Generals Uraga and Vidaurri. But the Emperor's moderation and conciliation were no more successful than Comonfort's had been in 1856 and 1857. The policy did not gain radical support, but it did alienate clerical supporters, thereby sacrificing a pillar necessary for the success of the Empire.[24]

Since Maximilian did not earlier adjust the Church question with the Pope, its settlement awaited negotiation with a papal agent. The nuncio, Monsignor Pietro Francesco Meglia, reportedly very conservative, finally arrived in Mexico early in December 1864, and Maximilian received him on the tenth. It was apparent at once that chances for an agreement were slight. The nuncio did not hide the fact that he

22. Marquis de Montholon, 20 June 1864, Díaz López, 3:406; and Toro, p. 412.

23. 31 July 1864, in José M. Iglesias, *Revistas históricas sobre la intervención francesa en México* (Mexico, 1867–1869), 2:435–36.

24. Bazaine to French Minister of War, 10 December 1864, in Achille François Bazaine, Correspondencia, 1862–1867, Latin American Collection, University of Texas, Austin, vol. 11.

had come to make demands, not concessions. General Bazaine accurately assessed the nuncio's attitude as contrary to everything that had happened in the country with respect to clerical prerogatives and immunities.[25] The Vatican's proposals brought by Meglia confirmed this assessment. The bases for a settlement of the Church question included: support of the Catholic Church to the exclusion of all others; complete freedom for the bishops to exercise their ministry; reestablishment of the religious orders; and protection of the patrimony and rights of the Church. The Pope further demanded clerical control of education, the independence of the Church from civil authority, and a prohibition against teaching or publishing false or subversive ideas. In sum, the Vatican insisted upon abrogation of the Reform laws and all others contrary to the rights of the Church and the repair of harm done to the Church.[26]

Faced with these formidable and apparently unexpected terms, Maximilian outlined his ideas to the nuncio on 13 December. The Emperor favored religious toleration, but the Catholic Church would be protected. Nationalization of property would not be reversed, but the Empire offered financial support to the Church in exchange for which the clergy were to administer the sacraments and perform other functions free of charge. Some religious orders could be reestablished. Finally, Maximilian demanded for himself and his successors the same broad rights of patronage exercised in America by the Spanish monarchs in the colonial period.[27]

The divergence was great between what Pope and Emperor considered a satisfactory settlement of this thorny matter. Monsignor Meglia informed Maximilian that he lacked the authority to negotiate on the basis proposed by the Emperor. His instructions were to secure abrogation of the Reform laws that injured the Church.[28] The irritated Emperor reacted on 27 December in a published letter to his Minister of Justice, Pedro Escudero y Echánove. The nuncio claimed, Maximil-

25. Ibid.

26. Arnold Blumberg, "The Mexican Empire and the Vatican, 1863–1867," *The Americas* 28 (July 1971):4.

27. Galindo y Galindo, 3:156–58. See Blumberg for the entire Imperial-Vatican diplomacy.

28. Bazaine to French Minister of War, 27 December 1864, Bazaine Correspondencia, vol. 11.

ian said, that he had to await new instructions from Rome, but the situation would permit no further delay. He therefore directed Escudero to propose the best means to assure justice, obedience to the laws, and protection of religion. The Emperor specifically instructed his Minister to draft a proposal on ecclesiastical property transactions with the object of ratifying those carried out according to the disamortization and nationalization laws.[29] Count Corti, the best biographer of Maximilian, attributes this proposed solution of the Church question to Maximilian's impulsive character. The instructions to Escudero certainly shocked all parties—the conservatives and clericals naturally, but also the liberals because the instructions signified revision of irregular operations.[30]

In any event, these instructions brought an open rupture with the nuncio. On 29 December Meglia informed the government that the Pope never imagined that Maximilian would present such a program, and he repeated that he lacked the authority to negotiate a settlement on those principles. Such a settlement had never been proposed to the Holy See; indeed, it had never been suggested to the Mexican bishops who, on the contrary, were led to expect something quite different.[31] On the same day, the bishops issued another in their long series of protests. There was little new in this latest declaration. As before, the prelates insisted on their purity of motives and nonpolitical posture. Remaining always aloof from party interests, with disregard for political ideas of incumbent governments, they had simply, but steadfastly, defended Church rights. The defect in this reasoning, as always, was that defense of Church rights meant condemning and excommunicat-

29. In Lares Correspondencia; and Segura, 3:285.

30. Egon Caesar Corti, *Maximilian and Charlotte of Mexico*, trans. Catherine Alison Phillips (New York: Alfred A. Knopf, 1928), 2:467.

Various contemporary accounts help convey the conditions under the Empire, including opinions of Maximilian and his intentions, comments on towns, sacked churches, poverty, uncertainty about the future, and views of the Church question. See Baron Maximilian von Alvensleven, *With Maximilian in Mexico* (London, 1867); William Marshall Anderson, *An American in Maximilian's Mexico, 1865–66*, ed. Ramón Eduardo Ruiz (San Marino, Calif.: The Huntington Library, 1959); Sara Yorke Stevenson, *Maximilian in Mexico: A Woman's Reminiscences of the French Intervention, 1862–1867* (New York, 1899); and J. F. Elton, *With the French in Mexico* (London, 1867).

31. Murray, p. 215.

ing all who in any way infringed those rights as defined by the episcopacy. Such an uncompromising stand divided Mexican society and inevitably meant interference in political affairs and, ultimately, bloodshed. Nevertheless, the bishops blamed the civil war on a hateful minority that attacked religion and the Church. The Emperor's outrageous letter of 27 December disappointed and pained the churchmen, and they urged him to await new papal instructions. The statement that the Emperor's present course could only aggravate the troubled situation sounded like a warning, if not a threat.[32]

Maximilian did not despair of an agreement, and, since Meglia lacked authority, the Church question was now taken up in Rome through the Imperial envoy to the Holy See and by a three-man commission specially appointed to explain the Mexican situation to the Pope and to remove obstacles to a settlement. Prospects for agreement seemed slight. Intransigent Imperial representatives matched equally unyielding papal negotiators.[33] Both parties appeared genuinely desirous of concluding a concordat, but the basic requirements of papacy and empire were such that, while points of disagreement might be narrowed, all obstacles to agreement could not be removed. Negotiations continued in Rome in the spring and summer of 1865. Of the twenty-one articles in Maximilian's proposed concordat, the papal representatives disputed eight. These were the most significant points, dealing with patronage rights, jurisdiction of ecclesiastical courts, tithes, State financial support of the clergy, and clerical property rights.[34]

In Mexico meanwhile, the Emperor acted. From December through the spring of 1865 a series of decrees upheld the major Reform measures. Among them, the most important dealt with religious toleration, elimination of separate courts, secularization of cemeteries, and civil registration of births, deaths, and marriages; for marriages, however, both civil and religious ceremonies were re-

32. Bishops to Maximilian, 29 December 1864, Lares Correspondencia.

33. José F. Ramírez, Imperial Minister of Foreign Affairs, to Imperial Envoy in Rome, 29 January 1865, García, 13:270–72. The commission consisted of the Imperial Minister of State and two Imperial Councillors. See also "Nota dirigida el 5 de Marzo de 1865 por su exmo. el Cardenal Secretario de Estado de Su Santidad al Sr. D. Ignacio Aguilar Ministro Plenipotenciario de S. M. el Emperador de Méjico, cerca de la Santa Sede," Documentos, 1850–1867.

34. García, 13:275–84.

quired. By decree Maximilian assumed imperial exequatur, by which all papal communications required his approval before circulation.[35] The bishops condemned these acts, and Meglia left Mexico late in May 1865. Maximilian's exasperation increased, although he did not despair of a satisfactory agreement with Rome. And in Mexico there was one faint hope that liberal support of the Empire would offset the alienation of conservatives.[36]

By early December 1865, the Mexican commissioners in Rome had proposed and dispatched a new twenty-nine point project for a concordat that was favorably received by the Emperor. But by the time the revised project was back in Rome on 9 March 1866, the Vatican had concluded that the Empire would collapse; the papacy procrastinated, and no agreement was achieved.[37]

Long before these events, however, the question of nationalized property demanded action. A definitive resolution of the matter had awaited the Emperor's arrival, despite the actions of the French and the Regency. Indeed, the provisional nature of the Regency and French control seemed to contribute to controversy and paralysis. The liberal *La Sombra* described the situation. Possessors of nationalized property were unable to put it on the market because prices could not be fixed. Promissory notes were generally uncollectable. Owners of the convent lots expected suddenly to see their homes reconverted into "cells." The paper, with considerable prescience, did not advocate revision of nationalization transactions because each property registry book that the government examined would produce hundreds of proceedings (*expedientes*), thus prolonging the tense and unstable situation. *La Sombra* simply proposed the ratification of all concluded operations.[38]

The vast numbers of transactions were an important consideration, but preference of rights disputes compounded the difficulties facing revision. There were many houses to which several individuals be-

---

35. J. Lloyd Mecham, *Church and State in Latin America: A History of Politico-Ecclesiastical Relations* (Chapel Hill, N.C.: University of North Carolina Press, 1934), p. 452; and Arrangoiz, *Méjico*, 4:71.

36. Corti, 2:468–69.

37. Blumberg, "Mexican Empire," pp. 18–19.

38. 6 January 1865, pp. 1–2 and 27 January 1865, p. 2. The paper later protested that the imperial law of revision was not revision but annulment.

lieved they had a just claim, for example, the original adjudicator, the purchaser after its return to the Church during the civil war, and the denouncer in Veracruz. Despite the courts' settlement of numerous cases, many people disagreed with the decisions rendered and appealed to the Empire.[39]

Warnings of the dangers of revision and the obvious dissatisfaction that such a measure would arouse notwithstanding, Imperial authorities, as the French before them, were committed to that uncertain course. Justice and the prospect of obtaining funds seemed to argue for revision. Considering the shades of political opinion supporting Maximilian, it is not surprising that adherents of the Empire included individuals who accepted many of the Reform measures as well as those who excoriated the liberals and all their works.[40] Similarly, the concept of revision enjoyed support in the Imperial camp from both opponents and supporters of the Reform in general.

A number of opponents of nationalization advocated revision. For example, one leading critic of the liberals, who saw no beneficial results from the expropriation of the Church, insisted that the Empire had to find a path between two extremes: the desire of the clergy for a total restoration of wealth and the demand of possessors of ecclesiastical property for reaffirmation of the Reform laws.[41] A foreign supporter of revision indicted the Juárez government's immoderate nationalization that had also deprived charitable and educational institutions of necessary resources. The sale of ecclesiastical lands had been conducted in a "scandalous" manner, making it important to revise the contracts for the benefit of the treasury and the dignity of the State.[42] Another critic lamented the squandering of the immense clerical wealth, which might have been used for necessary and useful projects. The penury of the government resulted from the considerable incentives granted by the laws of nationalization. Real estate and

39. *La Orquesta*, 21 January 1865, p. 1.

40. See, for example, "Un Mexicano," *México, el imperio y la intervención* (Mexico, 2 February 1867), pp. 58–59.

41. J. de J. Cuevas, *El Imperio, opúsculo sobre la situación actual* (Mexico, 1865), pp. 51–52. Cuevas believed that a concordat was essential.

42. Emile de Kératry, *The Rise and Fall of the Emperor Maximilian: A Narrative of the Mexican Empire, 1861–7, from Authentic Documents with the Imperial Correspondence*, trans. G. H. Venables (London, 1868), p. 33.

capital were disposed of at a fraction of their true value, and confusion reached such proportions that the same properties were sold by the government to three, four, and five different people. With all this, the government still faced bankruptcy.[43]

In contrast to these supporters of revision who had opposed nationalization stood the Abbé Testory, the French army chaplain in Mexico. He supported both the liberal property acts and a policy of revision. In a notable pamphlet, the Abbot acknowledged the State's duty to respect property, but assigned to government the further obligation to effect its just distribution because prosperity depended upon the more or less equal distribution of wealth. Monopolization of that wealth by the Church was contrary to the public good and had to be destroyed. In accomplishing this goal, the State had two obligations: to indemnify the expropriated, giving the clergy an annual subsidy; and to conclude an agreement with the Pope. The liberals, according to Testory, fulfilled neither of these requirements. Nevertheless, the Empire should respect the sale of ecclesiastical property. Property of the "poor" and of educational institutions should not have been sold, however, and the State should demand restitution of that property and indemnify those who had acquired it.[44] Testory's views did not pass unchallenged. Critics especially questioned the Abbot's allegations regarding Church wealth and defended the Church's right to possess property.[45]

Ysidoro Guerrero, a supporter of the Reform measures, wrote an especially comprehensive pamphlet in which he reviewed the history of the laws and offered suggestions for revision.[46] Little of novelty appeared in the pamphlet, but the very repetition of abuses added to the evidence of irregularity in property transactions. This kind of

43. Reprint of article from *La Nación* in *El Diario del Imperio* (Mexico), 17 January 1866, 3:78–79.

44. Abbot Testory, *El imperio y el clero mexicano* (Mexico, 1865).

45. See Basilio Arrillaga, *Cuartas observaciones sobre el opúsculo entitulado "El imperio y el clero mexicano" del señor Abate Testory (capellán mayor del ejército francés en México)* (Mexico, 1865); and Agustín de la Rosa, *Observaciones sobre las cuestiones que el abate Testory mueve en su opúsculo entitulado "El imperio y el clero mexicano"* (Guadalajara, 1865).

46. Guerrero. For an elaboration of Guerrero's analysis, see chap. 4, p. 109ff., *supra*.

analysis doubtless helped convince the Emperor of the need for revision.

While Guerrero focused on the confused, irregular, and groundless property transactions, another careful analysis that justified Imperial revision emphasized the financial aspects of the laws' operation. The detailed report prepared early in 1864 by a French lawyer, L. Binel, for the Marquis de Montholon, French Minister to Mexico, was certainly the best contemporary financial analysis of the property question.[47] Binel based his argument for revision on the relationship between property transactions and the amount or value of property involved. Careful scrutiny of a few available records for the Federal District in the years 1856 to 1861 proved to Binel that the overwhelming majority of transactions in clerical property in some way violated the laws to the detriment of the treasury. He concluded that regular sales represented relatively small amounts. In a revision of operations, scarcely 3 percent of the sales by value could be confirmed as regular. Validation of 19 percent more required some explanation of questionable points. But 78 percent would have to be voided as carried out in manifest violation of the letter of the law.[48] Binel believed revision

47. Montholon to French Minister of Foreign Affairs, 20 March 1864. Díaz López, 3:341–80. On previous occasions Binel had written reports on Mexican conditions that were known to the French Foreign Ministry.

48. Binel's major sources of data were a single register of property transactions available to him in the Ministry of Finance and two important, detailed government documents—the 1857 Ministry of Finance annual report and the 1861 report on disamortization operations in the Federal District by the special office in charge. The proof of irregularities found by Binel led him to extrapolate for the entire country. This generalizing perhaps led to some questionable conclusions, but the accuracy of his evaluation based on hard evidence was indisputable.

Binel made an undocumented estimate of Church wealth; he assigned an immense value of $600,000,000 to ecclesiastical movable and immovable wealth and calculated that one-quarter or one-third of the immovable property still remained directly or indirectly, through dummy purchasers, in clerical hands. Turning to specifics for which he did have data Binel distinguished four major categories of property transactions. The first group comprised regular operations. Complete legality required immediate payment of 60 percent of the amount in bonds of the national debt; the remaining 40 percent was payable in monthly promissory notes not to exceed 40 months. The register examined by Binel contained 944 transactions valued at about

of property transactions would be a measure of "reparation founded as much in right as imperiously demanded by the Mexican treasury."[49]

Although Binel based his conclusions on an analysis limited in area and time, he believed that his findings were valid for the whole country and that, if anything, fraud and illegality were greater in the years after 1861. Binel was aware, too, of some of the pitfalls of revision, but benefits far outweighed dangers. He discounted the insecurity of property and possible public disorders that extensive revision might cause, and he insisted that the process would secure great resources for the government. Annulment of irregular and fraudulent operations in the Federal District alone involved $40,000,000 worth of property, in his opinion. Properly handled, disposal of the property would prevent glutting the market and depreciating values, while widely distributing real estate among a large number of people.

The objectivity and detail of Binel's report were persuasive. A predominately statistical analysis, however, disregarded human nature and political realities. It underestimated the complexity of the property question; it overlooked the length of time revision would take, during which tension and insecurity would be rampant. Imperial authorities, too, overlooked or discounted these problems, precisely the ones on which the entire revision project foundered.

$8,300,000. There were 302 regular operations, approximately one-third of the total number, but the value of these, $216,000, was scarcely 3 percent of the total. The other dealings deviated in one way or another from legality: discounts in payments; alterations in proportions payable in bonds and cash or in time allowed for payment; simply fraud in making redemptions; or failure to redeem mortgages as agreed.

49. Díaz López, 3:374.

Chapter 6
Maximilian's Solution: Revision of Nationalization, 1865–1867

Maximilian's liberal philosophy basically determined his attitude toward the property question; his motives in decreeing revision were revealed in the law of revision and in various of the commentaries on the question discussed earlier. The Emperor accepted the liberal justification for nationalization that the clergy lacked the legal right to possess the property and that they should be subordinate to civil law. He believed that revision was an act of justice which assured that property had been acquired according to the legal provisions and that abuses and damage to individual interests would be corrected. Maximilian further hoped to benefit the propertyless of Mexico. Not the least of the considerations was financial. While serving the interests of justice, the Empire would obtain significant resources from revision, funds that the government greatly needed. The principles and interests that revision would serve thus outweighed the political dangers of such an act; but strenuous opposition from the Church and from the possessors of ecclesiastical property should certainly have been foreseen.

The Imperial law of 26 February 1865 ordered revision of disamortization and nationalization operations.[1] If not actually patterned after Binel's recommendations, it at least bore resemblance to

1. Segura, 4:194–98. In irregular operations on which there had been executive judgments or awards or transactions approved, the revisions were to be limited to the reimbursement of the treasury for the amount defrauded in the operation, the current owner of the property or mortgage being required to make this payment. When an operation was declared baseless, the amounts that had been paid in specie, credits, and interest were to be returned to the person who executed the operation except in cases of fraudulent transactions. If credits were not available to be returned, the Council was to issue certificates having the same legal effect. Real estate or mortgages of nullified operations were to be returned to the government with the income or interest that they should have produced. The regulatory law of 9 March established in greater detail procedures to follow in submitting transactions for revision. Segura, 4:222–27.

them and reflected many of the same concepts. The law entrusted revision to the Imperial Council of State, whose decisions were irrevocable. All transactions executed in accordance with the laws would be confirmed, irregular or fraudulent ones invalidated. Those irregular operations that the Juárez government had approved could, however, be confirmed by reducing them to the terms of the laws whenever no injury was sustained by a third party. Similarly, other irregular or fraudulent transactions could be confirmed by reducing them to the terms of the laws and by an immediate cash payment of 25 percent of the value of the real estate or mortgage in question. The law authorized the Council of State to ratify transactions concluded by the clergy during the civil war with property returned to them, as long as the previous possessor of the property did not contest it. Also, transactions would be confirmed that were carried out in conformity with the nationalization law but prior to the official publication of the law in the localities where the property was located.

The revision measure established an office of nationalized property that was to administer the real estate not yet alienated and mortgages not yet redeemed; the office would have control of mortgages regained by the government from revision and mortgages that resulted from the disposal of property, collecting the interest from them. In addition, those who were in the process of paying off mortgages were required to make a declaration to that effect within sixty days or the redemption would be invalidated, the mortgage then recovering its full value. The law provided for the sale of nationalized property not yet alienated and that reacquired under the revision law. The mortgages arising from these sales carried an annual interest rate of 6 percent and an eighteen year redemption period, payable in equal annual installments. The *Diario del Imperio* carried frequent announcements of the public auction of properties provided for by the law.[2]

Some of the most interesting provisions of the revision law reveal the Emperor's apparent desire to benefit the less fortunate classes and partially to counteract the impulse toward property concentration. The measure ordered the division of rural property prior to its dis-

2. See, for example, the issue of 5 January 1866, 3:27.

posal and its sale only to persons having no other land. Similar restrictions applied to urban property; preference was given to those who had no other real estate, and in no case could the same person acquire more than two properties. The following year, in June 1866, another law, reminiscent of the Lerdo law, further reflected Imperial concern. This act vested ownership of communal lands in the individual inhabitants of villages, hoped to guarantee each family sufficient land for its needs, and intended to protect their possession of the lands from encroachment by large landowners.[3]

The plan of imperial revision was commendable in theory. Based on a sense of fairness and justice, it also incorporated the praiseworthy goal to diversify proprietorship among the rural landless and urban propertyless. The prospect of obtaining important revenue, a critical need for the Empire, was an important motive as well. But it was immediately apparent that there would be many difficulties and that revision of all transactions was impracticable.

Difficulties arose either from genuine confusion or from deliberate desire to take advantage of the situation or both. Tenants and mortgagors (*censatarios*) refused to pay rents and interest. Tenants claimed they need not pay rents without proof that the owners had submitted their titles for revision. Mortgagors went even further, arguing that they did not have to make interest payments until after revision of the transactions. Furthermore, judges believed that judicial proceedings were suspended until the Council of State validated property acquisitions. The length of time required to carry out revision, and the effects of that long period, compounded difficulties. Revision would take years; meanwhile, proprietors and holders of promissory notes or mortgages faced financial ruin and were at the mercy of tenants and debtors. In sum, the revision law seemed to leave the nationalization issue where it had been for two years, ever since the French occupation of the capital: the only tenants paying rent were those inclined to do so, and signers of promissory notes

3. 26 June 1866, *Boletín de las leyes del Imperio Mexicano. Primera parte, tomo II comprende las leyes, decretos y reglamentos generales Números del 1 al 176 expedidos por el emperador Maximiliano desde 1° de julio hasta 31 de diciembre de 1865* (Mexico, 1866), 14, p. 138. Cited hereafter as *Leyes del Imperio*.

declined to redeem them; uncertainty, dissatisfaction, and confusion prevailed.[4]

On the issue of time, *L'Estafette* graphically, but perhaps with some exaggeration, made the point that revision would take many years. In Mexico City there were an estimated 10,000 transactions or cases (*expedientes*) and supposedly a like number in the states. That meant 20,000 cases to examine, verify, and judge. At the rate of one operation a day during a 300 work-day year, revision would take sixty-six years to complete! The result clearly would be continuous turmoil and insecurity. Another paper, *La Sociedad*, was not so pessimistic. A simple certificate showing that a title had been presented for revision was sufficient for an owner to be able to collect rent; it was not necessary to await the actual revision. In addition, the years to complete the revision process were few in comparison to the number of years proprietors would own the property.[5]

Indeed, as revision got underway, and throughout the one and one-half years it continued, there was no lack of commentary, especially in the periodical press, but also from Juárez officials. Criticism ranged beyond the law of revision itself to include the whole of disamortization and nationalization—principles, achievements, abuses, financial results. Much of the writing simply covered old ground, repeating old arguments. The interesting and useful comments revealed perceptions of the property issue with specific reference to Imperial revision. A principal liberal criticism of the law was that, in effect, revision would revalidate clerical sales of property returned to the Church during the civil war, in disregard of the disamortization law of 1856, which held such transactions illegal. Moreover, even though decisions of the Council of State were presumably final, no one would accept easily an unfavorable judgment; appeal to the courts was inevitable, but they were inadequate to handle such a task. Furthermore, the law protected fraud and inequities, while prohibiting legal proprietors from exercising their rights pending revision. Emphasis on the alarm, insecurity, and even paralysis in the exercise

---

4. *La Sociedad*; *Periódico Político y Literario* (Mexico), 8 March 1865, p. 2, and 16 March 1865, p. 2; and Bazaine to the French Minister of War, 10 March 1865, García, 27:18–21; and 10 March 1865, Bazaine Correspondencia, vol. 11.

5. *La Sociedad*, reporting from *L'Estafette*, 16 March 1865, p. 2.

of ownership rights was a common theme of critics regardless of political persuasion. This complaint was voiced early and remained a continuous one throughout the history of revision.[6]

In submitting a transaction for revision, the proprietor would typically review the history of his acquisition of the property. He might cite, for example, the original denunciation and redemption of a piece of land, noting the failure to pay the *alcabala* in the required time, thus necessitating a second payment in December 1863. Improvements made would be mentioned, such as erecting boundary markers and planting magueys. In conclusion, the owner would attest to his clear title; there were no encumbrances on the property and no litigation involving it.[7] A case in which Maximilian personally intervened to expedite matters substantiates the interminableness of the revision process as an operation moved through official channels. On 23 August 1866 Doña Gertrudis Escudero de O'Horan asked for the prompt revision of her case; she complained that the Administration of Nationalized Property "has delayed excessively in concluding this matter which was dispatched quite some time ago by the Minister of State."[8]

The administrators of the law faced problems that were not unique to the property issue in their time. Officials had to be ever watchful for dishonesty and fraud. One practice was the circulation of spurious promissory notes, the hope being to legalize them. Another problem, common as well to previous and later governments, was occult property. Maximilian's solution was to authorize denunciations of property and credits that properly belonged to the nation, offering sizeable rewards as an incentive. Denouncers received 25 percent of the sum entering the treasury if the amount denounced was less than $20,000;

6. 28 February and 30 April 1865, Iglesias, *Revistas históricas*, 3:190, 267–68; *L'Estafette*, reported in *La Sociedad*, 29 March 1866, p. 2.

7. "Departamento de Puebla, Distrito de Tepeaca, Expediente relativo al capital de sesenta y un pesos que valían un terreno y una noche de agua vertiente en el Pueblo de Santa María Actipan, y se adjudicaron y redimieron Don Manuel y Don Antonio Bautista, el cual pertenecía a la Parroquia de Acatzinco, y sujetan a revisión," Archivo Histórico de Hacienda, segundo imperio, leg. 275, exp. 24.

8. "Expediente relativo a la solicita de Doña Gertrudis Escudero de O'Horan en que se queja de la oficina de bienes nacionalizados," ibid., leg. 103, exp. 119.

as the amounts denounced increased, the percentage in payment decreased. Useful as this concession was, the zeal of denouncers caused a different problem for the Empire. The criterion that determined the denounceability of a property was clerical ownership or administration, not the pious objective of the property. Thus, denunciation of property with a pious or charitable end was not necessarily legal; specific cases had to be examined carefully and laboriously.[9]

The fact of Empire itself added complications to the already confused and difficult property question. Numerous court cases are available which, though often involving the wealthy and prominent, shed light on the complex operations and tergiversations under laws issued since 1856. José I. Limantour was one of those frequently-mentioned speculators who acquired many properties during the civil war.[10] In Mexico City Limantour denounced fifty houses valued at over $500,000. His ownership was not secure, however, and seemingly endless litigation involving various of the houses dragged on for years from the end of the civil war into the French Intervention, Imperial period, and beyond. In general, litigation developed because Limantour attempted to make good his claim to properties in conservative-controlled areas that he had denounced to liberal authorities at Veracruz. Allegedly, Limantour had not complied in some way with the provisions of the laws, by not properly fulfilling the

9. *La Sociedad*, 7 March 1866, p. 3; 5 April 1866, *Leyes del Imperio*, 11, p. 42; and *El Diario del Imperio*, 25 October 1866, 4:353.

10. There is considerable literature on litigation involving Limantour; the following represents a sampling only: *Ocurso que el doctor Don Antonio Fernández Monjardín presentó en 28 de abril de 1862 al juez 4° de lo civil, Lic. D. Agustín Norma, reclamando el despojo que se le infirió en 24 de mayo de 1861 de una casa de su propiedad, de la que se dió posesión a D. José Ibes Limantour* (Mexico, 1862); *Alegato de buena prueba que el Licenciado D. Manuel Siliceo, patrono y apoderado del Dr. D. Antonio Fernández Monjardín, ha hecho en el juicio posesorio promovido contra D. José I. Limantour, reclamando el despojo de la casa No. 6 de la calle de la Palma, ante el juez de lo civil Licenciado D. Antonio Aguado* (Mexico, 1863); *Sentencia pronunciada el día 28 de mayo por el juez 2° de lo civil, Lic. Don José María Barros, en el juicio posesorio promovido por el Dr. D. Antonio Fernández Monjardín contra D. José Ibes Limantour* (Mexico, 1863); and *Manifestaciones que José Ives Limantour, en cumplimiento del decreto de 26 de febrero del presente año, ha dirigido al Exmo. Consejo de Estado, relativas a la casa num. 6 de la calle de la Palma, y a la hacienda de Tenería, situada en jurisdicción de Tenancingo* (Mexico, 1865).

various requirements to validate denunciations, by not making proper redemptions, or by not concluding legal contracts.

A major source of dispute in these cases was that the properties had figured in sales by the Church during the War of the Reform. That circumstance had provided the basis for Limantour's denunciations and determined the liberal government's actions in awarding the properties to him. The courts, however, were interested in the strict legality of execution in the transactions: the circumstances surrounding the denunciation and redemptions, and particularly the activities of government officials in the operations. There is no doubt that strict legality was often not observed; it is not possible to judge, however, whether this was from deliberate dishonesty and collusion with speculators or simply from a desire to obtain resources for the war and to punish those who cooperated with the conservative government. Irregular operations were common in those years of crisis. In any event, the cases involving Limantour are indicative of the opportunities open to persons with wealth and connections to acquire numerous valuable properties for a fraction of their value, and they show how the government's need for resources made this acquisition even easier for speculators. Ample legal weapons were available as well to those whose interests were affected if they possessed the means to sustain lengthy and costly court battles.

These and other cases leave no doubt as to why Imperial revision seemed necessary and why it progressed slowly.[11] In addition to their sheer numbers, such complicated transactions required the careful study of many documents, claims, and counterclaims. The limited personnel responsible for revisions also precluded swift action. Meanwhile, ownership rights remained in a suspended and insecure state.

The Juárez government pursued much the same policy toward the Interventionist and Imperial regimes as it had toward the conservative administration during the civil war: in the fall of 1863 the Presi-

11. See, for example, *Esposición que presentó al respetable consejo de estado el lic. Anastasio Zerecero como representante de la señora Doña Agustina Guerrero de Flores en el espediente sobre revisión de las operaciones de desamortización practicadas sobre la casa no. 1 de la calle de Vergara* (Mexico, 1865).

dent declared all acts of Interventionist judges null and their decisions invalid in constitutionalist-controlled areas. The republican government also ordered the seizure of the property of prominent collaborators with the foreign invader. Francisco Mejía, as Superior Treasury Chief, carried out this order in 1864 in the states of Nuevo León and Coahuila, seizing the estates of the well-known and wealthy Sánchez Navarro family, among others. Such confiscations produced little cash; some grain and cattle were collected and then distributed to the troops.[12]

With regard to the Reform in general President Juárez received frequent complaints, as did the Interventionist and Imperial authorities, of flouting of the laws. Clergy continued to oppose and to incite hatred of the laws, while liberal officials infringed upon the laws, especially that on vital statistics. The law of 12 July 1859 had separated Church and State. Separation should have meant no government intervention in purely spiritual matters. But this precept was violated; governors required that the sacraments of baptism and marriage be administered only after the civil registration, while clergy continued to abuse the laws and to fight the Reform. In some localities, those who complied with the civil registry law were excommunicated or denied a religious marriage. Clergy even tried to convince people that the civil registry was not the institution that the Reform intended to establish. Because of such activities, the liberal government ordered prosecution of crimes against public order but respect for the independence of Church and State.[13]

With respect to nationalization, the republican government required that individuals who had signed promissory notes for property located in occupied territory and who continued to live in those areas were to appear before federal authorities to make their redemption payments; failure to comply meant loss of ownership of the property. Juárez naturally also nullified the Imperial law of revision. Therefore, revisions conducted under Imperial law were declared invalid by the republican government, and anyone dispossessed by Imperial revision of property legitimately acquired under federal laws could later de-

12. Decree of 15 October 1863, Labastida, p. 244; and Mejía, *Memorias*, pp. 83–84.

13. Ignacio Vallarta, Minister of Government, to the governors, 20 July 1865, Bassols, pp. 197–99.

mand the return of the property plus an indemnity for injuries. Furthermore, any unalienated nationalized property was denounceable, although denunciations could only be made before the federal government, which was the only legal authority.[14]

While Imperial laws substantially upheld the Reform and while the Juárez government prohibited cooperation with the invaders, ecclesiastical authorities provided for those who wished to come to terms with the Church, even though they had complied with liberal laws. Anyone holding mortgages who desired to make a settlement had to give the Church the mortgage and property deed and report the amount of redemption payments that had been made. Thus, for example, a $5,000 mortgage on which $2,100 had been paid had accrued interest due of $1,080. The $2,100 represented two-fifths of the mortgage in specie, or $2,000, plus three-fifths in bonds at 3 percent of their face value, or $90, and $10 for costs or expenses. In the agreement with the Church, the accrued interest was subtracted from the amount paid; this sum, $1,020, was then subtracted from the original value of the mortgage. That amount, or $3,980, plus interest on that sum, constituted the individual's obligation to the Church.[15]

In cases involving real estate rather than mortgages, clerical authorities required the proprietor to submit a secret document, signed by two witnesses, acknowledging the rights of the Church with a declaration stipulating the return of the property. The individual's executor or heirs also had to accept the document. The property, however, remained in the possessor's hands in the nature of a trust, with the obligation to turn over the net revenue to the Church. Only after such an agreement had been made would the Church remove the censure incurred by acquiring ecclesiastical property under the liberal laws. These provisions make it clear that the hierarchy, nearly a decade after disamortization, had not altered its initial policy or position. It still intended to retain or reacquire as much property as possible, flouting the laws of the country, and it remained quite willing to

14. Circular of 27 July 1863, p. 263; 11 May 1865, pp. 157–58; and Decree of 31 August 1866, Labastida, p. 230.

15. Circular of 18 June 1864, *Undécima pastoral que el Illmo. y Rmo. Sr. Obispo de León, Dr. y Maestro D. José María de Jesús Diez de Sollano y Dávalos, dirige a su Íllmo. y V. Cabildo, señores curas y V. clero* (León, 1872), pp. 41–42.

use its spiritual powers to this end. On the other hand, the insistence on secrecy was a formal departure, at least, from the earlier days when public retractions before authorities were necessary to regain the good graces of the Church. Clerical authorities not only maintained a substantially unaltered attitude toward property as such, they continued with little deviation their position on the Reform in general, whether emanating from Juarists, Interventionists, or Imperialists: the denial of sacraments to those who participated in the hated laws. Punishments, in fact, might stray from the spiritual to the physical. In one reported instance in Puebla state, the local priest conspired with the local judge to violate the laws. These officials demanded that villagers turn over to them the titles to lands adjudicated. Those who complied could keep and cultivate the lands if they shared the fruits equally with the Church. One of those who refused to relinquish his title or to work for the Church was allegedly "beaten up" by the priest.[16]

A major problem that should have been anticipated was the opposition the revision measure aroused. The United States Secretary of Legation, William Corwin, reported clerical dissatisfaction because of the confirmation of nationalization; possessors of property, on the other hand, complained because revision subjected them to unnecessary expenses and delays in the validation of their titles.[17] History repeated itself in the foreign reaction. The Empire in 1865, like the Juárez government in 1861, faced protests from foreigners who had purchased Church property. American citizens, unwilling to submit to so-called arbitrary decisions of the Imperial Council of State, sought the aid of their diplomatic and consular representatives.[18] Others doubtless shared the Americans' views. The dissatisfaction of possessors of nationalized property is only partially explained by the costs

16. *Idea Liberal* (Puebla), cited in *La Orquesta*, 15 March 1865, p. 2; and Circular of 29 May 1865, *Undécima pastoral*, pp. 34, 40.

17. Corwin to Seward, 28 March 1865, *Despatches from Ministers*, roll 31, vol. 30. For a case of revision of adjudications made by William Corwin, son of Thomas Corwin, former United States Minister to Mexico, see *Diario Oficial del Gobierno Supremo de la República* (Mexico), 4, 5, 6, and 9 January 1868, p. 3, and 8 January 1868, p. 4.

18. Marcus Otterbourg to F. W. Seward, Assistant Secretary of State, 28 March 1865, *Despatches from Consuls, Mexico City*, roll 6, vol. 11.

and delays and by their fears of revision. A related factor was the response of debtors, who were quick to take advantage of the situation, as noted above.

As revision progressed, statistics became available on the financial effects of the process. The results from this standpoint were undeniably disappointing. Whether because of the immensity of the task, or the loss of records, or the way in which nationalization had been conducted in the first place, or because of confusion and political instability, revision clearly did not produce the large revenue anticipated.[19] From 15 March, when revision actually began, until 31 December 1865 there were 4,230 cases (*expedientes*) representing a property value of $30,131,538 forwarded from the Council of State. The Administration of Nationalized Property had revised and returned to the Council only 2,859 of the cases, worth $20,831,401. The Empire collected from these revisions a total of $692,320.70, but only $50,095.06 was in cash. The bulk of the amount obtained was in the form of redeemable notes, bonds, and obligations payable in bonds.[20] By the end of July 1866, the Administration of Nationalized Property had received 6,834 cases valued at $42,314,812.53; the office dispatched 4,166 with a value of $28,475,788.89. By the time revision ended in August 1866, official reports showed that nearly $62,500,000 in property had been submitted to the Council of State. The total, broken down, was approximately: real estate—urban, $23,633,000, and rural, $5,772,000; mortgages—corporations and pious works, $26,000,000, and chaplaincies, $7,000,000. Not only did Imperial revision fail actually to revise the mass of transactions submitted to it, but it clearly failed as a financial expedient. Of total property of $62,500,000, the government obtained in the transactions revised probably only a little over $2,500,000, and of that amount only $150,000 was in cash. Furthermore, salaries and other expenses would have to be deducted to obtain a net profit.[21]

19. *La Sociedad*, 29 March 1866, p. 2.

20. Emmanuel Domenech, *Le Mexique tel qu'il est; La vérité sur son climat, ses habitants et son gouvernement* (Paris, 1867), pp. 149–51. Domenech was Maximilian's press director.

21. *Diario del Imperio*, 16 April 1866, 3:385, and 14 August 1866, 4:142; *La Sociedad*, 30 April 1866, p. 2; *Informe de Hacienda, 1872–73*, document 19; Bazant, *Alienation*, pp. 265–66; and Manuel Payno, *Cuentas, gastos, acreedores y*

In the spring of 1865 Maximilian toured some of the provinces of his Empire. The ovations that greeted him everywhere during the trip encouraged him. General Bazaine admitted, however, that Maximilian's enthusiastic reception belied the fact that the Empire was more unpopular than it had been at its inception; among the major reasons was the revision of nationalized property transactions, "a measure that has always been unpopular."[22] Revision not only was unpopular, it was a failure, a fact which the Emperor finally admitted. Revision did not eliminate obstacles to the free movement of nationalized property. It did not dispel the uncertainty surrounding ownership rights. It did not end the paralysis of property transactions. Instead, revision aggravated these problems by preventing the exercise of rights until the acquisition of the properties had been confirmed. The statistics revealed the extent of the failure: only one-fourth of the 16,000 transactions submitted to the Council of State had been dispatched in the sixteen months of the law's duration. At that rate, four more years would be needed to complete the process to the continuing detriment of the treasury and the individuals concerned.[23]

Like the Empire itself, a project so optimistically launched, with pure motives by and large, turned eventually into something approaching a disaster. The results, on the one hand, were insecurity and confusion for possessors of nationalized property, painfully slow revision of cases, and meager financial resources gained; on the other hand, there were argument, abuse of the law, and a great expenditure of energy, time, and newsprint.

Maximilian terminated revision on 23 August 1866. The decree upheld the decisions of the Council of State, but also ratified definitively transactions not yet revised by the Council and granted full ownership to current possessors of the properties except in case of disputes pending over preference of rights. The Emperor entrusted the Ministry of Finance with the collection of amounts still due the treasury by purchasers of properties and mortgages; the bonds were payable in two months, the cash in monthly installments of 1 percent

---

otros asuntos del tiempo de la intervención francesa y del imperio. De 1861 a 1867 (Mexico, 1868), p. 415.

22. Bazaine to the French Minister of War, 28 April 1865, Bazaine Correspondencia, vol. 12.

23. *Diario del Imperio*, 24 August 1866, 4:175.

each. However, the measure levied on the owners a tax of 15 percent of the value of the original property sale or of the nominal value of the mortgage. Those who acquired properties or mortgages through contracts directly with the clergy prior to the publication of the nationalization law were exempt from the tax, but if they had not yet paid the total price, they were to pay the tax on the part received by the government. The disamortization and nationalization laws remained in force insofar as they did not conflict with the new law. In addition, Maximilian authorized denunciations of occult property and the continuing revision of transactions with charitable, educational, and municipal property.[24]

Foreigners, as usual, objected. The advice given to complaining Americans was to pay the required tax under protest. Alphonse Dano, the French Minister, also refused to intervene on behalf of French citizens, although he believed the law was unjust.[25] The press, too, was highly critical of the new edict. *L'Estafette*, a constant critic, pointed out that acquirers of nationalized property benefited greatly, even with the imposition of a 15 percent tax. None of the purchases had cost even 50 percent of the value of the property, and by payment of the tax, the possessors received definitive titles and need have no fear of future revisions. On the other hand, they could abrogate the contract, return the property or mortgage, and receive in exchange the amount they had actually paid. To prove its charges, the newspaper posed several hypothetical cases to show how cheaply and on what easy terms property could be acquired.[26]

The press alleged another probable injustice arising from the decree ending revision. A dutiful, law-abiding person who submitted to revision and lost his property for failure to fulfill various requirements received no repayment for the cost of the property or for improvements he had made. Another person in the same situation

---

24. *Diario del Imperio*, 24 August 1866, 4:175. A regulatory law on the 23 August decree, issued on 5 April 1867, established rules for operations revised and not revised by the Council of State, proceedings relative to questions of arbitration, and settlements made to regularize the operations. *Diario del Imperio*, 6 April 1867, 5:283.

25. Otterbourg to Seward, 29 August 1866, *Despatches from Consuls, Mexico City*, roll 6, vol. 11; and 26 September 1866, Díaz López, 4:390–91.

26. Cited in *La Sociedad*, 26 August 1866, pp. 2–3.

and in no hurry to comply with the law did not submit his acquisition for revision. With the law's annulment, he remained in possession of a property of which he would have been deprived under the revision law, and by paying a 15 percent tax he kept it with a secure title. Thus, the new law penalized those who had obeyed the law of revision and benefited those who had resisted it.[27] In any case, one source records that the effect of the new law was such that the office established to receive the sums still due for revised operations functioned with such activity that it resolved the majority of its transactions in twenty-four hours. These operations, however, yielded only a little more than $10,000.[28]

Still, it is unlikely that the law of 23 August was widely obeyed. Money was scarce and the Empire was crumbling. The decision to withdraw French forces had already been made, troops were being evacuated, and the French financial support of the Empire was, for the most part, at an end. The termination of revision may, therefore, be viewed in the context of the worsening political and fiscal condition of the Empire and Maximilian's need to turn to internal sources, taxation, to finance the government.[29]

During the period that revision was being pursued, Maximilian turned his attention as well to the allied matter of charitable and educational institutions. On at least two occasions Maximilian received information on the plight of those establishments: once through the highly colored presentation at Miramar in October 1863 and again in a more accurate and detailed report, written in December 1863, devoted exclusively to charities in Mexico City.[30]

This later analysis clarified the impact on the institutions of liberal

27. *La Sociedad*, 30 August 1866, p. 2.

28. *Diario del Imperio*, 26 April 1867; 5:344; and Rivera Cambas, *Historia de la intervención*, 2:343.

29. See Bazant, *Alienation*, pp. 272–74.

30. Joaquín García Icazbalceta, "Informe sobre los establecimientos de beneficencia y correción de ésta capital; su estado actual; noticia de sus fondos; reformas que desde luego necesitan y plan general de su arreglo, presentado por José María Andrade, Méjico, 1864. Escrito póstumo de Don Joaquín García Icazbalceta, publicado por su hijo Luis García Pimentel," in *Documentos históricos de Méjico* (Mexico: Moderna Librería Religiosa, 1907), 5:81–239.

anticorporate property legislation and the French Intervention. The real estate of charities, mostly urban, was sold as the Lerdo law provided, but the advantages of allowing corporations to retain the capital value of the real estate were deceptive. The capital realized was far less than the actual value of the property because of the system of public auctions adopted by the government and because the capital value was based on the low rents charged by the corporations. Thus, the institutions lost their real estate, while the income from the capital that replaced it was far from reflecting the true worth of the real estate. For example, houses which cost the Hospital of San Juan de Dios $80,000 were auctioned for $18,100. The customary manner of redemption of mortgages, a large proportion in bonds and a smaller percentage in specie, signified further loss. In effect, houses worth $80,000 were sold for about $5,500. Furthermore, debtors resisted payment of the interest due on the mortgages. Even though the nationalization law respected charitable property, in mid-1862 because of needs arising from the French invasion, the Juárez government appropriated the capital remaining to sustain those establishments. The government thus ended by completely absorbing the wealth and destroying the work of charities in aid of the poor.

The point made by the author of this report, José María Andrade, that charities lost wealth through the operation of the disamortization law, might have been extended in scope. All corporate property could suffer the same fate. For example, property sold at auction was usually for amounts below valuations. Losses were by no means universal, however. Even though the Church charged low rents, in some cases these still were capitalized at inflated values. For example, in Zacatecas the worst rental housing yielded $13 annually. The law established that the rent equalled 6 percent of a property's value, or $200 in this case. In fact, the value was only $70 or $80.[31] Thus, the corporation would realize in the redemption of a mortgage more than the actual worth of the property.

In any case, the deterioration in the financial condition of charities is undeniable, although there is evidence that in the pre-Reform era the existence of some, at least, was precarious. Benito Juárez as Governor of Oaxaca, for example, with the blessing of the bishop, sought

31. Scholes, "A Revolution Falters," p. 13, footnote 35.

to consolidate the resources of three hospitals in the state capital in order to provide adequate income for one hospital. Nevertheless, information is available showing the decline of charities' fortunes in the decade after 1856. One gauge of this decline is the reduced income through loss of real estate and capital during those years; another gauge is the figures that show expenses far exceeding income from all sources. For example, José María Andrade reported current monthly expenses of the charitable establishments in Mexico City for salaries, clothes, food, etc. as $19,008, while income from all sources—raffles, alms, government donations, etc.—was only $13,938. Another source lists redemptions of charitable capital in Mexico City of $2,163,175.08 to obtain funds to repel the French invaders. The capital that remained, $91,939.10, yielded only $5,534.10; against this income there was an annual budget of $186,100.22. Equally dismal statistics could be cited for other cities in Mexico.[32]

Schools, like charities, suffered from the trying political conditions. Foreign invasion brought closure of schools, sale of school buildings at a fraction of their value, and disposal of property supporting schools to pay government salaries and to reward service to the Nation, or simply to obtain resources to defend the country.[33] As the enemy progressively occupied Mexico, the liberals continued to draw on wealth of charities and schools. Government decrees made a pretense of maintaining income from nationalized charitable and educational property for the support of those institutions. The sincere desire

32. "Noticia de los capitales de beneficencia redimidos por orden del Supremo Gobierno y para auxilio de los gastos de la guerra," in Vicente Riva Palacio, *Miscelánea sin fechas*, Latin American Collection, University of Texas, Austin; and *Memoria que el ayuntamiento popular de 1868 presenta a sus comitentes y corresponde al semestre corrido desde el 1 de enero al 30 de junio* (Mexico, 1868), p. 17.

For other statistics, see Albert S. Evans, *Our Sister Republic: A Gala Trip through Tropical Mexico in 1869-70* (Hartford, Conn., 1870), pp. 121-26; and Mariano de Jesús Torres, *Historia civil y eclesiástica de Michoacán desde los tiempos antiguos hasta nuestros días* (Morelia: Tip. part. del autor, 1914), 1:373-76.

33. See, for example, Mariano de Icaza, *Exposición sobre la nulidad de las operaciones practicadas en los años 1861 y 62 con los bienes pertenecientes al Colegio de Niñas y a la corporación que lo fundó* (Mexico, 1864).

notwithstanding, inevitably the needs of the time meant the sacrifice of both education and the property sustaining it.[34]

Prior to Maximilian's arrival, General Forey hoped partially to remedy the damage done to these institutions and, at the same time, to reduce the heavy demands that support of charities made on the government. In May 1863 the General ordered the revision of sales of real estate belonging to charitable corporations in Puebla. Following appraisal, purchasers could keep the properties by paying the difference between the original purchase price and the new appraised value. They could, on the other hand, return the property to the corporations and receive what they had paid. Shortly thereafter, in July 1863, the French extended this order to the whole country and finally expanded its coverage to include mortgages as well as real estate. That the affected parties did not hasten to comply with these directives is shown by the extension granted for revision of the transactions. French policy apparently was no more successful in this specific area than it was in the general property issue.[35]

In order to aid the institutions, Maximilian exempted from nationalization the property of charities, public instruction, *ayuntamientos* (municipal governments), and other civil corporations. The Emperor nullified transactions involving such property. A later law did, however, validate, following revision, alienations of real estate of civil, charitable, and educational corporations made in conformity with the 1856 disamortization law. Even if revision proved a transaction irregular, the property was not returned to the corporation unless the irregularity specifically was a violation of the exemption that was granted to property that was directly and immediately destined for the purposes of the corporation. The law further nullified all redemptions of mortgages of such institutions executed in error or in malice under the 1859 nationalization laws. The affected mortgagor

34. *La Victoria. Periódico del Govierno de Oaxaca*, 3 January 1864, p. 4, and 28 January 1864, p. 1.

35. 22 May and 11 December 1863, Segura, 1:19–20, 113. Although it is not clear, these orders apparently covered only property destined for charitable ends that had been owned previously by *ayuntamientos* and other civil corporations. See 20 April and 3 May 1864, Segura, 2:169, 185, and 25 February 1865, 4:191.

could reclaim the amount paid in redemption, but then was to remain indebted for the mortgage.[36]

By a law of 27 May 1865, Maximilian left the administration of charities under individual councils of charity while *ayuntamientos* continued to pay their expenses and administer the funds. A change in 1866 placed the direction of charities exclusively under a general council. Charitable establishments were permitted to acquire real estate, but only that necessary for their own objectives, and their funds derived from property recovered through revision, funds administered by *ayuntamientos*, and donations.[37] Whatever the efforts and good intentions—and certainly no government, whether liberal, conservative, or imperial, wished deliberately to disable these institutions—charities and schools continued to be inadequate for the needs of society, both in the number and in financial resources. In the most peaceful or normal of times this was true, and these years were far from normal or peaceful. A decade of strife—civil war followed by foreign intervention—wreaked havoc on charities and schools. The end of that extraordinary era did not immediately bring an improvement. Indeed, improvement could not be expected, given the nature of liberal reforms, the state of the nation's finances, and the traditional paucity of local resources. The inadequacy of these important institutions continued to be a festering problem, partly the legacy of the troubled times.

Circumstances forced Napoleon III to withdraw the French Expeditionary Army from Mexico in stages during 1866 and early 1867. Among the considerations were the growing unpopularity of the adventure in France and increasing political pressure that could be brought to bear on Napoleon III as his regime "liberalized." The mounting pressure for liquidation of the intervention by the United States after the Union victory in the Civil War also influenced the French Emperor, and the unexpected, swift, and complete Prussian

36. 22 March 1865, Segura, 4:295; and 5 July 1865, *Leyes del Imperio*, pp. 12–16. Maximilian aided the Sisters of Charity specifically by cancelling the mortgages owed by them to various corporations. He did this because of the "noble charitableness" of the Sisters and the bad state of their finances. 22 May 1865, Segura, 4:617–18; and *Diario del Imperio*, 29 May 1865, 1:501.

37. *Diario del Imperio*, 7 June 1865, 1:533, and 20 June 1866, 3:591.

military victory over Austria in the summer of 1866 led to an accelera-
tion in the timetable for French evacuation.[38] This withdrawal,
coupled with the French appropriation of the customs revenues in an
attempt to recoup part of her heavy financial investment, meant that
the days of the Empire were numbered: Maximilian could not sustain
his throne financially or militarily. His direction of affairs was indeci-
sive, even inept. Liberal policies and conciliation failed to consolidate
Maximilian's position, and he seriously considered abdication. A
confidant, Father Agustín Fischer, apparently convinced him that a
solution to the ecclesiastical problem and hope for the throne—the
only solution and hope—lay in an agreement with the conservative
and clerical forces. After some hesitation, he decided to remain in
Mexico and place himself in conservative hands. In September 1866
Maximilian formed a conservative cabinet.[39] But without the French
army, the Empire quickly disintegrated, and Maximilian, with his
grand and well-intentioned plans, was sacrificed with it. President
Juárez' second and last forced absence from Mexico City was over. In
mid-1867 the liberals again occupied the capital. The road was open
to the long-promised reconstruction of the country; nationalization
could be consummated.

38. Napoleon definitely decided by January 1866 to withdraw French
forces from Mexico. The withdrawal was originally to be made in three
stages—in October 1866, the spring of 1867, and October 1867. The outcome
of the Austro-Prussian War apparently caused him to accelerate his timetable.

39. N. Andrew N. Cleven, "The Ecclesiastical Policy of Maximilian of
Mexico," *Hispanic American Historical Review* 9 (August 1929): 357.

Chapter 7
Nationalized Property under the Restored Republic, 1867–1876

After the collapse of the Empire, the victorious government confronted conditions and tasks similar to those following the defeat of the conservatives in the civil war: an empty treasury, a paralyzed economy, and destitute agriculture and commerce. The fissures in society had to be closed, the wounds healed. Once again a law was needed to redefine the rules for transactions with nationalized ecclesiastical property.[1]

President Juárez in 1867, as in 1861, cleaved insofar as possible to the Lincolnian concept of charity toward all and malice toward none. A radical liberal element made difficult the pursuit of a conciliatory policy toward the Church, as did some clerical-conservative activities, but Juárez in 1867 considered the revolution achieved and the principles vindicated for which he had steadfastly fought for a decade. Conciliation did not, however, signify surrender to the clergy. It meant looking to the future, not clinging to the past. Progress for Mexico was a task for all. Divisions of the past, if maintained, would only be an obstacle to progress and prosperity.[2]

The Zapotec Indian insisted as he always had that separation of Church and State be respected by both sides. Nevertheless, civil encroachment in religious affairs and, conversely, clerical opposition to the laws constituted a perennial problem. There were complaints that judges ordered priests not to baptize, marry, or bury without prior evidence of the civil registration of those acts. Priests had even been imprisoned, fined, or banished for failure to comply. The federal government prohibited such meddling in purely religious matters as

1. For the condition of the country in 1867–1868 according to the principal advisor of President Juárez, see *Memorias de Sebastián Lerdo de Tejada*, preliminary study by Leonardo Pasquel (Mexico: Editorial Citlaltépetl, 1959), pp. 11–12. Pasquel believes that Adolfo Carrillo was the real author of the *Memorias*, basing them on interviews with Lerdo.

2, Karl M. Schmitt, "Evolution of Mexican Thought on Church-State Relations, 1876–1911," (Ph.D. diss., University of Pennsylvania, 1954), pp. 26–31.

contrary to the Reform laws, but adherence to, or obstruction of, the laws depended largely on attitudes of state and local officials rather than on dictation from Mexico City. Thus, actions varied considerably at the local level, and the problem continued.[3] For their part, clergy in some areas opposed the laws to the point of excommunicating those who complied with civil registration. Clergy refused religious marriage to those who had a civil ceremony; a priest denied confession to a dying girl because she had been married civilly and not canonically. In certain localities religious processions held in defiance of the law were well attended, especially by women, and cemeteries remained illegally in clerical hands. Clerical activities affected nationalization of property as well. For example, a parish priest presented a dying man with a paper to sign restoring to the Church a plot of land that he purchased for $60, while another priest intervened to prevent the signing. Allegedly, many people, fearing threats of damnation, returned property to the Church, thereby leaving their families destitute. Thus, the republican government faced the question of nationalized property in an atmosphere of obstruction and conflict that made its task more difficult.[4] In view of such actions the Ministry of Government repeated an earlier order to governors concerning separation of Church and State—because of the "daily complaints" received about the "reprehensible" means used by the clergy to evade the Reform laws. The Ministry emphasized its continuing efforts to prevent authorities from interfering in purely religious matters but insisted that clerical acts contrary to the civil registry and other Reform laws had to be punished.[5]

Early in the Intervention the Juárez government had voided all acts of the usurpers and established harsh penalties for anyone cooperating with them. After the victory neither policy appeared entirely practicable. There were some executions—Generals Miramón and Mejía who died with Maximilian at Querétaro, Santiago Vidaurri, and a few others. There were some confiscations of property and many fines.

3. 20 December 1868, Bassols, pp. 192–93.

4. *Diario Oficial*, 22 July 1868, p. 1; 22 March 1868, p. 3, citing *El Observador* of Matamoros; 24 March 1868, p. 3; and 4 November 1870, p. 2.

5. 5 October 1871, repeating the circular of 20 July 1868, in *Memoria que el Secretario de Estado y del despacho de Gobernación presenta al sexto congreso constitucional* (Mexico, 1871), document 10, pp. 79–81.

Surprisingly soon, however, Imperial supporters found their way back into republican government service, and persecution was relatively slight. With regard to Imperial laws, Juárez found it impractical and injurious to nullify all judicial acts of the invaders. Actions begun under the Empire continued under republican judges, and the republic confirmed many Imperial court decisions. In civil cases, a formal written protest was necessary to nullify a decision, except for actions contrary to the Reform laws or executed in fulfillment of the laws. Decisions of French military courts were annulled, as were criminal judgments based solely on loyalty to the Juárez government.[6]

The relatively lenient policy toward Imperial collaborators and judicial proceedings was one thing; the attitude toward property revision was a different matter. Imperial revision was undone and nationalization vigorously pursued. A decree issued immediately following the republican victory ordered the restoration of property to those deprived of it through Imperial revision. A special office for nationalized property established in the Ministry of Finance was responsible for revising Imperial proceedings as well as other matters relative to administration and disentailment of former clerical real estate and the redemption and disposal of mortgages.[7] These were only preliminary, stopgap measures, however.

A new and more comprehensive law on nationalized property soon followed these first steps on 19 August 1867.[8] The two major aspects of that act concerned denunciations and redemptions. Denunciations had to be of occult ecclesiastical real estate or capital, defined as property unknown to government offices or courts. As under the Empire, sizeable rewards were offered for denunciations on a sliding scale: from one-third of the amount obtained by the government under $10,000 down to 8 percent to the denouncer for anything over $200,000. Following a new appraisal, real estate, as in the past, was redeemable by payment of 40 percent in cash and 60 percent in bonds or credits. Convents and other buildings destined for public use, however, were not adjudicable; nor were mortgages redeemable that sus-

6. A decree of 15 October 1863 nullified all acts of interventionist judges; the law of 20 August 1867 allowed all pending civil actions started under the usurpers to be completed by republican judges. Labastida, pp. 244–46.

7. 21 June and 12 August 1867, Labastida, pp. 487, 304.

8. Labastida, pp. 160–61.

tained educational or charitable institutions. The redemption of mortgages varied with the circumstances; terms depended on whether or not the mortgage was occult or interest payments were in arrears, whether the mortgage contract had expired and, if not, the length of time remaining. The provisions in this regard were especially important. Expired mortgage contracts, those within a year of expiration, and those with interest payments in arrears were collectable entirely in cash; if between one and two years remained on the contract, 75 percent was redeemable in specie and 25 percent in bonds. The scale of cash payment continued to diminish to contracts with more than four years to run, redeemable with 40 percent in cash, 60 percent in bonds.

The objectives of the new law were clearly to increase federal revenue from nationalized property and to eliminate abuses. The increased stringency provided both the basis for criticism and the major reason for the law's failure. The government justified the new measure on the basis of altered circumstances. In the early days of nationalization the primary goal was political, to implement the laws quickly and to defeat the country's enemies. By 1867–1868, it was no longer necessary to sacrifice the financial possibilities of nationalized property. The government believed that real estate no longer sold for a fraction of its value, a circumstance that earlier made it in no hurry to obtain sums due. The administration also believed that little occult property remained.

The new law, especially the denunciation and redemption provisions, reflected the government's perception of the changed conditions. The law of 19 August 1867 restricted denouncers' privileges by granting them only a fixed percentage in proportion to the amount accruing to the treasury. No longer could a denouncer's portion be exorbitant, nor could he designate which part of a property, always the choicest, he wanted as his reward. The law eliminated two abuses by limiting denunciations to occult property and defining it as property unknown to the authorities. It was unjust to permit denouncers to use information supplied by government employees with knowledge of the properties as it was to accept denunciations of properties already known to public officials. Republican authorities expected to take advantage of the new information available as a result of transactions submitted for Imperial revision. The government hoped to avoid disputes and conflict over rights that often arose by the denunciation of the same property by different individuals in different offices. Henceforth, state offices of finance recorded the hour and date of each denunciation and forwarded this information to the Ministry in Mexico City. With regard to redemptions, the law not only required immediate payment but also prohibited the substitution of bonds for specie. This common practice was detrimental to the treasury because bonds were so cheaply bought on the market.[9]

The desire to increase income from nationalized property is understandable, but the government seriously misjudged the situation. A simple perusal of the official newspaper reveals that many properties were denounced in late 1867 and early 1868. For example, one issue alone listed 240 urban properties. It would seem, too, that ordinary real estate was available for 30 percent of its value; it was thus unrealistic to expect the immediate payment in specie of 40 percent of the value of nationalized property. Moreover, a major objective of the law, putting an end to the sacrifice of nationalized property for a fraction of its worth, was a patent failure.

The hope of obtaining important resources from the disposal of remaining wealth, or at least significantly reducing the public debt, proved unfounded. Nevertheless, although the law tightened the rules, the terms were even then not entirely unfavorable for the acquisition of nationalized property, and the difficulty at times of disposing of real estate increased the advantageous terms. Thus, houses confiscated from Imperial collaborators and put up for auction found no bidders, so the asking price had to be reduced at a later auction. One house confiscated from General Juan N. Almonte valued at $14,700 was reduced to $9,800, and a house of Joaquín Velázquez de León was reduced from $7,860 to $5,120. The auction announcement indicated that the minimum acceptable bid on traitors' property was two-thirds of the amount in cash.[10]

9. "Memoria que el secretario de Estado y del despacho de hacienda y crédito público presenta al Congreso de la Unión," of 20 February 1868, reprinted in *Diario Oficial*, 16 and 18 July, p. 1, and 19 July 1868, pp. 1–2.

10. *Diario Oficial*, 6 February 1868, p. 3. See also issues of 9 November 1867, p. 4, 3 and 4 January 1868, p. 4; Gutiérrez and Alatorre, vol. 2, pt. 2,

In general, the income from the rental or sale of confiscated properties was negligible, and the amounts obtained from nationalized property represented a small percentage of total federal income, and most of that was not in cash.[11] Unfortunately, official government reports do not reveal the specific activity under the 1867 law, but they do provide totals for income from nationalized property, which included continuing redemption of mortgages, payment of promissory notes, and sales of real estate. Thus, for example, the office of nationalized property reported income, apparently gross income, between 1 January and 30 June 1866 of about $367,000. This total included approximately $112,000 in cash, $210,300 in bonds and credits, and $19,000 in promissory notes.[12] The total income from nationalized property during the next fiscal year, 1868–1869, was about the same, $371,806.[13]

The hope that expired mortgages were collectable totally in cash succeeded no better than the expectations for auctions, denunciations, or debt reduction. The first admission was the acceptance of sizeable sums in credits, as had been the practice earlier. Then on 1 July 1869 the government discontinued that procedure and suspended all operations of nationalized property pending issue of a new law. In fact, operations under the 1867 measure had virtually ceased before this. Ministry of Finance officials, from Minister Matías Romero down to those in lower echelons, recognized that the 1867 law was too harsh. More favorable bases for the acquisition of property had to be established or reinstated, notably by accepting a considerable proportion of redemptions in bonds or credits. Furthermore, absolute security of possession had to be given to purchasers of property.[14]

Congressional critics, less concerned with financial considerations,

pp. 705–6, 718–19; and Session of 5 November 1868, in Pantaleón Tovar, *Historia parlamentaria del cuarto congreso constitucional* (Mexico, 1872–1874), 2:474–75.

11. See, for example, *Memoria de Hacienda, 1869–1870* (Mexico, 1870), pp. 763–64. Since most of these annual *Memorias* (*Informes* for 1872–75) have roughly the same title, hereafter they will be cited as *Memoria (Informe) de Hacienda, 18   –18*

12. *Memoria de Hacienda, el 28 de setiembre de 1868*, p. 18.

13. *Memoria de Hacienda, 1868–1869*, p. 62.

14. *Memoria de Hacienda, el 31 de enero de 1868*, pp. 16–17; and *Memoria de Hacienda, 1868–1869*, pp. 16, 30–31.

found the law in violation of the spirit and intent of the original disamortization and nationalization measures. A major objective of the legislation was to make property accessible to many people. Any obstruction of that goal thwarted the spirit of the liberal program. The 1867 law did just that; indeed, it virtually paralyzed operations by its redemption and denunciation requirements. Another obstacle to the fulfillment of nationalization was the inconvenient, if not impossible, requirement that acceptable denunciations be accompanied by innumerable data from registry books. These data were virtually unobtainable by the general citizenry, and treasury officials should have investigated the existence of occult property from information supplied by a denouncer, however incomplete it was. Deputy Ramón Fernández, supported by the Coahuila delegation, proposed a law that would have eased the legal requirements for denunciation and facilitated redemptions. A new law in 1869 did relax the payment requirements, and much later, in December 1875, the government finally eased the requirement that an acceptable denunciation needed the presentation of all pertinent property records; instead, the government insisted only on sufficient data to demand from the possessor his title or other proof of legal ownership. In any event, the discovery of so-called "hidden" property was a serious problem only partly attributable to the legal requirements. The decade of political upheaval was more to blame. During the years of turmoil many federal and state archives and notarial registers disappeared. At the end of the civil war in 1860 many employees in the state of Mexico fled with records, a number of which were later lost or destroyed. President Juárez, in evacuating the capital in 1863, took with him many documents relating to nationalization; many of these did not survive his "travels." The loss of records made it difficult to collect amounts owed and prevented the government's having knowledge of property.[15]

While the authorities continued to process nationalization cases, they faced problems of types long familiar, such as the perennial difficulty in collection of amounts due on promissory notes. A single notice in the official periodical listed ninety-two persons in arrears on

15. Session of 5 November 1868, Tovar, 3:474–75; "Un Progresista," *Los moderados y el estado de México* (Toluca, 1861), pp. 24–25; Pallares, pp. 216–17; and *Diario Oficial*, 16 January 1876, pp. 1–2.

their notes. To cope with the matter, the government ordered that when it was necessary to use force to collect the sums due, movable property would be seized first, and, if that were insufficient to cover the debt, then the income and produce of the real estate would be taken. Eventually the authorities levied a fine not to exceed 10 percent of the debt. Collection of promissory notes due the government was only one aspect of this question. Another involved claims against the treasury for repayment of the value of notes redeemed in operations later nullified by the government. These notes represented a continuing threat to the treasury; therefore, the government, when it voided transactions, established a time limit of eight months for presentation of claims, after which the notes were without value.[16]

Inadequate information created problems. The government lacked knowledge of the status of many transactions. As noted earlier, the years of political upheaval were a primary reason for the lack of data on clerical wealth—occult property; political conditions also accounted for the misplacement of information on mortgages. The Ministry of Finance published lists of mortgages about whose redemption it had no information and ordered possessors to prove their redemptions or face payment of the capital value plus interest. The government also required notaries to forward all data in their notarial and mortgage registers. One published list included 120 mortgages ranging in value from $73 to $100,000. Another listed 119 mortgages, with a composite value of more than $750,000 on 45 haciendas, 19 *ranchos*, and assorted houses, lands, and mills.[17]

Denunciations were another common source of dispute, particularly of property legally exempt from denunciation. These actions sometimes resulted from a legitimate ignorance of the law or uncertainty over the inclusion of a particular property under nationalization. At times, however, there was a deliberate intent to circumvent the law. Disamortization had specifically excluded civil and ecclesiastical corporate property destined immediately and directly to the purposes of the institutions. Therefore, denunciation of a parish residence was illegal as long as it continued to serve as the priest's home.

16. *Diario Oficial,* 9 October 1867, p. 4; 20 May, 18 November 1869 and 11 December 1871, Labastida, pp. 269, 290–91.
17. *Diario Oficial,* 27 May 1871, pp. 1–2 and 10 June 1869, p. 1; and *Memoria de Hacienda, 1870–1871,* pp. 596–601.

Other cases were not so clear-cut. For example, the government voided the denunciation and adjudication of the Puebla botanical gardens—a denunciation in which the head of the state office of the Finance Ministry apparently abused his office. Also disallowed was denunciation of a bequest to a priest, the government basing its decision on an individual's right to reward clergy for services rendered as long as the payment was not in real estate.[18]

While the Ministry of Finance struggled with a multitude of problems, the property question as well as many others, the failure of the 1867 law became apparent. Therefore, the administration submitted a bill to Congress on 25 September 1869 designed to facilitate nationalization operations. The congressional committee that examined the bill heartily endorsed it as a necessary corrective to the 1867 law, which had made it more costly to acquire nationalized property than private property. This allegedly was the reason so much property remained occult. There was insufficient advantage in seeking out and denouncing the property, thus depriving the treasury of resources and evading the Reform. Evidently, there was not as much nationalized property remaining as had been assumed, nor did it enjoy the expected market value.[19]

The new law of 10 December 1869 was designed to correct the shortcomings in the earlier measure and to end the near-paralysis in operations by dividing redemption payments for all unalienated nationalized property into three parts: one part payable over a period of time in bonds of the public debt; the second in so-called "liquidation certificates"; and the last part in cash, with a maximum of twenty months to pay. As a result of the relaxation of redemption terms, dealings in nationalized property revived, and redemptions, or payments to the government, accelerated. Income from this source more than doubled, rising from a low of about $295,000 in 1869–1870 to $779,000 in 1870–1871. For the next two years the figure remained well over $700,000 annually.[20]

While federal authorities grappled with nationalization, ecclesiasti-

18. 7 May and 27 March 1868, Bassols, pp. 193–95; and 30 March 1868, Labastida, p. 231.

19. *Diario Oficial*, 27 September 1869, p. 2; *Siglo*, 10 October 1869, p. 1; and *Memoria de Hacienda, 1870–1871*, p. 72.

20. Labastida, pp. 163–64; and *Memoria de Hacienda, 1869–1870*, pp. 981–

cal authorities, as during the civil war and Empire, provided guidance to the faithful. Soon after the collapse of the Second Empire, an episcopal circular reminded the people of the official position vis à vis the liberal laws. With certain specific exceptions, Catholics could not participate in the laws' implementation. Renting an adjudicated property was not permissible inasmuch as that act implied recognition of the purchaser's ownership and at the same time acknowledged the legality of the Church's despoilment. On the other hand, in the eyes of the Church, legitimate pré-Lerdo law tenants who had refused to adjudicate the property did not lose their rights and could in good conscience continue in tenancy. Furthermore, in case of extreme need, determined according to the person's class, clerical authorities permitted temporary rental of an adjudicated property until another could be found.[21]

Several years later, presumably because many purchasers wished a reconciliation, the episcopacy established detailed procedures for an accommodation with the Church. The petitioner first applied to the parish priest, who required an oath accepting the validity of the various Church protests against being deprived of its property and acknowledging the obligation to return all the property he had usurped. The priest next obtained a statement that included: the property's value and current condition; the corporation to which it had belonged; the amount due the corporation since the usurpation and the one to whom payment had been made; and the name of anyone else involved in the usurpation. The priest then heard the proposal for restitution of the property. This proposal had to include the above information as well as the return of the property, if it was in the applicant's hands, and his agreement that it could be sold if it suited Church interests. The proposal also had to contain a declaration that the penitent made this accommodation voluntarily and freely in order to come to terms with his conscience. Also required were a humble supplication for absolution from the censure incurred and a request for pardon for injury done to the Church. The bishop received this agreement between priest and applicant; if the ecclesias-

82. See also *Memoria de Hacienda, 1870–1871*, and *Informe de Hacienda, 1872–1873*.

21. Circular of 28 October 1867, *Undécima pastoral*, p. 38.

tical *cabildo* consented, removal of the censure followed the execution of the agreement's terms.[22]

During the Porfirian regime, agreements, called *contentas*, also restored an undetermined amount of wealth to the Church. Through a *contenta* a person who had acquired clerical property obtained a renunciation of all Church ownership rights in exchange for a sum of money. These transactions were conducted secretly, and it is not known how much wealth the Church acquired as a result, but presumably many of the faithful desired to make peace with the Church.

Although the effects of the 1869 law encouraged the administration, it soon became evident that operations were not proceeding as quickly as desired, that still more favorable terms had to be granted. As lenient as the government made redemption terms, there remained outstanding obligations for bonds, the new liquidation certificates, and the ubiquitous promissory notes that purchasers had signed but not redeemed. To deal with these delinquencies, the government ordered the sale of properties on which obligations were outstanding. The appointment of special investigators (*visitadores*) further aimed at the discovery and prevention of irregularities in nationalization dealings. These federal agents checked deeds, promissory notes, and denunciations and reviewed transactions in general to prevent defrauding the treasury and to assure fulfillment of all legal requirements. For example, they searched out unpaid interest and redemption terms confirmed for less than the value of the property. They investigated denunciations to ascertain that there had been no earlier ones on the same property; they made certain that the denouncer received his proper reward and that the denounced property was in fact occult, unknown to government offices.[23]

The Congress in April 1873, as in November 1868, sought to eliminate nationalized property once and for all as a factor disturbing economic and social tranquility. The Finance Commission of the Chamber of Deputies reduced the various proposals it examined on the issue to four main principles that revealed the major concerns a

22. Circular of 2 January 1871, ibid., pp. 35–37.
23. *Memoria de Hacienda, 1870–1871*, p. 72; Circular of 29 March 1872, Labastida, p. 270; and *Diario Oficial*, 29 August 1871, pp. 1–2.

decade and a half after nationalization took place. These were that: current possessors of "undisputed" property be freed from future denunciations; disamortizable property be alienated in conformity with the laws; a time limit be placed on denunciations, litigation, and pending claims; nationalized mortgages and real estate be granted to municipalities for the support of charities and education. The Commission proposed a law embodying the first three of these points. The fourth was excluded because of the enormous federal deficit and in the belief that such an action would simply transfer pending complaints to municipalities.[24]

Clearly, uppermost in the legislators' thinking was the disposal of the entire interminable matter as expeditiously as possible. More than that, the deputies reflected the very real concern that existed over the continuing insecurity of ownership and the depressed value of property. Their commentary amounted to a catalogue of factors that had complicated nationalization from the beginning and frustrated the termination of the process. Legislators pointed to the continuing denunciations and litigation. Religious beliefs and clerical attitudes also contributed to the inferior status of nationalized property in the market. The government, although equally interested in security of ownership and property values, was reluctant to terminate denunciations because it was unwilling to sacrifice resources that might be obtained to retire the debt and defray costs of public programs. Thus, the laws simply delayed and muddled completion of disamortization. In addition, personal rivalries between the department of the Finance Ministry responsible for nationalization matters, Section 6, and the Ministry itself seemed to preempt public interest. For example, the accusations of infractions of the law brought by Juan Zambrano, head of Section 6, against the Minister, Matías Romero, derived from personal animosity and perhaps political factionalism—Zambrano was a Porfirista and Romero an old Juarista. Furthermore, the department acted as a revising body, which alarmed proprietors, and it acted as a mock court with pleas, allegations, and suits taking place as though before real tribunals and judges. Indeed, deputies alleged that government offices were a "hotbed of complaints" and an "arsenal that

24. Report of the Finance Commission of the Chamber of Deputies, 4 April 1873, in *Diario de los debates. Sexto congreso constitucional de la unión* (Mexico, 1887), 4:58–61. Cited hereafter as *Diario-sexto*.

contrivers" exploited against proprietors. Some otherwise "respectable" men submitted contracts to perpetual revisions. Unfounded denunciations and transactions arose. Interminable and sterile proceedings continued, based on proprietors' desires to make their possession secure. All of these scandalous activities produced incalculable difficulties; they deprived some people of property and placed the ownership of others in doubt.[25]

The Chamber of Deputies was not the only forum for criticism of the government as it struggled with the monumental nationalization issue. *El Monitor*, a Porfirian paper, charged federal authorities with carrying out an impossible but nonetheless alarming and threatening revision of nationalization operations, including those which had been definitively terminated. The government, in the *Diario Oficial*, did not deny the charge of revision as such but insisted that only a few transactions were involved and that those were pending, not concluded, transactions. Some revision was necessary to prevent treasury losses from irregular operations. The legislation itself distinguished between dealings. On the one hand, there were those carried out in conformity with the laws or, although irregular, approved definitively by the government. On the other hand, there were those operations whereby property did not legitimately pass to private hands because of occultation or other reasons. The former transactions were irrevocable. The latter were pending and denounceable and thus subject to revision.[26]

While press and congressional criticisms made the unsatisfactory status of nationalization clear, the administration itself supplied further evidence, though with a different focus. Government officials emphasized especially technical problems hindering progress toward liquidation of nationalization. A multitude of proceedings (*expedientes*) were initiated after 1867, many of which remained unresolved. In addition to old transactions, in fiscal 1872–1873, 545 new petitions were filed dealing with denunciations, deed cancellations, debts for

25. 4 April 1873, *Diario-sexto*, 4:58–61. See also *Expediente informativo formado por la sección del gran jurado del congreso de la unión, con motivo de la acusación presentada por D. Juan Andrés Zambrano contra el C. Ministro de Hacienda y Crédito Público, Matías Romero* (Mexico, 1868).

26. *El Monitor*, cited in *Diario Oficial*, 24 September, 3 and 21 October 1874, p. 1; and 12 November 1874, pp. 2–3.

promissory notes, and claims against the treasury arising from nationalized property or nuns' dowries. The property in denunciations alone involved 243 pieces of real estate and mortgages worth $1,576,102.81. The next year there were 699 new proceedings, including denunciations of 482 pieces of real estate and mortgages valued at $2,188,751.90. There were more than 500 new transactions in 1874–1875, denunciations involving 285 properties and mortgages valued at $1,959,476.24. The various transactions, old and new, in 1872–1873 produced 4,506 resolutions, but only 636 were definitive. Little absolute progress was made, as terminated operations barely kept ahead of new ones. An unfortunate practice contributed to this situation: those who disagreed with the decisions could request revocation of their agreements, making a new examination of the case necessary, including hearing allegations and reviewing all the relevant documents.[27]

Other circumstances hindered the nationalization process, some of which were perhaps minor concerns of the government but especially important for individuals. One of these, which also contributed to depressed real estate values, was the single mortgage that covered several properties. Since the mortgage applied to all the properties, a partial cancellation for one property, leaving the others encumbered for the remaining amount, apparently required special congressional authorization. Second was the matter of the many mortgagors who were unable to redeem their promissory notes either because the holders of the notes did not present them for payment or because the whereabouts of the notes were unknown. In these circumstances the debtors could not negotiate for their payment. This led to an illegal practice; a debtor deposited a cash amount in the treasury equivalent to part or all of the missing promissory notes, and in exchange he obtained the cancellation of the debt or part of it.

Further complications related to denunciations and their relationship to mortgages and the condition of records. For one thing, denunciations seldom referred to only one property or mortgage. Generally, several were involved—one covered fifty-five mortgages—and

27. *Informe de Hacienda, 1872–1873,* pp. 147–48, 150; and *Informe de Hacienda, 1873–1874,* pt. 1, p. CCLXXVII; and *Informe de Hacienda, 1874–1875,* pp. 290–91.

as many as two or three hundred had been the object of denunciation. In addition, the information submitted by denouncers to support their cases was filed alphabetically or numerically in a notebook to facilitate examination—one case contained over 2,000 pages—but the archives that had to be searched by Ministry officials were chaotic. Records were an agglomeration from republican and imperial regimes. There was no inventory and no order. Daily searches had to be made for antecedents of transactions that sometimes dated back 100 years. Often the archives of the extinct Juzgado de Capellanías, the primary pre-Reform ecclesiastical lending institution, or other corporations had to be searched; these documents were voluminous and strangely arranged. Furthermore, the use of the depositories by inexpert personnel and the scattered locations of various archives posed other difficulties. At times the files were even multilated and useless. At least, however, the archivist had at his disposal the indispensable registry of denunciations to aid his search for antecedents. This registry indicated whether a property or mortgage had previously been denounced. If it had, then a new denunciation claiming that the property was occult was inadmissible. Finally, a lack of personnel contributed to the slow processing of cases. Lamentably, to discharge its many tasks the responsible Ministry department employed only a chief, four officials to substantiate proceedings, four secretaries, and an archivist.[28]

Not the least of the difficulties obstructing a definitive conclusion of nationalization related to the amount of ecclesiastical wealth subject to the laws. In order for the government confidently to close the door on nationalization and achieve the much desired goal of secure ownership, it was important to determine a total value for ecclesiastical wealth and the amount of nationalized property that still remained available. Such calculations posed a difficult, in fact an impossible, task.[29] The accumulation of transactions in the Ministry, the haste with which the first ones were made, disorder in the archives, bad faith—all these factors impeded formation of statistics on Church property. Records and documents had been lost or destroyed so that necessary data on only a few areas were available. Moreover, during

28. *Informe de Hacienda, 1872–1873*, pp. 148, 150.
29. Ibid., pp. 151ff.

most of the colonial period, mortgage registration took place in the mortgage office issuing the deed, even when the location of the property was in some other district. The same mortgage might also be repeated several times over the years because of renegotiation of a debt when the interest became too burdensome; perhaps the mortgages had passed to other individuals. Calculating the amount of nationalized property still obtainable by the government was as elusive as determining total ecclesiastical wealth—lack of information, fraud, and confusion, facilitated by the political changes, attended redemption operations and mortgage cancellations. A long-standing fraud was simply changing dates on documents, including altering the dates of mortgage cancellations to avoid the penalty of double payment for having been carried out during the civil war; also registry books carried certain mortgages as active simply because interested individuals advancing claims presented documents dated prior to the expiration of the time limit for payments.

Various reasons aside from fraud accounted for the confusion. For example, mortgage and registry books recorded transactions in which both parties were ecclesiastical corporations. In such cases the government was both creditor and debtor, but the mortgages had not been cancelled or stricken from the active list because of lack of information regarding their status. Another source of confusion was the failure to cancel instruments with the completion of operations. For example, only the first monthly cash payment might be recorded as satisfied (*tildado*) or only the part in bonds; at times there was no explanation for a cancellation, except perhaps that it was by judicial order. In some cases newspapers carried notices to creditors to make a claim within a specified time; after that date the record of the operation was marked cancelled just as if it had been completed, disregarding the nation's right to future collection of the debt. Indeed, cancellations had been recorded without the express order of a competent authority, or of any authority, but simply because the interested parties presented the series of promissory notes to an official in charge or informed the government office that the debts had been paid.[30]

These and other practices attest to the chaos in the records and offices. Even without such practices it would still probably have been impossible to determine the extent of nationalized property available

30. Ibid., pp. 156–57.

because of the lack of necessary data. This problem was traceable in part, though not entirely, to the indolence of officials. In many areas of the republic, officials had not determined the number of mortgaged properties; in others, they did not know the value of the contracts. Furthermore, the federal government lacked information from the vast majority of mortgage offices in the country. Data had been requested but was available from only 97 of the 324 offices; the government did not even know who was in charge of 51 of the offices. Those responsible for mortgage and registry offices thus failed to forward notices of corporation mortgages. Aside from the damage to statistics, this meant—and this was more serious and compounded the existing confusion—that the government inadvertently accepted denunciations of properties as occult when in reality the mortgages appeared in registers not yet made available to the authorities. Part of the trouble, consistently admitted by Ministers of Finance, was the peremptory and careless way in which civil war governors and military commanders carried out property transactions. These officials did not register the dealings in state finance offices; they exchanged nationalized property or demanded redemption of mortgages on the spot, either directly or through *ad hoc* commissions, in order to obtain resources for the war. Of necessity, federal authority approved these operations, but their extent or value was unknown.[31]

Government employees from national to local levels, in so many ways an impediment to processing nationalization cases, seemed especially irresponsible in localities far from the watchful eye and power of superior authority. The state offices of the Finance Ministry were responsible for reporting to Mexico City on all matters relative to nationalized property, such as denunciations, controversies, settlement of debts, and the issuance of deeds. The state offices placed officials in various towns, but outside the large ones where the chief offices were situated, a notable lack of cooperation prevailed in fulfilling the requirements of each transaction; therefore, the collection of sums due lagged. Even an honorarium of 10 percent of the amount collected in specie as an inducement failed to secure the employment of effective collection agents.[32]

31. *Informe de Hacienda, 1873–1874,* pt. 1, p. CCLXXXIII; and *Memoria de Hacienda, 1870–1871,* pp. 71–73.
32. *Informe de Hacienda, 1874–1875,* p. 289.

In the 1870s speculation remained a durable aspect of the property question. Some denouncers obtained the required governmental declarations, accepting their denunciation as admissible, and then approached the mortgagor, proposing that he pay the denouncer a part of the amount owed. In return, the denouncer promised not to continue with the denunciation proceedings. A little later, the same person, using an intermediary, denounced the mortgage again, requesting that the previous denunciation be invalidated because no action had been taken on it. The Minister of Finance, Francisco Mejía, like his predecessor Matías Romero, proposed solutions to the wide-ranging problems afflicting nationalization, and he attempted to bring order out of the chaos hindering the processing of cases, but with little success in the decade of the Restored Republic.[33]

As mentioned previously, of abiding concern to the administration and to the Minister of Finance in particular were security of proprietorship and retirement of the public debt; both were intimately related to nationalization of clerical property. Matías Romero believed that by 1870 most of the property had been alienated and that it was important to close the books on nationalization, giving security of ownership to those who had acquired property. As matters stood, they feared the loss of their properties through administrative action or unfounded denunciations. Romero recommended two policies. The first was to accept total payment for the property in bonds of the public debt. The second was to terminate irrevocably administrative actions on nationalization, leaving the courts as the only recourse to disputants. The President did declare that preference of rights disputes should be decided by the courts rather than by administrative offices. The courts, in fact, did exercise jurisdiction over those questions; the result was conflict between governmental departments and the tribunals. The courts, with strict legalism and seeming disregard for the rectitude of the government's actions, jealously guarded their prerogatives to deal with such cases. The Supreme Court, especially, overturned lower court decisions and supported with writs of *amparo*, or injunctions, individuals who claimed violation of constitutional rights when administrative decisions deprived them of property and

33. *Informe de Hacienda, 1873–1874*, pt. 1, pp. CCLXXXI–LXXXII.

awarded it to others.[34] Romero believed that the measures he recommended would benefit individuals in the acquisition of property at a low price, the treasury would benefit by retiring part of the debt, and the length of time to complete an operation would be shortened. The Minister suggested another simple and useful method to dispose of the property—allow municipalities to obtain nationalized mortgages for the support of public education. This recommendation was not adopted at the time, but it was revived in 1873 and discussed by the Finance Commission of the Chamber of Deputies, which rejected the idea as noted previously. Finally, in 1876, shortly after his successful revolution, Díaz did issue a decree granting to municipalities the remaining nationalized property, the income from which was to be divided equally between support of public education and charities.[35] In any case, Romero hoped by these various recommendations to provide absolute security to possessors of nationalized property, while at the same time making certain that all, or nearly all, property had been discovered and sold.[36]

The problem of the national debt was of longstanding concern, and the retirement of that debt was an objective of the nationalization laws. The government, in providing for payment partly in cash and partly in bonds, certainly intended to amortize the internal debt. In addition, those who obtained the property received an advantage, inasmuch as the bonds could be bought at a fraction of their face value. In fact, the value of the bonds acceptable in nationalization operations showed little appreciation over the years. Miguel Lerdo reported in 1857 that they temporarily brought 12 or 15 percent of their value shortly after the decree on disamortization. Thereafter, they were generally worth 5 percent. In 1873 the bonds still sold for only 7 percent of their value.[37] If the laws had been rigorously adhered to, perhaps nearly all of the legally issued bonds could have been retired. Romero, at least, believed that $24,250,000 out of a total

34. See, for example, *Diario Oficial*, 2 November 1871, p. 1, and 10 November 1871, p. 2.

35. *Memoria de Hacienda, 1876–1877*, p. 11, Decree of 30 November 1876.
36. *Memoria de Hacienda, 1869–1870*, pp. 982–83.

37. Ibid., pp. 565–68; and Juan Velasco to Villada, 8 January 1873, in José Vicente Villada, *Correspondencia, 1871–1879*, Latin American Collection, University of Texas, Austin.

$29,250,000 in outstanding bonds of the internal debt could have been amortized by 1870, largely through nationalization operations.[38] Several factors defeated that objective. For one thing, the government accepted a larger proportion in cash and less in bonds than stipulated by law. For example, on 13 August 1862 an additional 3 or 4 percent of the amount due in bonds was accepted in cash. This was a wartime measure that made sense when money was desperately needed to fight the foreign invader. A second unfortunate practice was the acceptance of security (*fianza*) for the payment of bonds. The disorder in public accounting and the government's change of residence made it simple for this evidence of obligation to be lost accidentally or intentionally. Finally, the policy of returning bonds to circulation that had already entered the treasury impeded retirement of the debt.

The failure to retire most or all of the internal debt via nationalization is thus easily understandable in terms of unwise practices dictated largely by political or military need. Nevertheless, nationalization operations did account for a significant proportion of the debt amortized. Naturally, as these dealings declined in importance so did their significance in reduction of the debt. In the early 1860s one could speak of millions of pesos; a decade later, of hundreds of thousands; at the turn of the century, nationalization accounted for a few thousand pesos of the debt retirement and other means tens of millions. After 1902 nationalized property no longer figured at all in liquidation of the debt.[39]

The plight of charitable and educational establishments was another enduring problem facing the republic. Whatever else the

38. In contrast to Romero's statistics, the internal debt in 1867 has been estimated recently at about $78,700,000 and the foreign debt at $375,500,000. Francisco R. Calderón, *La república restaurada: La vida económica*, vol. 2 of *Historia moderna de México*, ed. Daniel Cosío Villegas (Mexico: Editorial Hermes, 1955), p. 235.

39. José María Mata's *Memoria de Hacienda* of 4 May 1861, reprinted in *Diario Oficial*, 30 January 1868, pp. 3–4; *Memoria de las operaciones que han tenido lugar en la oficina especial de desamortización del Distrito, desde el 7 de enero en que se abrió, hasta el 5 de diciembre de 1861, en que cesaron sus labores, para continuarlas la Junta Superior de Hacienda* (Mexico, 1862), pp. 150–51; *Memoria de Hacienda, 1870–1871*, pp. 55–56, 91; *Memoria de Hacienda, 1891–1892*, p. 202; and *Memoria de Hacienda, 1903–1904*, p. 437.

restoration of the republic in 1867 meant, it did not signal an improvement in the condition of charities. One reason was that so much damage already had been done to their resources in fighting the invaders; in addition, for a time after the Empire's collapse the government continued to use charitable mortgages to indemnify individuals whose property had been appropriated. Another reason was the chaotic condition of records, already mentioned, which was partly attributable to past political instability. This condition made it difficult to ascertain the existence of property destined for the support of charities. The municipal government of Mexico City, entrusted with the city's charities between 1862 and 1877, attempted to regularize this area of responsibility. It attempted to recover unpaid back interest on properties that had been sold by concluding new contracts with mortgagors and by taking care in new sales to guarantee the future payment of interest. On the other hand, in 1877 when a special board took over the administration of charities, the accusation was made that the *ayuntamiento* was indolent, that it mixed up records, and that it generally made a mess of the job.[40] In any case, the measures taken by the city were not likely to meet the financial needs of charities.

Federal authorities, however, did help in various ways. The law of 19 August 1867 prohibited the redemption of charitable and educational mortgages. When, five years later, the government reversed this policy, the redemptions were to benefit the institutions. An aid to some establishments were subsidies, granted in compensation for the use of their funds during the foreign intervention. Conversion of many ecclesiastical buildings into schools was beneficial. In part, this decision came because of the difficulty of finding buyers for the structures, such as monasteries. The government also complied with local requests to divert income from nationalized properties it held to support schools or hospitals. The Congress, too, devoted attention to the problem. One suggestion was to transfer to municipalities unalienated episcopal palaces and priests' houses. The proceeds from their disposal would be applied to primary education in each municipality. Another proposal called for the government to reimburse charities for their losses with nationalized real estate and mortgages. Since the

40. Labastida, p. 379; and *Memoria de la corporación municipal que funcionó de agosto a diciembre de 1867* (Mexico, 1868), pp. 10–11.

federal government had alienated the property, it was responsible for seeing to charitable needs; municipal governments with very scanty resources could not continue to bear the expense.[41] Furthermore, as mentioned above, on different occasions the administration and the Congress both considered turning nationalized property over to municipalities for the support of schools and charities, and such a proposition was briefly implemented at the beginning of the Díaz regime.

In the midst of continuing difficulties with nationalization—one of many serious problems facing the administration—the President, Benito Juárez, died suddenly in July 1872. So passed from the scene the man so long the symbol of Reform, Constitution, and Law. Sebastián Lerdo de Tejada, a close associate of Juárez during the difficult years of foreign intervention and Empire, succeeded to the presidency since he was President of the Supreme Court.

In his later years President Juárez had been more conciliatory toward the Church, but apparently the clergy expected his successor to be even more accommodating. Instead, Lerdo insisted upon strictly enforcing the laws. He reiterated the prohibition against religious acts or manifestations outside churches, excepting only ceremonies in cemeteries. The Lerdo government also suppressed clandestine convents, expelling seventy Jesuits, friars, and servants, and two hundred nuns and servants from illegal religious houses in the Federal District. Others who infringed the Reform laws suffered expulsion from the republic as well. The President also took the unpopular step of expelling the Sisters of Charity. They had been excluded from previous measures against religious orders because they were dedicated to charitable works and did not live communally. Now Lerdo decided

41. Decree of 14 December 1872, Resolution of 9 January 1873, and Decree of 29 September 1876, Labastida, pp. 395–96, 378; 12 August 1868, in M. Riva Palacio Correspondencia.

For a list of converted buildings in Mexico City, see Juan E. Pérez, *Almanaque de las oficinas Guía de Forasteros para el año de 1871* (Mexico, 1871), pp. 32–122.

See *Memoria de Hacienda, 1870–1871*, pp. 72–73, 654–55; and *Memoria de Hacienda, 1868–1869*, pp. 862–63. See also Session of 16 March 1868, and Session of 16 November 1868, Francisco Zarco, in Tovar, 1:588 and 3:536.

that they lived by certain rules peculiar to themselves and were subject to one or more superiors and, therefore, fell under the prohibitions against monastic vows and orders.[42]

More significantly, Lerdo, little more than a year after becoming president, aroused clerical animosity and prompted a storm of protest and controversy when the Reform laws for which the liberals had fought so long were incorporated into the Constitution. Debate on the bill in the Chamber of Deputies in the spring of 1873 was not uniformly favorable. Criticism, however, did not center on the Reform measures as such but on fears of the centralization of power and the incompatibility of both disamortization and nationalization as constitutional precepts. The former, already a constitutional article, left Church wealth intact; the latter deprived the Church of its property. The response to those who feared an increase in federal power was simply that nationalization of clerical property meant that the nation, as represented by the federal government, should legislate on the question. To allow the states to do so might undermine the Reform laws.[43]

Despite some misgivings the radicals had their way. On 25 September 1873 the measure passed, thereby committing the "gravest mortal sin," according to the Jesuit historian Mariano Cuevas. The law prohibited religious institutions from acquiring real estate or mortgages on real estate except that property immediately and directly destined for the purpose of the corporation. It declared Church and State separate and stipulated that marriage was a civil contract. Uncompensated personal service and any contract depriving the individual of liberty whether by reason of work, education, or religious vows were forbidden. A year later the organic law of 14 December 1874 expanded on and refined these principles. Religious associations

42. Frank Averill Knapp, Jr., *The Life of Sebastián Lerdo de Tejada, 1823–1889: A Study of Influence and Obscurity* (Austin: University of Texas Press, 1951), p. 215; Schmitt, p. 34; 13 May 1873, and 27 November 1874, Bassols, pp. 200–202; Ricardo García Granados, *Historia de México desde la restauración de la república en 1867, hasta la caída de Porfirio Díaz* (Mexico: Librería Editorial de Andrés Botas e Hijo, n.d.-1928), 1:118, 120; and Hubert Howe Bancroft, *The Works of Hubert Howe Bancroft*, vol. 14, *History of Mexico*, vol. 6, *1861–1887* (San Francisco, 1888), pp. 404–5.

43. Session of 28 April 1873, *Diario–sexto*, 4:275–77.

had the right to receive alms or donations, but these could under no circumstances be in real estate, and they could not be solicited outside churches. Direct ownership of church buildings resided in the nation, but their exclusive use and maintenance was left to the religious institutions, which were tax exempt The organic law prohibited religious instruction in public schools, the wearing of clerical garb in public, and the holding of religious activities outside the church; the ringing of church bells was restricted.[44]

The move against the Sisters of Charity and the constitutionalization of the Reform laws inspired the Cristero Rebellion of 1875–1876, as well as forceful protests from the pulpit, in newspapers, and in pastoral letters. There were disorders and uprisings that involved some clerics in Morelia, Dolores Hidalgo, León, and elsewhere in the republic. The hierarchy, as in earlier years, urged the faithful to obey legitimate civil authorities and the law; simultaneously the bishops condemned the Reform laws and Church-related articles of the Constitution and reaffirmed their censure and punishments for those who complied with those laws.[45]

It is clear that, in nearly two decades, the bishops' position on the Constitution and liberal acts had not changed. In October 1873 the Church dusted off its original declarations on the Constitution. Because of the objectionable provisions in the charter, the faithful could not take the oath to support it. If abstention proved impossible, the oath might be taken by adding "yes, as a Catholic," as long as the official before whom the act took place accepted that qualification. Otherwise, prior to the oath-taking a communication should be directed to the official stating that it was taken "without prejudice to

44. Cuevas, *Historia de la iglesia*, 5:391; *Diario de los debates. Sétimo congreso constitucional de la unión* (Mexico, 1885), 1:1267; and Bassols, pp. 201–2, 205–10.

45. *Instrucción pastoral que los Illmos. Sres. Arzobispos de México, Michoacán y Guadalajara dirijen a su venerable clero y a sus fieles con ocasión de la ley orgánica expedida por el Soberano Congreso nacional en 10 de diciembre del año próximo pasado y sancionada por el Supremo Gobierno en 14 del mismo mes* (Mexico, 1875); *Exposición del obispo de León contra el proyecto de elevar a constitucionales las leyes de Reforma* (León, 1873); *Manifestación que hace el obispo de León a su Venerable Clero, fieles diocesanos y a todo el mundo católico, contra el proyecto de ley orgánica que se discute en el congreso general* (León, 1874); Toro, p. 446; Prieto, p. 441; and Knowlton, "Clerical Response," pp. 509–28.

[one's] beliefs." The Church permitted governmental employees to take the oath if they had nothing to do with implementing the Reform laws; clerks and archivists were in this category. The penalty for swearing the oath without heeding these requirements was denial of the sacraments of Penance and Extreme Unction until a retraction had been signed before the confessor and two witnesses. The penitent had also to resign his position when it was incompatible with his duties as a Catholic.[46]

Early in 1875, the Archbishops of Mexico, Michoacán, and Guadalajara protested the organic law of December 1874.[47] They objected particularly to the absolute ban on religious teaching in public schools, the many obstacles to the exercise of the Faith, the prohibition on collecting alms outside churches, and the injury done schools and charities by the suppression of the Sisters of Charity. The prelates left the faithful only two options in following their consciences in these difficult circumstances: "Between the two means . . . that is, between that of respectful petition [to secure changes in the laws] and that of suffering there was no other. . . ."[48] The hierarchy thus urged obedience to the laws and peaceful petitioning to secure the revocation of obnoxious provisions. At the same time, however, it denied the sacraments necessary for peace of mind and salvation to those who swore to uphold those laws. Some clergy, at least, saw their duty in more actively promoting alteration of the hated measures. In the 1870s, as in the late 1850s, there was a basic inconsistency—an incompatibility—in the position of different members of the Mexican Church.

Aside from the renewed protests and controversy that the constitutional additions caused, and this is not the place to deal extensively with the controversy, there was as always confusion or uncertainty over what the property provisions meant. There were denunciations of property that had been and continued to be excluded from such action. One denouncer thought the exemptions in the Lerdo law had been annulled by the new organic law and so sought property belonging to a parish residence. Another denounced some buildings of a

46. 18 October 1873, in Vera, *Colección*, 3:222–23.
47. *Instrucción pastoral*, pp. 3–37.
48. Ibid., p. 37.

parish devoted directly and immediately to the service of the Faith. The authorities, however, quickly disabused these individuals of their mistaken opinions, disallowing the denunciations.[49]

Contemporaries and modern writers alike believed that the constitutionalization of the Reform laws marked the end of an era in ecclesiastical history, that it signified the victory of the Reform and the end of open clerical attempts to dominate politics.[50] The subsequent laxity of the Porfirian regime notwithstanding, the continued existence of the laws acted as a deterrent to "extravagant clerical pretensions." While these judgments may be valid, the official Church position on the Reform remained one of opposition. The disaster that befell the institution did not bring a mellowing in clerical attitudes. And throughout the country many faithful still listened to the counsel of their priests. There was, in fact, considerable diversity in the implementation of the laws. The liberals demanded enforcement in the principal centers, but elsewhere authorities often did not exact compliance. They reputedly tolerated frequent clerical infractions of the laws, including the existence of religious communities. Liberals alleged that the very people who fulminated the most against the laws took advantage of them to obtain clerical property. These included the Bishop of León and many pious women whose families did well in acquiring property.[51] Thus, constitutionalization reopened old wounds, revived earlier arguments and conflicts, and compounded difficulties in the settlement of the property question.

Sebastián Lerdo was overthown in late 1876 while seeking to continue in office after his first four-year term. General Porfirio Díaz,

49. Both of these took place in small towns: the former in Cuautitlan and the latter in Tlalmanalco. 6 September 1875, and 9 February 1876, Bassols, pp. 218–19.

50. Mecham, p. 455; Matías Romero, "The Philosophy of the Mexican Revolutions," *North American Review* 162 (1896): 47; and *Las memorias diplomáticas de Mr. Foster sobre México*, vol. 29 of *Archivo Histórico Diplomático Mexicano* (Mexico: Publicaciones de la Secretaría de Relaciones Exteriores, 1929), p. 44.

51. John Lewis Geiger, *A Peep at Mexico: Narrative of a Journey across the Republic from the Pacific to the Gulf in December 1873 and January 1874* (London, 1874), pp. 301–6; Rodolfo Menéndez Mena, *The Work of the Clergy and the Religious Persecution in Mexico* (New York: Latin American News Association, 1916), pp. 15–16; and *Diario Oficial*, 2 February and 12 March 1874, 4 February 1875, p. 1, and 6 April 1875, p. 3.

perennial aspirant to the presidency and rebel against the incumbent government, was at last successful in taking advantage of other revolts against the President. If Lerdo's anticlericalism did not assure positive clerical support for Díaz in his machinations, neither did the President enjoy that support in his attempt to retain office. A different policy, such as the one Díaz or at least Juárez in his later years pursued, might have won Lerdo the support of the Church; but that support still might not have assured his victory under the circumstances.[52] In any event, the policy of Don Porfirio during his long tenure in power was one of "conciliation" toward the Church. Enforcement and respect for the Reform laws were only superficial. On the other hand, operations in nationalized property and the attendant problems continued to a final liquidation.

52. Schmitt, pp. 45–47.

Chapter 8
Epilogue and Prologue: The Díaz Era, 1876–1910, Nationalization Concluded

The major impact of the liberal attack on ecclesiastical wealth occurred in the two decades between 1856 and 1875. The main focus of this study has been, therefore, on those crucial years. This history would be incomplete, however, without some attention to the Díaz period. In a sense, the Porfiriato represented an epilogue and a prologue in the history of Church and State in Mexico: an epilogue to the Reform and a prologue to the 1910 Revolution. Porfirio Díaz brought the nationalization process to a conclusion. His government grappled with the same problems that his predecessors had faced. The policies pursued were those established earlier. The dictator-president did, however, relax the constitutional restrictions on the Church, making possible its revival. The Church regained influence and wealth, while maintaining anachronistic political attitudes. The flouting of the Reform laws created one more basis for indicting the Díaz regime, one more justification for revolution. Twentieth-century revolutionaries found they had to rewage the battles of the nineteenth-century reformers, rewin the victory against a wealthy, influential, and political Church.

There was an apparent contradiction between the consummation of nationalization and the relaxation of anticlerical restrictions. The contradiction was, however, more apparent than real; the two policies were not incompatible. Politically and practically, it was not possible to reverse nationalization. The important thing was to end the multitude of problems associated with the transfer of property—to have done with the interminable business. On the other hand, the Díaz conciliation policy toward the Church permitted the reacquisition of wealth, in particular apparently, forms of wealth not strictly prohibited by law. The intent of this chapter is, however, to trace the liquidation of nationalization; to see, primarily through official and public documents, how the government coped with the problem it inherited.

A policy suggested on different occasions some years before by the Minister of Finance and federal deputies to dispose of the remaining but as yet unalienated nationalized property was to cede it to municipalities. These recommendations were rejected, in part because of the loss this policy presumably would have meant to the treasury and because the cession would simply transfer problems from national to local authorities. Nevertheless, immediately following his successful rebellion, General Díaz implemented a similar plan; on 30 November 1876 the government ordered all unalienated nationalized property ceded to municipalities. The municipalities were to divide the income from the disposal of the property equally between schools and charities.[1]

The effects of these good intentions were in no way advantageous to the federal government, and only eight months later, on 1 August 1877, the administration revoked the concession. Implementation of the 1876 decree encountered great difficulties that paralyzed nationalization and redemption transactions: the directive raised preference of rights questions, and it encouraged municipalities to undertake litigation contesting property rights that had been guaranteed by administrative and court decisions. In addition, federal income from nationalization plummeted. In the years after 1867, federal revenue from that source was measured in hundreds of thousands of pesos, but in 1876–1877 the treasury obtained only about $31,500; of that paltry sum only a bit over $5,000 accrued between 1 December 1876 and 30 June 1877. The decree had also abolished the office responsible for nationalization matters, transferring jurisdiction to another department (Section 2) of the Finance Ministry. This new duty overburdened that office, and before long more than 300 transactions and petitions piled up awaiting dispatch. Furthermore, Ministry files had to be consulted in order to prevent abuse, and the lack of data in the files delayed action by municipalities.[2] Finally, the government found that the cession to municipalities did

1. Labastida, p. 310.
2. *Memoria de Hacienda, 1876–1877,* pp. 46, 56–57, 85–86; and Circular of 1 August 1877, *Memoria de Hacienda, 1877–1878,* document 19, p. 168. For difficulties and conflicts in the operation of the order in San Juan de los Lagos, Jalisco, see Santos González in San Juan to Díaz, 4 and 9 June 1877, in Carreño, 24:17–19, 112–13.

not relieve the treasury of a multitude of obligations that could now be met only by levying new taxes.

Understandably, the government could not withdraw the boon granted to municipalities without complaints. The Governor of Zacatecas, Trinidad García de la Cadena, for example, insisted that the 1876 order was a "legislative resolution" that had granted to municipalities "invulnerable rights" of property ownership that no authority could revoke. It was illegal and even unconstitutional to do so. The government denied such allegations, affirming its respect for private rights and its duty to annul orders that were impractical or detrimental to social order. Despite the scattered protest, the government remained firm in its abrogation of the 1876 decree.[3]

The well-meant attempt to benefit municipalities was ill-conceived; circumstances required a law both broader in scope and written in greater detail. The administration did propose, in September 1877, a bill that sought to solve outstanding and long-standing problems of nationalization. Had it become law, the measure would have safeguarded the interests of the federal treasury and aided municipalities. On the one hand, part of the income from nationalized property would be applied to amortization of the public debt and to other obligations such as the unpaid nuns' dowries and reimbursement for nullified transactions. The municipalities, on the other hand, would have received part of the income for education and charities. The bill also was intended to prevent jurisdictional questions between local and federal authorities, and, by terminating denunciations, the expectation was that proprietorship would be made secure. Increasingly, this question gained importance and demanded action.[4]

The newly-installed government's early essays into the maze of nationalization matters were thus not notably successful. Operations continued under the new as under former administrations, but the "new broom" did not sweep any cleaner than the old—nationalization matters were no more efficiently handled than they had been earlier. In mid-1879 the organization of records continued to be chaotic—the

3. Trinidad García de la Cadena, Governor of Zacatecas, to Matías Romero, Minister of Finance, 30 August 1877, and Romero to the Governor, 24 September 1877, in *Memoria de Hacienda, 1877–1878*, pp. 235–38.

4. 24 September 1877, ibid., document 1, pp. 233–35.

lack of any alphabetical register made it virtually impossible to know what was owed the treasury and by whom. A year and a half later, however, President Díaz expressed satisfaction with the functioning of the responsible department, now called the Department for Remaining Nationalized Property (Rezagos de Bienes Nacionalizados). The efforts of the Department to organize the files meaningfully and to collect sums owed the treasury were presumably meeting success.[5]

Unquestionably, this Ministry Department had broad responsibilities; its tasks were many and diverse. Many problems remained to afflict nationalization more than two decades after that momentous action. The Department's authority encompassed four major, separate areas.[6] One task was to bring some order to the disorganization that prevailed. Different offices had handled nationalization cases or transactions (*expedientes*), and from the beginning the arrangement of the documents was careless and unsystematic—not even all papers relating to a single operation were kept together. It was essential, therefore, to organize a file of nationalization transactions. A second responsibility was the collection of sums still owed the treasury. A third function was disposal of property that did not involve denouncers' rights. Finally, the Department disbursed income from nationalized property destined for specific objectives, such as payments of dowries to former nuns and rebates for nullified transactions. These disbursements alone were no small task. For example, the roster of former nuns was inexact—sometimes their family names were known, at other times only their religious appellations. The government had not even been able to establish which nuns had died since suppression of the nunneries in 1863 or whether they had left heirs. Still, some progress had been made toward a list of those who qualified for repayment of dowries with a notation as to whether

5. Report of the Department for Remaining Nationalized Property, July 1879, Labastida, pp. 312–17; and "Informe que en el último día de su período constitucional da a sus compatriotas el Presidente de los Estados Unidos Mexicanos, Porfirio Díaz, acerca de los actos de su administración," 30 November 1880, in *Informes y manifiestos de los poderes ejecutivo y legislativo, de 1821 a 1904, publicación hecha por J. A. Castillón de orden del Señor Ministro de Gobernación Don Ramón Corral* (Mexico: Imprenta del Gobierno Federal, 1905), 2:508 (cited hereafter as *Informes, 1821–1904*).

6. Luis G. Labastida to the Minister of Finance, 3 August 1881, in *Memoria de Hacienda, 1880–1881*, pp. 278–81.

nationalized mortgages were earmarked to satisfy that obligation. The issue of rebates for nullified transactions, on the other hand, might be complicated by involvement of judicial authorities. This complication arose because the government had disposed of many mortgages without considering factors that might later lead the courts to render decisions against the purchasers.

Weaknesses in legislation, differing interpretations of the laws, lack of clarity or oversight, and deliberate evasion added complexity to the Department's tasks. For example, the liberals in Veracruz issued an act on 3 November 1858 forbidding mortgagors to redeem clerical mortgages on penalty of a second payment. The law could not be published in conservative-held territory where implementation was most desired, and it was not generally obeyed. Following the liberal victory in the civil war, mortgagors resisted demands for payment on the ground that the law was inoperative inasmuch as it had not been officially published and because they had, unlawfully under liberal laws, already redeemed the mortgages by paying the religious corporations holding them. In resisting a second payment, the "injured" parties charged infringement of constitutional guarantees of persons and property and added that the courts rather than the administration possessed authority to determine such cases. It is not likely that the government could accept such charges or sympathize with objectors. Yet, incredibly, as late as 1880 such complaints were being made.[7]

Other hoary problems concerned redemption provisions, denouncers' rights, and the meaning of occult property. By this time the definition had changed. Hidden property was that on which no formal and continuing gesture for recovery was officially made, even though some government office had knowledge of the property. In order for a denouncer to be eligible for his reward, one-third of the amount in specie received by the treasury, he had only to show that the property was occult and prove the government's right to it.[8]

Far more serious than these complaints and technicalities were the continued instability of ownership and the depressed real estate values. Some small progress had been made by canceling mortgage contracts that appeared as active in the public registers even though they

7. See, for examples, ibid., pp. 329–43.
8. Ibid., p. 280.

had actually been totally paid off and by giving possessors of property the title deeds which had been left in the Ministry. Operations imperfectly concluded by state governors were also rearranged to conform to the laws. On the other hand, the last general law on the subject, that of 10 December 1869, discouraged owners of mortgaged property from voluntarily approaching the authorities to liquidate their debts because they believed the law obligated them to pay in specie the principal as well as the interest due since 1 January 1861. They preferred to conceal the existence of their mortgages. This situation deprived the government of sizeable amounts in bonds or certificates that would have considerably reduced the public debt. It also contributed to the depreciation of real estate, because possessors of the property could not use it for credit purposes. Furthermore, purchasers in those circumstances were open to future denunciations and fiscal inquiries.

While at that late date the owners of former ecclesiastical property remained insecure in their ownership and real estate values still sagged, local official opposition and noncooperation—by design, overwork, or lassitude—contributed to the tardy termination of nationalization. A circular of 5 August 1877 directed state offices of finance to forward to the Ministry a detailed report on the promissory notes and obligations for bonds that remained outstanding. Nearly two years later only the Oaxaca office had complied with this order.[9]

Other requests for information were equally unproductive. On different occasions in 1877 and 1880 the government asked state finance offices for the status of nationalization operations and local mortgage offices about mortgages formerly held by ecclesiastical corporations. The response in 1881 revealed both a lack of cooperation and the intervention of unavoidable circumstances.[10] Aguascalientes' finance office possessed no information because the archives had been destroyed during political disturbances. Campeche forwarded a report, but it did not contain the requested information. Coahuila's archives were not founded until 1876. The notaries in Colima reported that

9. *Memoria de Hacienda, 1877–1878*, document 21, p. 169. Circular of 2 June 1879, in *Memoria de Hacienda, 1878–1879*, p. 53.

10. Circular of 9 August 1877, in *Memoria de Hacienda, 1877–1878*, document 23, p. 169; 31 January 1880, *Memoria de Hacienda, 1880–1881*, p. 282; and report to the Minister of Finance by J. E. Hernández y Dávalos, 30 July 1881, in *Memoria de Hacienda, 1880–1881*, pp. 283–84, 286, 297–304.

their registers contained no mortgages affected by nationalization, but the mortgage offices failed to answer the request. Chihuahua did not answer either the original request or a follow-up. Durango responded that the information could not be given because there were no account books on nationalized property and the archives were in disorder. Guanajuato, Guerrero, and Hidalgo did not answer at all. Chiapas and Jalisco submitted partial reports, and the state of Mexico sent data from a number of notarial and mortgage offices covering only certain years. The other states supplied either fragmentary information or none at all. These reports in all provided information on mortgages from 87 mortgage offices out of a total of 327.

In sum, in 1881 incomplete records and disorder in existing archives continued as a major obstacle to the successful and speedy conclusion of nationalization. The lack of a general registry of mortgage redemptions carried out since 1867 enabled mortgagors to make unfounded claims that they had paid their debts. Disorder in state finance office files and insufficient personnel made the compilation of data difficult. Yet that information was indispensable for the collection of outstanding debts and for the consummation of nationalization. Registers that did exist were incomplete in that they did not note claims against nationalization, such as those for ex-nuns' dowries and amounts assigned to states and municipalities for charities and public instruction. An examination of each case file was necessary to compile a registry of these debts.

In spite of the chaos and gaps in the documents, slow and painstaking progress was made. By mid-1881 the massive accumulation of papers originating from Church and Imperial offices had been divided into two groups: the old, pre-1867 records and the current proceedings, including terminated cases. The former remained in some disorder for another three years, hindering the search for antecedents that was necessary in each case. As compilation of data and organization of records proceeded, several things became clear. The obvious, of course, was that many valuable documents had disappeared from the archives, lost during political upheaval. But, also, it was clear that there still remained a large number of unredeemed debts. It appeared, too, that disamortization and nationalization had been completely implemented only in the Federal District and a few state capitals; in the states in general, they had not been. Therefore, the majority of operations dispatched in these later years logically were in the states—this was true of denunciations as well as mortgage redemptions and real estate sales.[11]

In the mid-1880s the exemption of certain buildings from denunciation was one of several matters that continued to be a source of abuse, dispute, and misunderstanding. This problem was the subject of careful analysis by an astute and important official in the Ministry of Finance, Luis G. Labastida.[12] His historical study and recommendations are indicative of the concern and dedication of some civil servants in untangling and settling issues surrounding nationalized property. As late as 1885 there continued to be denunciations of property legally exempt since the very beginning. Pending denunciations of atria, parish priests' homes, ruined chapels, even of churches open to worship bespoke the need for clarification and definite, invariable, uniform rules; not only cupidity but diverse, often contradictory, resolutions issued over the years gave rise to these groundless denunciations.

Both the 1856 disamortization law and the 1857 Constitution explicitly exempted and protected buildings directly and immediately destined to the service of religious and civil corporations; these included convents, municipal and episcopal palaces, schools, hospitals, residences of parish priests, and nuns' chapels. In addition, the disamortization law permitted the renting of parts of these buildings; the Constitution, however, omitted this provision. This inconsistency was a source of confusion and danger to the implementation of the laws. The intent of the legislation was to exempt only those buildings strictly necessary for the object of the institution, so a precise determination was necessary on renting and on the parts of the buildings that could be rented. Without such a stipulation, exemption could be interpreted to include all clerical real estate on the assumption that the income was destined to the service of the Faith. The authority to rent parts of buildings also involved acts of administration, which the

11. *Memoria de Hacienda, 1883–1884*, pp. XCII–XCIII. For figures on denunciations, see *Memoria de Hacienda, 1878–1879*, document 266, pp. 980–81; *Memoria de Hacienda, 1879–1880*, document 40, p. 88; and *Memoria de Hacienda, 1880–1881*, document 2, pp. 119–21.

12. *Memoria de Hacienda, 1884–1885*, pp. 44–48; and Labastida, pp. 52–55.

law prohibited. Under these conditions the principles of disamortization might be destroyed.

Nationalization in 1859 brought a change. By that act all buildings passed to the dominion of the nation, which henceforth was the only authority that could rent them. The law limited a corporation's right to the use of those buildings designated by the state governors. Episcopal and parish priests' residences and other buildings annexed to churches entered the national domain, but possessors could continue to occupy them with the government's permission; that is, the relevant laws granted religious bodies only the use of churches and annexed buildings for so long as they remained destined for the service of the Faith.

The law of 14 December 1874 elevated these principles to constitutional precepts in an explicit way. That measure repeated the general prohibition on ownership of real estate by religious institutions and vested ownership of churches and dependencies necessary for the Faith in the nation. At the same time, it granted the exclusive use, maintenance, and improvement of the buildings to the ecclesiastical institutions until such time as "consolidation" was decreed. Thus, the corporations might acquire a kind of ownership of specified real estate, and they were entrusted with the use, maintenance, and improvement of that property. In this way the law divided ownership, granting control of use (*dominio útil*) to the churches while the actual ownership (*dominio directo*) remained in the nation. The only solution to this division, Labastida believed, was that proposed by the law, "consolidation," that is, the reunion of both rights in one party, either the nation or the corporation.

In any case, Labastida asserted, no one had the right to denounce or adjudicate churches at the service of the Faith. They could not be denounced because they were not occult property. They could not be adjudicated because they were devoted to a public service and were distinct from property that the nation was obliged to alienate. Although the 1874 law referred to churches exclusively, atria, sacristies, baptistries, etc. were integral parts of churches. Thus, churches open to worship and associated or dependent buildings could only be alienated if the Minister of Government, who had the authority to declare consolidation, revoked the right of use granted to the institution.

Until such time, denunciations or requests for adjudication were not admissible. Abandoned churches, however, were in a different category because their abandonment implied loss of the use right (*dominio útil*) and hence their consolidation. They could, therefore, be alienated.

Residences of parish priests and nuns' chaplains were in another special category. Though considered individual private property under the terms of the 1874 law, both lent themselves to abuse by the occupants. Priests and chaplains frequently rented them in order to obtain income, or they allowed relatives and friends to live in them without charge. Since religious bodies only enjoyed the use of those buildings, they could not possess the right to rent them. Chaplains' houses in fact should have been alienated because after suppression of the nunneries in 1863 it was impossible to fulfill their intended object. Even though the use of the buildings destined directly for the Faith was left to the religious institutions, logically, if they were used in an unlawful manner, consolidation should be ordered and the property auctioned.

Resolutions adopted in January 1885, based on Labastida's analysis and recommendations, clarified property exemptions, refined the rules for denunciations and disposal of the relevant real estate, and ended abuses. After the turn of the century, another law repeated the distinction between "dominio útil" and "dominio directo" and maintained governmental supervision of the buildings. This authority meant that no repairs or alterations could be made without governmental permission if they affected the buildings' solidity or historical and artistic value. Conversely, the government could require alterations it deemed useful or ornamental. Governmental authority encompassed, as well, opening churches to worship. Finally, the federal executive could decree consolidation whenever he believed that would serve public order or interests. This would be the case, for example, if the clergy did not fulfill their obligation to repair and maintain the churches or other buildings or if worship was suspended for more than one year without just cause.[13]

Pious bequests were related to real estate exemptions and, like that matter, were the subject of disputes and abuses for three decades; the

13. *Memoria de Hacienda, 1902–1903*, pp. 194–95. Articles XXXVII–XLIII dealt with churches and their dependencies.

government finally resolved this problem in the 1880s. The disamortization and nationalization laws had both encompassed real estate and capital bequeathed for pious ends. The lack of a good legal interpretation, however, had produced many contradictory judicial and administrative resolutions. Two notable cases resulted over provisions in the wills of Cayetana Echevarría and the conqueror Hernán Cortés, both of whom bequeathed property for pious and charitable purposes. Because of these and similar cases, the government made it clear that under the laws only property actually administered by the clergy entered the dominion of the nation and could be acted against. Denunciations of pious legacies under individual, private administration were inadmissible. In the future, substantiation of a denunciation required proof that a pious legacy existed, that the property was occult, and that a religious corporation administered it.[14]

A third area of controversy settled in this period centered on the competence of federal courts in certain nationalization cases. The question was: did or did not federal courts have jurisdiction in disputes between individuals over nationalized property once the federal government ceased to have an interest in the property, that is, after it had passed to an individual and/or the government no longer had a financial interest in it? For example, did federal courts or local courts have jurisdiction if the government ceded a nationalized mortgage to an individual, liquidating its financial interest in the mortgage, and then litigation resulted when the new mortgagee tried to collect from the debtor? The lack of consistency in several decisions may have prompted the order affirming the competence of federal courts in cases in which the federal government had ceded its rights to an individual or "substitute" and a controversy arose over payment of the nationalized mortgage.[15]

14. *Memoria de Hacienda, 1883–1884*, pp. XCIV–XCVI; Pallares, pp. 208–9; Labastida, pp. 464–65 and Circular of 6 April 1885, p. 484.

15. Labastida, p. 254. For specific cases on this matter, see: *Alegato presentado a la Suprema Corte de Justicia por el Lic. Ignacio L. Vallarta en representación de los herederos del licenciado Don Jesús Navarro en el amparo promovido por D. Miguel Estrada contra la ejecutoria del tribunal de Michoacán que lo condenó a pagar un capital nacionalizado* (Mexico, 1883); *La prescripción respecto de los bienes nacionalizados. Pedimento fiscal. Apuntes del informe pronunciado por el Lic. Luis G. Labastida y sentencia de segunda instancia que causó ejecutoria en el juicio iniciado por el Sr. Lic. Pedro Azcué, como subrogatorio de la Hacienda Pública Federal, contra los*

While there was significant progress in the resolution of several of the remaining property issues, these tended to be the more minor irritants. Far more important and unsettled were those two hardy perennial effects of nationalization: the collection of all amounts due the government from nationalization and the need to assure security to possessors of nationalized property. The latter was becoming ever more imperative, the former gradually receding in significance, but it was apparent that the two objectives were mutually exclusive—both could not be accomplished. For years the desire to obtain resources and assure that all relevant property came under the effects of the legislation had taken precedence over secure ownership. At this time federal authorities still believed that ownership could not be guaranteed until the definitive settlement of all questions concerning payment for the property.

The government knew that there were promissory notes (*vales*), representing sizeable amounts, that had been misplaced by treasury offices. For the most part, mortgages on real estate secured these notes. Consequently, the treasury had not received the sums owed it, and the mortgagors could not free their property from encumbrances. In the 1880s the government acted to recover the value of the misplaced notes and at the same time gave some security to proprietors. On the one hand, mortgagors were ordered to present themselves to the Finance Ministry to satisfy their debts or suffer forced collection. This threat, however, excluded those who had not paid because they were awaiting a summons for payment from their creditors. On the other hand, the order permitted the holders of promissory notes three months to record them at the Ministry and thus validate their claims; thereafter, the government, upon request, absolved mortgagors from payment of amounts still owing on unrecorded notes.[16]

---

poseedores de la casa esquina de la Plaza del Carmen en San Angel, sobre pago de un capital nacionalizado (Mexico, 1887); and *Fuero competente en los juicios sobre bienes nacionalizados. Informe a la vista pronunciado por el Lic. Ignacio L. Vallarta en el recurso de súplica interpuesto por D. Atenógenes Llamas contra la sentencia del tribunal de circuito de Guadalajara que declaró incompetente a la jurisdicción federal para conocer de la demanda contra los dueños de la hacienda de Huacasco, sobre pago de un capital nacionalizado* (Mexico, 1891).

16. Circular of 15 July 1884, and 22 December 1885, Labastida, pp. 273–75; and *Memoria de Hacienda, 1883–1884,* p. XCIII.

The significance of this measure was that it eliminated the constant threat to holders of nationalized real estate whose titles were encumbered by promissory notes for which no one had claimed payment. Prior to this alteration in December 1885, proprietors in such a situation had two choices: they could wait some years before requesting cancellation of the debt based on the prescription period specified in the mortgage contract; or they could initiate judicial proceedings to obtain a declaration that the notes had expired. Either course meant great inconvenience to the owner. Meanwhile, the property was liable to pecuniary claims from holders of promissory notes who might demand payment at any time. Many of the notes originated from contracts between the government and individuals. Because it felt responsible for the notes, the government some years earlier permitted the cancellation of debts only after the adjudicator had deposited in the treasury a sum equivalent to the value of the promissory notes encumbering the property. In this way, any time the holder of the notes claimed payment, the amount was available on deposit. This practice protected the treasury, which, in authorizing cancellation with notes still outstanding, might be liable later for their payment. On the other hand, the deposit of sums harmed the owner of the nationalized property by depriving him of the use of the money for other purposes. The December 1885 circular eliminated these problems. Thereafter, to obtain cancellation of that part of the encumbrance corresponding to promissory notes, the possessor of the nationalized property only had to worry about those notes presented by the holders in fulfillment of the circular and those in process of collection by the Ministry of Finance. In all other cases cancellation occurred at once.[17]

To accelerate and facilitate the collection of sums due from nationalization operations, the government appointed temporary, special investigators or commissioners (*visitadores*), resuming a previous practice to good advantage. The agents achieved good results because they devoted their entire energies to nationalization affairs, while the regular finance officials, occupied with other tasks, could not. The special investigators reviewed files to find data and to prove the existence of occult property. They investigated the concealment

17. *Memoria de Hacienda, 1885–1886*, pp. XIII–XIV; and Labastida, pp. 271–72.

of debts and activated their collection. They regularized imperfect operations. In all, the efforts of the agents led to the collection of considerable sums for the nation. For example, activities of Luis G. Labastida, the agent in Guanajuato, and apparently the most successful of them, resulted in collection of $223,363.79 from 1885–1886 through 1889–1890, an overwhelming portion of which was in cash rather than credits.[18]

Another rewarding practice in the late 1880s was the conclusion of agreements with individuals who for some reason possessed detailed information on nationalized property proceedings. In these agreements the government generally guaranteed to the "contractor" one-third of the amount in specie received by the treasury. In these years denunciations increased noticeably as did income received from nationalization. The Minister of Finance, Manuel Dublán, attributed the increase to the confidence the government inspired in persons with information about former clerical property and to the efficiency with which the authorities dispatched matters. Despite improvement, the Minister concluded that not even 75 percent of nationalized ecclesiastical property had yet been redeemed.[19]

Although much remained to be accomplished, the 1880s were noteworthy for progress in collecting debts due from nationalization and in giving security to the possessors of the property. Early in the next decade the government acted to resolve the remaining problems of the thirty-five year old nationalization process. But the dilemma remained a formidable one for the administration, despite the passage of years and the progress made. It was essential to safeguard proprietorship and legitimate rights without flouting the principles of the Reform, but the door could not be permanently closed on denun-

18. *Memoria de Hacienda, 1885–1886*, p. XIII and document 209. Agents were sent to Orizaba canton in Veracruz state, to Guanajuato, San Luis Potosí, and one to Jalisco, Colima, and Tepic. For the results of their efforts, see *Memoria de Hacienda, 1886–1887*, pp. XXXV–XXXVI; *Memoria de Hacienda, 1887–1888*, chart 2 on income from nationalization in documents sections; *Memoria de Hacienda, 1888–1889*, p. XXVII; and *Memoria de Hacienda, 1889–1890*, p. LV.

19. *Memoria de Hacienda, 1887–1888*, p. LII; and "Informe del C. General Porfirio Díaz, Presidente de los Estados Unidos Mexicanos, a sus compatriotas acerca de los actos de su administración en el período constitucional de 1° de Diciembre de 1888 a 30 de Noviembre de 1892," *Informes, 1821–1904*, 3:664.

ciations for fear of clerical reacquisition of a considerable part of the real wealth of the country. In order to achieve these twin objectives, the government promulgated a new law in 1892.[20]

The law of 8 November 1892, with the regulatory law of the same date, was comprehensive.[21] Its objectives included overcoming debtors' resistance to payment and the termination of possible persecution of owners because of hidden encumbrances on their property by making payment terms so alluring that debtors would have a powerful incentive to fulfill their legal obligations. Furthermore, to forestall ecclesiastical reacquisition of property, the law maintained the old prohibitions while continuing to permit denunciations. The denouncer, however, was to receive only one-ninth of the amount actually obtained by the treasury. In addition, the law authorized the redemption of mortgages, regardless of the status of collection proceedings, by payment of one-third of the amount due in cash and two-thirds in bonds; in some cases, it waived payment of the interest due altogether. If debtors did not take advantage of these terms by 30 June 1893, then denouncers or others could receive the same terms. In order to secure their ownership forever against government claims for debts arising from nationalization, proprietors could purchase low cost "certificates of liberation" that terminated fiscal claims on their property. And, finally, the law empowered the Finance Ministry to adjust transactions with debtors under special circumstances and to declare valid, even though they contained some irregularities, operations that had been approved by the federal executive, state governors, or constitutional military chiefs up to 5 February 1861. Operations confirmed by governors and military commanders after that date might even be accepted if they had been revalidated by the federal government or its agents.

There was considerable activity under the 1892 law. By the end of the fiscal year, 1892–1893, the new Finance Minister, José I. Limantour, reported numerous requests for certificates of liberation, and he was confident that these would increase when the law was fully publicized throughout the Republic and when proprietors realized the

20. *Memoria de Hacienda, 1891–1892*, p. 21.

21. Law of 8 November 1892, Labastida, pp. 170–72, 517–22, 527–33 and Reglamento of the law, pp. 173–80.

advantages of securing their ownership of property by means of the inexpensive certificates.[22] Governmental income from the execution of the law, however, was always less than it should have been, in part because the executive allowed reductions to individuals in the settlement of their debts: sometimes by waiving interest due, or by accepting an amount in credits that should have been paid in cash, or by discounts given on the amount due in cash. In many cases the government thus concluded agreements with debtors for far less than should have been paid, but in all cases the purpose was to free real estate from encumbrances arising from nationalization. Concessions notwithstanding, during the 1890s the government repossessed a number of properties for failure to pay debts; often because of a lack of bidders at public auctions, properties reverted to the treasury for payment of the debts.[23]

Denunciations of considerable value continued under the new law, but in many cases the government did not have to pay to denouncers the reward of one-ninth of the amount collected by the treasury because they failed to supply the required data justifying their denunciations within the allotted one month time limit.[24] Cancellations of various types of deeds also declined as a result of the law—deeds of adjudication, of substitution, and of redemption. The decline occurred because, by purchasing certificates of liberation, a proprietor freed his property from any future fiscal claims, and he did not need to request a special cancellation of those debts.[25] The government

22. *Memoria de Hacienda, 1892–1893*, pp. XI–XII.

23. *Memoria de Hacienda, 1896–1807*, p. X. In 1894–1895 there were eight urban and twelve rural properties in this situation (*Memoria de Hacienda, 1894–1895*, p. XXIII). In 1896–1897 there were sixteen urban and fifteen rural properties (*Memoria de Hacienda, 1896–1897*, p. XI); in 1897–1898, twenty-one urban and twenty-four rural (*Memoria de Hacienda, 1897–1898*, p. VII). And in 1898–1899, twenty-eight urban and eleven rural (*Memoria de Hacienda, 1898–1899*, p. XI).

24. In 1893–1894 denunciations amounted to $413,931.09 (*Memoria de Hacienda, 1893–1894*, p. XXIV), and in 1894–1895, $191,949.69 (*Memoria de Hacienda, 1894–1895*, p. XXII).

25. *Memoria de Hacienda, 1893–1894*, p. XXV. Before the law, there were: in 1888–1889, fifty-eight cancellations (*Memoria de Hacienda, 1888–1889*, p. XXVIII) in 1889–1890, sixty cancellations (*Memoria de Hacienda, 1889–1890*, p. LV).

successively extended the deadline to apply for certificates of liberation from the original 30 June 1893 date eventually to the turn of the century. The cost of the stamps of liberation was based on the price of the property, ranging from $1 for property under $500 to $25 for that over $20,000. From the issuance of the law on 8 November 1892 until the end of fiscal 1893–1894, there were 30,108 requests for liberation, representing a total value of $195,458 in stamps of liberation. In succeeding years, income from the stamps decreased dramatically: from $89,090 in 1894–1895 to only $7,331 in 1900–1901. Despite definite strides made in the 1890s to make proprietorship secure while assuring government collection of sums due from transactions, the 1892 law did not completely fulfill expectations.[26]

Minister Limantour submitted a bill to Congress on 17 September 1900 that invoked the principle of prescription to end the government's claim for payment of sums still owed it from nationalized property. Limantour explained that despite the benefits offered by the 1892 law, a relatively small number of people had taken advantage of its terms. The proposed new measure would remove the cause of depreciation of nationalized real estate and the factors making the property unuseable for certain transactions. The time was opportune because all mortmain property was presumably in the hands of individuals, excepting that destined for public service. Besides, more than forty years had elapsed since nationalization, so that the government, without compromising political purposes already achieved, could ignore the scanty fees that the treasury might obtain from as yet un*dis*covered or un*re*covered property. The bill, however, retained the prohibition against the acquisition or administration of real estate by religious corporations, it continued to allow denunciations of such property, and it authorized continued fiscal action against clandestine administration and simulated acquisitions by the clergy. Otherwise, the bill renounced governmental rights to reclaim nationalized real estate and encumbrances on it under the principle of prescription;

After the law, there were: in 1893–1894, thirty-seven cancellations (*Memoira de Hacienda, 1893–1894*, p. XXV) and in 1896–1890, fifteen cancellations (*Memoria de Hacienda, 1896–1897*, p. XI).

26. *Memoria de Hacienda, 1893–1894*, p. XXVI; *Memoria de Hacienda, 1896–1897*, p. 321; *Memoria de Hacienda,* 1900–1901, p. 222; and Reglamento of law of 8 November 1892, Labastida, p. 177.

prescription applied twenty years from the date of the title of purchase of the nationalized property or from the date the obligation on the property fell due. The new measure also confirmed the validity of the certificates of liberation purchased under the 1892 law. Two months after its submission, the bill became law, on 16 November 1900.[27] In effect, it closed the lid on the Pandora's box opened more than forty years before with nationalization; it terminated a source of doubts, discomfort, and agitation among proprietors. In that respect, the law marked the passing of a relic of an earlier era, that shattering, turmoil-filled, chaotic period, *La Reforma*.[28]

President Díaz, from the beginning to the end of his long rule, consistently supported in official pronouncements and directives the anticlerical legislation of the Reform. Soon after achieving power, the new government resolved to implement fully and strictly the laws of 1873 and 1874 that constitutionalized the major Reform measures. Several years later, a directive ordered scrupulous obedience to the Reform laws, which were being neglected in various localities. Among other things, processions and other religious ceremonies were taking place outside the churches, and priests wore their clerical garb in public. Although there were complaints about the flouting of the laws in some towns, such as Querétaro, in other places, like Zacualtipan, Hidalgo, the laws were vigorously enforced.[29]

27. *Memoria de Hacienda, 1900–1901*, pp. 180, 227–28. Prescription could not be invoked: (1) when in litigated claims a sentence favorable to the treasury was dictated that had not been revoked; (2) when the possessor of the encumbered property had expressly acknowledged in writing his debt to the treasury or made some contract concerning it to the effect that fiscal action would not be prescribed by the passage of twenty years; or (3) when the debt had been transferred to an individual by substitution or redemption.

28. A law of 18 December 1902, classified and established rules for federal property. The law divided the immovable property of the government into property of public dominion or of common use and public property (*bienes propios*) of the federal treasury. The latter included property that arose from nationalization. After 31 December 1904, the time limit for prescription of these properties passed and the individual societies or corporations that possessed the property on that date could acquire them by means of prescription. *Memoria de Hacienda, 1902–1903*, pp. 189–99.

29. Circulars of 15 January 1877, and 12 April 1881, Bassols, pp. 219–21, 222–23; T. Montiel in Querétaro to Díaz, 19 February 1877, in Carreño,

As explained previously, the Díaz regime, like preceding governments, disallowed denunciations and adjudications of property exempt under the laws, and it legislated to deal with the remnants of nationalized property and to terminate operations arising under the law.[30] On the other hand, there is evidence that under Díaz' policy of conciliation toward the Church, the Reform laws were openly evaded with the encouragement or acquiescence of the President and that the clergy reamassed extensive wealth.

The aging radical, Ignacio Ramírez, complained in 1898 that the Catholic Church was slowly but surely regaining all the power it had lost earlier and that far from being submissive to the laws, it violated them and infringed Mexican institutions. The laws prohibited convents, but the Church secretly maintained them. The laws prohibited processions outside churches, but they were held even though they cost the Church heavy fines. The laws prohibited distinctive clerical garb in public, but such clothing was visible daily on the streets. An ecclesiastical official himself announced that Church coffers contained $100,000,000.[31]

Other sources suggested that the Church regained wealth during the Porfiriato, in both pre-Reform forms of mortgages and real estate and newer types with holdings in railroads, mining, telegraph systems, and manufacturing.[32] Revolutionary political figures, though

---

18:131; *Memoria que el jefe político de Zacualtipan, Felipe Angeles, presenta al C. gobernador del estado sobre los ramos de la administración del distrito por lo relativo al año anterior de 1888* (Mexico, 1889), p. 12; and Schmitt, pp. 55–56.

30. 24 July 1891, and 18 August 1892, Bassols, pp. 225–26.

31. "El Nigromante" [Ignacio Ramírez], *El partido liberal y la reforma religiosa en México* (Mexico, 1898), pp. 4–6. See also the reminiscences of José F. Vérgez, *Recuerdos de Méjico* (Barcelona: Imp. de Henrich y Ca., 1902), p. 255. Occasionally, action was taken against the illegally existing regular orders, as in the closing of two convents in Mérida in 1891. Moisés González Navarro, *El porfiriato: La vida social*, vol. 4 of *Historia moderna de México*, ed. Daniel Cosío Villegas (Mexico: Editorial Hermes, 1957), pp. 477–78.

32. Juan N. Navarro, "Mexico of Today," *National Geographic Magazine* 12 (1901): 154; José C. Valadés, *El porfirismo, historia de un régimen*, vol. 2: *El crecimiento* (Mexico: Editorial Patria, 1948), p. 161, quoting from *El Monitor*, 14 April 1887; *El Insurgente* (Mexico), 12 January 1908, p. 2 Luis C. Balderrama, *El clero y el gobierno de México, apuntes para la historia de la crisis en 1926* (Mexico: Editorial "Cuauhtemoc," 1927), 1:6; and Menéndez Mena, pp. 18–19.

suspect, support these allegations. For example, the Liberal Party program of 1906 of Ricardo Flores Magón promised that all the Church lands that had been turned over to "puppets" to prevent their nationalization would be confiscated by the government. And a later revolutionary president, Emilio Portes Gil, insisted that the Church reacquired wealth and influence: through the conciliation policy of Díaz; through the agency of prelates, priests, and laymen who were relatives of clerics, in whom the clergy had complete confidence; through the establishment of business corporations in which clergy were the principal and controlling stockholders; and from *contentas*, individual bequests to clergy, alms, tithes, nuns' dowries, real estate, and mortgages. In addition to the material wealth, the Church increased its influence through control of schools and charities.[33]

Whether the Church did or did not reacquire its wealth during the Porfiriato is a moot point. Professor Karl Schmitt insists that there is no real evidence that the Church reacquired wealth and that accusations that it did, without further evidence, are malicious fabrications and/or simple and somewhat natural suspicions of enemies of the clergy.[34] Certainly, the charges emanated from either old anticlericals like Ramírez, or twentieth-century revolutionaries like Flores Magón, Luis Cabrera, and Portes Gil, or scholarly writers like W. H. Callcott and Ernest Gruening, who perhaps did not sufficiently investigate the point to uncover firm evidence.[35] Elusive as the point may be, evidence presented in this study is sufficiently substantial to conclude that the Church did not, in fact, lose all of its wealth in the Reform and that it did reacquire some wealth through agreements with pious individuals. It seems likely, too, that donations and bequests added to the wealth, but these were not unconstitutional as long as they did not

33. Charles C. Cumberland, "An Analysis of the Program of the Mexican Liberal Party, 1906," *The Americas* 4 (January 1948); 300; and Emilio Portes Gil, *The Conflict between the Civil Power and the Clergy: Historical and Legal Essay* (Mexico: Press of the Ministry of Foreign Affairs, 1935), pp. 82–85. The work of Jesús Romero Flores appears to be a reproduction of the Portes Gil statements; see his *Anales históricos de la revolución mexicana* (Mexico: Ediciones "El Nacional," 1939), 1:49–52.

34. Schmitt, pp. 80–81.

35. See Ernest Gruening, *Mexico and Its Heritage* (New York: The Century Co., 1928), p. 227; Luis Cabrera, *The Religious Question in Mexico* (New York: Las Novedades, 1915), p. 11; and Callcott, p. 144.

consist of real estate or mortgages on real estate. Nor did the law of the land prevent the clergy from organizing stock companies and investing in industrial enterprises. Such activities, the acquisition of property in those forms, may have violated the spirit of the Reform; they did not violate the letter of the law. More solid evidence of the extent of clerical wealth during the Porfiriato must await careful examination of primary materials of the period, an issue beyond the scope of this study.

The Porfirian policy of conciliation toward the Church—a policy described as one not designed to strengthen the Church but to secure peace, order, and prosperity—had implications other than that of wealth. The years after 1876 were years of reconstruction for the Church. New bishoprics and archbishoprics were created and the number of churches increased, more than making up for losses during the Reform. New religious societies were established dedicated to charitable work; one of these at least, the Congregation of the Servants of the Sacred Heart (Congregación de las Siervas del S. Corazón), in 1888 took vows of poverty, chastity, and obedience. The Jesuits reestablished themselves and grew in numbers and prestige. President Díaz and other high-ranking government officials showed their regard for Archbishop Labastida, and in 1910, during the centenary celebration of Independence, the Virgin of Guadalupe was carried through the streets in a procession.[36]

From the standpoint of consolidating political power and establishing tranquility, the conciliation policy was unquestionably wise. Díaz gained clerical support, healed the rift in society created by the Reform, and at the same time maintained the laws on the books as a veiled threat to the Church. The policy did not enjoy universal support, however. On the one side, individuals denounced clerical infractions of the laws, as did newspapers and some congressmen, but with little success. On the other side, the Church could not be completely satisfied.

36. Schmitt, p. 60; Antonio García Cubas, *Cuadro geográfico, estadístico, descriptivo e histórico de los Estados Unidos Mexicanos* (Mexico, 1885), pp. 33–35; Mecham, pp. 457–58; *Cuadro estadístico de las seis provincias que componen la iglesia mexicana el año de 1893* (Querétaro, 1893), chart at the beginning; Murray, 1:319–20; M. Cuevas, *Historia de la iglesia*, 5:409–20 and *Historia de la nación*, 3:514; and Valadés, *El porfirismo*, 2:188.

As long as the 1857 Constitution remained in effect, the clergy never adjusted to the restrictions surrounding external discipline—friction and disputes disturbed the peace in many towns over such matters as the ringing of church bells, wearing of clerical garb in public, and prohibition of public religious processions.[37] And the continuing legal disability to acquire and administer real property aroused occasional public complaint. Arguments advanced to establish the juridical personality of the Church and its right to possess and administer property were the same as those used by clerical supporters half a century earlier.[38] Such arguments did not move the Díaz government any more than they had previous administrations, but it was not necessary to alter the laws. The Church circumvented them—with due allowance for enforcement by local authorities—and regained much of its former influence during the seemingly eternal rule of Don Porfirio. Partially as a result of the permissive unofficial policy toward the Church, revolutionary governments of the twentieth century felt impelled to redo the work of the mid-nineteenth century reformers—to reconfiscate ecclesiastical property and reimplement Reform legislation—acting at times even more radically than their liberal predecessors.

37. M. Cuevas, *Historia de la nación*, 3:514; Schmitt, pp. 86–87. For other comments and summaries on the conciliation policy, see; Mecham, pp. 456–60; González Navarro, *El porfiriato*, pp. 458ff.; J. Pérez Lugo, *La cuestión religiosa en México* (Mexico: Centro Cultural "Cuauhtemoc," 1927), p. 33; Helen Phipps, *Some Aspects of the Agrarian Question in Mexico: A Historical Study* (Austin: University of Texas Press, 1925), pp. 29ff.; Toro, pp. 454–57; Luis Lara y Pardo, *De Porfirio Díaz a Francisco Madero: La sucesión dictatorial de 1911* (New York: Polyglot Publishing & Commercial Co., 1912), pp. 70–74; and Arturo M. Elías, *The Mexican People and the Church* (New York: n.p., 1926?), pp. 46–47.

38. See the thesis presented by Emilio Sedas Rivera for examination for attorney, printed in *El País. Diario Católico* (Mexico), 2 July, p. 3; 16 July, p. 4; and 18 July 1909, p. 3.

Chapter 9
Summation and Conclusion

The Reform of the mid-nineteenth century represented the violent culmination of the long-standing and increasingly bitter conflict between the proponents of liberal doctrine and the adherents of conservatism. The movement's antecedents may be traced to Spain and France, and its principal ideas found expression during the struggles for independence. Liberalism experienced brief national success in 1833–1834, reached full force in the 1850s, and consolidated its gains only after a decade of civil war and foreign intervention. A fundamental tenet of the liberal philosophy was individualism: a firm belief that Mexico could only take her rightful place in the community of nations through the liberation of the individual from the chains binding him to the past; that her economic and political development depended upon freeing the individual from deadening corporate restrictions and privileges. Because privilege and inequality were so deeply entrenched, the individual could achieve the freedom to realize his full potential only with the intervention and assistance of the government.

One institution that stifled progress was the complex of individuals and corporations that comprised the Catholic Church. The Church possessed incalculable wealth in real estate and invested capital, which allegedly stagnated in its corporate hands. The Church enjoyed a privileged legal and social position in the country. The Church used all its resources, spiritual and material, to maintain its status and thus to retard the country's development. Completely valid or not, the liberals reasoned in this manner.

Assuming the pervasive and hampering nature of the Church, liberals sought to limit it to what they considered its legitimate sphere, the purely spiritual. It is doubtful that they realized the Pandora's box they were opening when they issued their reforms at mid-century; certainly they did not foresee the consequences of the disamortization of corporate real estate in 1856 or of the subsequent laws on ecclesiastical property. The anticipated effects of the measures were not realized. The principal intent of the 1856 measure, to create a large class of middle- or small-scale owners and to promote prosperity through pride of individual proprietorship, failed of achievement. Some tenants of the Church and some enterprising mestizos did benefit, but the bulk of the property passed ultimately to the wealthy or relatively well-to-do middle class who could afford the acquisition and ownership costs. Often these were foreigners unconcerned about Church anathemas.

This law and other anticlerical measures precipitated a devastating civil war, which in turn aroused liberals to more drastic decrees, such as the nationalization of all Church property in July 1859. The Juárez government took this action to punish the Church for its opposition, to obtain resources to fight the conservatives, and to maintain its leadership of the Reform. The civil war and the foreign intervention that followed did much to prevent the orderly disposal or constructive use of the nationalized ecclesiastical property. Even much property, the income from which sustained schools and charities, had to be disposed of to the detriment of those institutions.

With the reestablishment of relative internal peace, the government in 1867, as in 1861, faced the task of regularizing operations and correcting the worst abuses in earlier alienations of property. It acted to discover hidden ecclesiastical property and to collect sums formerly owed to Church corporations on terms that would not place too great a burden on debtors. Federal authorities allowed denunciations because the loss, destruction, and occultation of records prevented knowledge of the location of much property and the identity of debtors, and because many transactions had not been consummated in strict accordance with the laws. Proprietorship thus remained insecure, and real estate values depreciated for decades.

It is difficult for a people accustomed to political stability and sanctity of property ownership fully to appreciate the conditions facing Mexicans during and after the Reform. This study has explained the dilemma confronting acquirers of Church property during the civil war. It is possible to lack sympathy for the problems of those who speculated in property, but besides that handful, there were the legions of common, ordinary citizens caught in the gigantic clash of the temporal and spiritual powers of the land. Both demanded the allegiance of the people: the former punished them if they did not obey governmental decrees; the latter damned them—threatened them with far greater punishment beyond this life—if they did obey.

Property holders, having somehow survived the holocaust that ravaged the Republic for three years, then faced the hardly less difficult years of Intervention and Empire that followed. For a decade between 1857 and 1867—although certainly not in all sections of the country—the original adjudicator of an ecclesiastical property was insecure in the possession of his property. He faced revocation of the laws under which he had acted, revisions, and denunciations; he was threatened by more revisions and administrative decisions that might menace or uphold his ownership and even litigation in the courts. Then, while relative political peace may have followed 1867, tranquil possession of property did not—again there were revisions, denunciations, administrative and judicial decisions. A proprietor could never be certain that denunciation of his property might not be his lot the next day, week, month, or year. Not even the man who scrupulously fulfilled all legal requirements and obligations was secure—and such confidence was not easily attained. Unfounded, illegal denunciations were not rare, but to prove an action groundless might require a lengthy, costly court fight. To be sure, this was not the only problem arising from nationalization and political turmoil—preference of rights to property and jurisdictional disputes were others—but the insecurity of ownership and the allied problem of denunciation of real estate became the most important concern of the government as the years passed. These were among the varied and unforeseen results of nationalization of clerical wealth and its distribution according to Reform principles. The achievement of liberal goals was complicated and frustrated by factors beyond the control of well-meaning and best-intentioned men. These problems were only resolved late in the Díaz regime, which finally ended nationalization dealings and gave security to proprietors some forty years after the issuance of the first laws.

The Reform laws, thus, caused Mexico, directly or indirectly, much bloodshed, anguish, and turmoil. The Catholic hierarchy never ceased its opposition to and condemnation of the laws and the Constitution and of those who took advantage of them. However, once active opposition had failed, the Church made the best of the situation by concluding special agreements with those who had acquired Church property.

The nineteenth-century liberals as agrarian reformers were failures. Under the laws, most corporate property passed to individuals.

Unfortunately, this often meant, particularly in the case of rural estates, the creation of a new, lay entailment. Failure resulted not from the liberals' grand conception, but from the execution of their design and the principles on which they operated. Their faith in individualism and their belief in private property obstructed the creation of a rural middle class. They defeated themselves by the refusal to touch lay latifundia, which, though individually owned, constituted as much an entailment as corporate ownership; the economic and social effects of this concentration were as bad as, if not worse than, that which they attacked. The liberals defeated their aim as well by not insisting on division of rural estates and by not limiting the amount of property acquired by any one person.

In effect, then, the anticorporate property legislation—civil as well as ecclesiastical—did not broadly redistribute rural or urban real estate; it did transfer most of that property from ecclesiastical to a limited number of lay owners. Whatever the virtues of this transfer, the new owners were less sympathetic and easygoing landlords than the clergy had been. The highly touted economic benefits of the circulation of landed wealth and the individualization of landholding failed to materialize.

Generalities such as these, to be sure, are always belied by specific cases. There is no doubt that just as the generalities are true, so, too, many cases can be found in contradiction; many former tenants of the Church acquired and held a house or plot or ranch with the result envisioned by the reformers. In addition, from the laws' operation, the government obtained some millions of pesos, retired part of the national debt, and restricted the economic and political influence of the clergy.

An accurate estimate of ecclesiastical wealth or of the resources obtained by the government from the expropriation of Church property will never be known. A fair educated guess would place the value of the property affected by the laws—real estate, mortgages, ecclesiastical buildings—at about $150,000,000 and federal income at approximately $25,000,000.[1] But the resources that went to the government hardly offset the costs of effecting the laws—in lives lost, property destroyed, or resources expended to achieve victory. Even the hard-

1. See the Appendices at the end of this work.

won victory turned out to be largely a hollow one, in some measure because of Porfirian policies. During the long rule of Porfirio Díaz an accommodation was reached between Church and State, and the Church gradually regained influence and prominence in the country. Federal relaxation of the laws and the authorities' favorable attitude toward the clergy provided a freer atmosphere that permitted the Church to regain a role in education, for it to carry on social action programs, for regular orders to reappear, and apparently for the Church to acquire some wealth.

Looking back over Mexican history, the Reform appears as a halting step, a hope and a promise, an unfulfilled dream. It was a catastrophe that shifted, to a degree, the base of power in the country and benefited some Mexicans, while leaving the lot of most unimproved. The successes and the failures alike, in the long run, did not have a measurable impact on the masses. The secularization of life could have meant little to most, equality before the law was an illusion for most, individualization of property was more harmful than beneficial to most. The ideals and goals of the reformers remained to be achieved by a later generation imbued with other objectives as well. In some respects, indeed, the revolutionaries of the twentieth century returned to the corporatism that the nineteenth labored to destroy as the means to achieve dignity and justice for all. The Porfirian one-third of a century represented a reaction to the Reform, but one in tune with the prevalent concepts of order and material progress. It may perhaps be viewed in retrospect as a hiatus, an interruption in the progress of Mexicans from their colonial past to modern nationhood. Such a view, however, implies a deterministic interpretation of history that unjustifiably ignores the importance of men and their struggles, achievements, and failures. Nevertheless, although the great Revolution had much to redo, it built on and benefited from the ideas, the failures and mistakes, as well as the successes and achievements of the Reform.

Appendix 1
Ecclesiastical Wealth and Nationalization

Two of the most difficult problems, and perhaps un-answerable questions, concerning Church property are to estimate the value of ecclesiastical property prior to the Reform legislation and to calculate the value or amount of the wealth disamortized and nationalized. In reading nineteenth-century materials, it sometimes seems that virtually every writer on the Reform, at the time and since, estimated Church wealth, though some in greater detail and some more accurately than others. The estimates vary widely. In part this variation stems from the precise meaning of Church wealth, what was included and excluded; in part it results from the lack of reliable information on clerical holdings.

The estimates arrived at here for total ecclesiastical wealth and for the value of nationalization are not definitive. At best they are "educated guesses" based on other published and unpublished calculations of various kinds and on archival research by this writer. Even the most minute and painstaking examination of records in every part of Mexico, in major depositories and in small, out-of-the-way places, would not yield a completely reliable, accurate figure. Aside from the lifetime required to accomplish such a task, the necessary documents are simply not extant. The writer believes, however, that a reasonably accurate figure can be arrived at on the basis of the available information. The estimate obtained for the value of nationalization compared with that on total ecclesiastical wealth helps support, in a tentative way, the accuracy of the figures. Although at the outset, the ideas and estimates of various other authors will be summarized and will include the diverse categories that they did, for the purposes of the writer's estimate, only that property subject to nationalization will be considered.

At the close of three centuries of colonial rule, the Mexican Church by all estimates was extremely wealthy. It was rich in all forms of material wealth: urban and rural properties, mortgages on real estate, religious buildings, jewels, furnishings. The Church possessed great wealth despite significant losses sustained in years past. For example, the property of the expelled Jesuits—at least 128 estates in New Spain—was offered for sale, and the Crown obtained $10,000,000 to $12,000,000 from the alienation of real estate and the redemption of mortgages of certain religious corporations. Still, Lucas Alamán, historian and conservative statesman of the early national period, estimated that at the end of the colonial era the Church owned or held mortgages on one-half of the real estate in the viceroyalty, or about $300,000,000.[1] Enrique Olavarría y Ferrari pegged total ecclesiastical income at $50,000,000 in 1809.[2] Genaro Raigosa, on the basis of operations during the Reform, valued clerical real estate in 1810 at $120,000,000 minimum, invested capital at $80,000,000, and annual Church income from all sources at $12,000,000.[3]

A decade after Independence and the losses and destruction resulting from that lengthy struggle, the liberal José María Luis Mora proposed a detailed statement of ecclesiastical wealth.[4] Mora arrived at productive clerical capital and the annual income produced therefrom in the following way:

Source	Income	Capital
Tithes in 1829	$ 2,341,152[5]	$46,823,040
Parish fees (1,204 parishes at $600 each)	722,400	14,448,000
Primicias (1,204 parishes at $10 each)	12,040	240,800

1. Lucas Alamán, *Historia de México* (4th ed.; Mexico: Editorial Jus, 1942), 1:70. Jan Bazant has estimated that total Church wealth, about $100 million in 1856, represented one-fifth of the total national wealth. Jan Bazant, "The Division of Some Mexican *Haciendas* during the Liberal Revolution, 1856–1862," *Journal of Latin American Studies* 3 (1971):25.

2. Enrique Olavarría y Ferrari, *México independiente, 1821–1855*, vol. 4 of *México a través de los siglos*, ed. Vicente Riva Palacio (Mexico, n.d.), p. 317.

3. G. Raigosa, "La evolución agrícola, breve ensayo sociológico," in *México. Su evolución social*, ed. Justo Sierra (Mexico: Imp. de Ignacio Escalante, 1902), 2:18.

4. José María Luis Mora, *Obras sueltas* (Paris, 1837), 1:372–73.

5. While income from tithes in the five-year period from 1806 to 1810 was $10,691,300, in the five years from 1829–1833 when civil coercion in their collection ended, it was only $5,211,628. *Memoria del Secretario de Estado y del despacho de Justica e Instrucción Pública leída a las cámaras del congreso nacional de la República Mexicana en 12 de enero de 1844* (Mexico, 1844), Appendix, Chart 2.

Source	Income	Capital
129 rural properties of monks	147,047	2,940,940
1,738 urban properties of monks	195,553	3,911,060
1,593 urban and rural properties of nuns	436,209	8,724,180
Capital of regular clergy	800,000	16,000,000
Capital of *capellanías* and *obras pías*	1,425,000	28,500,000
Real estate of *obras pías* not belonging to regular clergy	150,000	3,000,000
Alms and annual perquisites received by regular clergy	162,192	3,243,840
155 monasteries and 58 nunneries at a price of $100,000 each	1,065,000	21,300,000
Total	$ 7,456,593	$149,131,860

In addition to a total productive capital of over $149,000,000, Mora estimated unproductive capital, that is, sacred objects, furniture, jewels, churches, clerical residences, and lands on which they stood at $30,031,894, for a grand total of more than $179,000,000.[6]

Among the critics of Mora, Porfirio Parra, an early twentieth-century student of the Reform, asserts that his figures were exagerated, hypothetical, and misleading; they included unproductive wealth, and Mora assumed that the convents would be suppressed and converted to private dwellings or tenements, which would yield an income equivalent to that from capital of $21,300,000. Also, the capitalized income of the parishes should not be regarded as productive wealth. Nor should a study of clerical wealth include voluntary or fortuitous income such as alms and offerings. Thus, Parra, deducting

6. Mora, *Obras sueltas*, 1:372–73. Elsewhere, Mora compared ecclesiastical wealth with the total wealth of the Republic, which, including agricultural production, family income, precious metals, and commerce, amounted to $1,776,787,862; at 5 percent this yielded an income of $88,839,393. "Revista política," *Obras sueltas*, 1:clxxxi. Mora, like the generation of liberals that followed him, favored taking clerical property to pay the interest on and amortize the public debt. *Obras sueltas*, 1:clvii. The internal debt was $82,364,978, and the foreign debt was $45,349,504. José María Luis Mora, *Disertación sobre la naturaleza y aplicación de las rentas y bienes eclesiásticos* (Mexico: Talleres de la Secretaría de Hacienda y Crédito Público, 1957), first published in 1833, p. 462.

everything that was hypothetical and that did not represent real estate or invested capital, reduced the total to $100,000,000.[7]

In the nineteenth century, a few years after Mora's analysis, the moderate liberal Mariano Otero wrote that in 1829 the clergy's productive wealth was $18,000,000 in real estate and $44,500,000 in invested capital, plus $61,500,000 derived from "forced" exactions and $3,000,000 from alms and perquisites, for total productive capital of $127,000,000. Unproductive wealth amounted to $52,000,000, so that total ecclesiastical wealth was $179,000,000, a figure virtually identical to Mora's, reflecting Otero's apparent reliance on Mora's work.[8] Relying in turn on Otero to some extent, Brantz Mayer, the United States Legation Secretary in Mexico in 1841–1842, arrived at a total of between $90,000,000 and $100,000,000. He believed this a sum sufficient to pay off the public debt with enough remaining to support the clergy.[9]

In contrast to these estimates, the Bishop of Michoacán calculated the value of clerical real estate and invested capital at $23,500,000.[10] The religious writer Regis Planchet calculated the Church's productive property in the 1850s at $58,000,000.[11] Pérez Verdía set the figure at the time of nationalization at $45,000,000.[12] High estimates,

7. Porfirio Parra, *Sociología de la Reforma* (Mexico: Empresas Editoriales, S.A., 1948), pp. 80–83; see also Aquiles P. Moctezuma, *El conflicto religioso de 1926. Sus orígens. Su desarrollo. Su solución,* 2d ed. (Mexico: Editorial Jus, S.A., 1960), pp. 166ff.

8. Mariano Otero, *Ensayo sobre el verdadero estado de la cuestión social y política que se agita en la República Mexicana* (Mexico, 1842), pp. 38–43. Otero apparently added the first three items in Mora's list to get his $61,500,000 and added the final item to Mora's unproductive capital figure to get $52,000,000; he added together Mora's two items called "capital" to arrive at his $44,500,000 figure.

9. Brantz Mayer, *Mexico as It Was and Is* (New York, 1844), pp. 328–31. Mayer declared that this sum was $88,000,000 less than the pre-Independence value. The nunneries alone possessed capital of more than $4,500,000, producing an income of $250,000, and 1,700 properties, producing about $560,000 annually.

10. Parra, p. 81.

11. Regis Planchet, *La cuestión religiosa en México o sea vida de Benito Juárez* (Rome: Librerías Pontificias de Desclée, Lefebvre & Cía., 1906), p. 29.

12. Luis Pérez Verdía, *Compendio de la historia de México,* 11th ed. (Guadalajara: Librería Font, 1951), p. 450, footnote 1. The author added that in the

however, far outnumber the low. Jacinto Pallares, writing of the same period, estimated clerical capital at more than $150,000,000, yielding income of $8,000,000 annually.[13] At the time of the victory of the Ayutla Revolution in 1855, another commentator calculated minimum ecclesiastical wealth at $100,000,000.[14]

Even higher estimates include one of $300,000,000, providing income of $20,000,000.[15] A clerical writer, lamenting the losses of the Church, stated that prior to nationalization the Church's real estate alone was worth $184,614,530.[16] Pérez Hernández, the probable source for this statistic, added $30,000,000 more as the value of the convents, churches, chapels, and other immovable property, and $40,000,000 as the value of mortgages held by the Church, for a total of $254,000,000.[17]

previous 100 years the government had received $150,000,000 from the Church in donations and exactions. After Independence, Church wealth also suffered through the suppression of the Inquisition and sale of its property, through termination of civil coercion in tithe collection, and from depreciation of real estate values resulting from political turmoil. In 1849, for example, the Carmelites of Mexico sold fourteen haciendas, mostly situated in the state of San Luis Potosí, for $450,000 when one of them alone was worth $200,000 at the time and another was valued at $80,000. José María Pérez Hernández, *Estadística de la República Mexicana, territorio, población, antigüedades, monumentos, establecimientos públicos, reino vegetal y agricultura, reino animal, reino mineral, industria fabril y manufactura, artes mecánicas y liberales, comercio, navegación, gobierno, hacienda y crédito público, ejército, marina, clero, justicia, instrucción pública, colonias militares y civiles* (Guadalajara, 1862), p. 205.

13. Jacinto Pallares, ed., *Legislación federal complementaria del derecho civil mexicano* (Mexico, 1897), p. xl. The author adds, by way of comparison, that the federal budget was never more than $24,000,000 annually.

14. Y. O. [Manuel Payno], *La reforma social de Méjico deducida del aspecto político que él presenta, y fundada en la esperiencia de cuarenta y cinco años* (Mexico, 1855), p. 18.

15. George E. Church, *Mexico. Its Revolutions: Are They Evidences of Retrogression or of Progress?* (New York, 1866), p. 15. This is probably based on a figure from Miguel M. Lerdo de Tejada's *Cuadro sinóptico de la República Mexicana en 1856 formado en vista de los últimos datos oficiales y otras noticias fidedignas* (Mexico, 1856), p. 83. For another contemporary estimate, see Charles Lemprière, *Notes in Mexico in 1861 and 1862: Politically and Socially Considered* (London, 1862), p. 247.

16. Fortino Hipólito Vera, *Catecismo geográfico-histórico-estadístico de la iglesia mexicana* (Amecameca, 1881), p. 12.

17. Pérez Hernández, *Estadística*, pp. 250–57. The statistics were restated in

Miguel Lerdo de Tejada, author of the law of disamortization, took considerable pains in analyzing the sources and yield of ecclesiastical wealth in his *Cuadro sinóptico* of 1856.[18] On the basis of figures on agricultural production and vital statistics, Lerdo concluded that income from tithes, parish fees, alms, masses, ecclesiastical functions, and the sale of devotional objects was at least $6,000,000 to $8,000,000 a year, while the total wealth of the Church in 1856 was $250,000,000 or $300,000,000.[19] In Mexico City alone, he wrote, the churches, public buildings, and the 5,000 houses had a value of at least $80,000,000, more than half of which belonged to the clergy.[20] The return from these and its other properties, together with other sources of income brought total Church revenue to more than $20,000,000 a year in Lerdo's opinion.[21]

While Lerdo's estimate is a high one, it was by no means the highest. One contemporary placed Church wealth in 1859–1860 at $520,000,000.[22] And Francisco Mejía, a future Finance Minister and

1875 in 3:440ff. of his *Diccionario geográfico, estadístico, histórico, biográfico, de industria y comercio de la República Mexicana* (Mexico, 1875). They were also given by Feliz Ramos y Duarte in 1899 in *Diccionario de curiosidades históricas, geográficas, hierográficas, cronológicas, etc. de la República Mejicana* (Mexico, 1899), pp. 82–86. The 861 ecclesiastical rural estates were worth $71,373,270, and the 22,649 urban properties were valued at $113,241,530. Pérez Hernández also itemized annual ecclesiastical income of $21,477,813 which was balanced by expenses of $15,301,962. Some of the items at least are very much inflated for the mid-nineteenth century: income from tithes, for example, is listed as the amount received earlier in the century before the end of civil coaction.

18. Lerdo de Tejada, pp. 81–83.

19. Lerdo estimated (p. 43) the value of the rural real estate in the Republic at $720,000,000 and urban real estate at $635,000,000, or a total value of $1,355,000,000, which, however, he considered a low estimate.

20. In 1813 the house rents in Mexico City yielded about $1,911,000 according to one writer; of this, about $1,061,000 belonged to corporations, principally clerical. Almost all of the houses of individuals were encumbered for more than one-half of their value with mortgages held by the clergy or other corporations. Luis de La Rosa, *Observaciones sobre varios puntos concernientes a la administración pública del Estado de Zacatecas* (Baltimore, 1851), p. 94.

21. Lerdo de Tejada, p. 83. Government income, both state and federal, at that time was about $15,000,000. Ibid., p. 86.

22. This was Gaulot's estimate in *Maximilian*, pp. 103–5, cited by Ulick

one intimately involved in nationalization, claimed that in 1856 he saw a book that computed clerical wealth in the Republic at $500,000,000, excluding gold, jewels, and worked silver in churches.[23] Years later, however, as Minister, Mejía had occasion to estimate ecclesiastical wealth in an official report, and he arrived at a much lower figure, $233,500,000. He obtained this amount on the basis of percentages of mortgages, from the limited number of mortgage and notarial records available to him, to total real estate value in several of the states. He found the average percentage of encumbrance on real estate in those states to be about 68.50, and he generalized from that—not a very trustworthy procedure.[24]

During the Empire a careful analysis was made of disamortization and nationalization for purposes of considering the prospects for revision. The author was a French lawyer, L. Binel; he extrapolated from the admittedly fragmentary archives at his disposal and from earlier published statistics. He came up with the astounding total of more than $600,000,000: $460,000,000 to $470,000,000 in immovable property and more than $150,000,000 in movable.[25]

In the twentieth century two conservative estimates have been made in some detail, although neither attempted the kind of analysis that Binel or Mejía did, based on available original documents; both relied on Mora's basic classification. The one, earlier in this century, was by the noted Jesuit historian, Mariano Cuevas; the other, in the late 1950s, was by Manuel Loza Macías. Most recently, the economic historian Jan Bazant, mentioned throughout this study, has published an exhaustive analysis and interpretation of disamortization and nationalization.[26]

Ralph Burke, *A Life of Benito Juárez, Constitutional President of Mexico* (London, 1894), footnote on p. 97.

23. Franciso Mejía, *Memorias* (Mexico: Ediciones del Boletín Bibliográfico de la Secretaría de Hacienda y Crédito Público, 1958), p. 41.

24. *Informe de Hacienda, 1872–1873*, pp. 151–52.

25. Report by L. Binel, "Property of the clergy, March 17, 1864," Díaz López, 3:365–68.

26. See his preliminary article "La desamortización de los bienes corporativos de 1856," *Historia Mexicana* 16 (October–December 1966): 194–212 and his *Alienation of Church Wealth in Mexico. Social and Economic Aspects of the Liberal Revolution, 1856–1875*, ed. and trans. Michael P. Costeloe

Loza Macías, with some modification of Mora, arrives at an annual income of nearly $4,000,000, representing real estate and productive capital of $30,000,000; he added unproductive property of $30,000,000, for a total of slightly more than $60,000,000. The author, in calculating capital, deletes Mora's categories of tithes, first fruits, parish fees, alms, and perquisites as not capitalizable. This deletion was justifiable in a sense, but he also makes no allowance for property of the Juzgado de Capellanías, *cofradías*, chaplaincies, and pious works; he apparently assumed that there was none, since the Royal Order of 1804 had suppressed such corporations and used their property to pay off royal debts.[27] Also disregarded is property of charitable and educational institutions administered by the Church; this property should properly be included in any estimate of total clerical wealth. And while Mora used an average of $100,000 in calculating the value of convents, Loza Macías uses $10,000, which seems excessively low even if Mora's average was high.

Loza Macías, as earlier writers, cites the losses sustained by the Church from before Independence, but he makes no mention of increases in Church wealth over the years. He, thus, implies that entering nuns no longer paid a substantial dowry, that the Church no longer loaned money at interest, acquired mortgages, bought or inherited real estate, or received other pious gifts; all of these indeed did occur. In any case, $60,000,000 would not appear to reflect accurately total wealth of the Church.[28]

Father Cuevas, in his history of the Church in Mexico, first sought to demolish a whole host of earlier commentaries: Lerdo's figures were vague and untrue; Almán's statements false; and Callcott's conclusions the result of a mistranslation and misunderstanding of Ote-

---

(Cambridge: The University Press, 1971). See also the comments of Michael Costeloe with particular reference to the wealth of the Juzgado de Capellanías in his excellent study, *Church Wealth in Mexico: A Study of the 'Juzgado de Capellanías' in the Archbishopric of Mexico, 1800–1856* (Cambridge: The University Press, 1967).

27. Loza Macías disregards the real estate of pious works on the theory that the income was destined for pious works and that the clergy did not directly use the property.

28. Manuel Loza Macías, *El pensamiento económico y la Constitución de 1857* (Mexico: Editorial Jus, S. A., 1959), pp. 200–205. The author's classification and figures are:

ro.[29] Mora, he argued, failed to allow for the reduction of tithes after civil coercion was ended in 1833, and, even so, the Church did not receive all of the tithes collected.[30] He exaggerated the number of parishes, and surely many of the properties that he counted did not belong to the Church. Nor did Mora allow for expenses of repair or improvement of property; he listed amounts for alms and perquisites which were not capitalizable; and the sum representing the value of the convents was unproductive wealth for which the government would have had to pay if the buildings were taken from the true owners. Vera's figures lacked reasoning or proof and Ramos y Duarte's statistics were unsubstantiated by any source, besides including thirty-four nonclerical properties, such as the silversmiths' guild.[31]

Source	Income	Capital
Tithes	$ 1,800,000	
Parish fees (1,204 parishes at $600 each)	722,400	
Primicias (1,204 parishes at $10 each)	12,040	
201 rural properties of monks	122,944	$ 2,458,880
1,740 urban properties of monks	169,352	2,387,040
2,174 ιrban and rural properties of nuns	625,820	12,162,320
Capital of regular clergy in 1846	371,446	10,947,940
Alms and perquisites	162,192	
147 monasteries and 57 nunneries at an average value of $10,000 each		2,060,000
Total income per year	$ 3,986,194	
Total real estate and productive capital		$30,016,160
Total unproductive property (based on Mora)		30,031,894
Total clerical property		$60,048,054

It will be noted that the amount of capital listed for the monasteries and nunneries does not agree with the total of 204 such establishments and that the total for real estate and productive capital is $20 short of what the figures actually total.

29. M. Cuevas, *Historia de la iglesia en México* (El Paso: Editorial "Revista Católica," 1928), 5:288–99.

30. Mora did state that his figure was for 1829, several years before the end of civil coaction.

31. Cuevas apparently did not make use of Pérez Hernández's *Estadística*, written in 1862, which Ramos y Duarte copies verbatim, though he lists no source. Cuevas may be correct about the inclusion of civil property. Antonio Peñafiel lists the *cuerpo de plateros* as a civil corporation. *Boletín Semestral de la*

After criticizing the efforts of others, Cuevas attempted to establish a more accurate statistic, though admitting the impossibility of arriving at an exact total value of ecclesiastical wealth. With some exceptions, he, too, followed Mora's pattern, but made a point of the number of people who had to be supported by the income: annual tithe income of $1,170,576 supported about 1,200 people; the regular clergy's income of $1,014,141 supported a total of 5,422 people.[32] The total productive wealth of the clergy, ideally capitalized at 5 percent, was $42,694,340.[33] Cuevas excluded the value of jewels, artwork, and other precious objects, which were unproductive wealth and not indicative of the wealth of the clergy, but rather of the piety of the donors; nor did he allow for any real estate or capital held by the secular clergy, an omission which is misleading and unrealistic. He ignored the value of the churches and convents themselves, as well as property of chaplaincies, *cofradías*, and pious works. All of these were affected by the Reform measures, and their wealth should properly be calculated in any estimate of total ecclesiastical wealth, even though they might be excluded for particular reasons by a given writer.[34]

The few statistics cited, though by no means exhausting the possibilities, do include the most notable and serious efforts to arrive at an accurate figure. They include as well the opinions of proclericals, anticlericals, and presumably dispassionate scholars. The samples cited cover a long time period—from the early nineteenth century to the present. The great disparity evident in the estimates results

---

Estadística de la República Mexicana, a cargo del Dr. Antonio Peñafiel, Minsterio de Fomento, no. 1 (Mexico, 1888), p. 9. On the other hand, a clerical writer in 1863 listed the *cuerpo de plateros* as an ecclesiastical group. Luis Alfaro y Piña, *Relación descriptiva de la fundación, dedicación, situación geográfica, etc. de las catedrales, parroquias, conventos y demás iglesias del arzobispado y obispados de la República Mexicana con una indicación del estado que guardan desde el año de 1861 en adelante* (Mexico, 1863), p. 30.

32. This included, for the former figure: 10 bishops, their *curias*, 187 prebendaries, nearly 700 seminarists and professors, servants, and managers of various kinds; for the regular clergy, the income supported 1,194 friars and their 250 servants, 1,609 nuns, 26 novices, 988 girls, and their 1,345 servants.

33. Cuevas apparently capitalized income from tithes as well as property to arrive at his total; the figure is $1,000,000 less than it should be, perhaps due to a printing error.

34. Cuevas's breakdown was:

from the partisan interests of the authors, categories of income included, and differing opinions as to acutal values; perhaps more than anything else, the disparity arises from the lack of sufficient information on which to base an estimate with any real degree of accuracy.

It is relatively easy to be critical of others' efforts, to reject some aspects or all of the earlier estimates for one reason or another. Even the more painstaking analyses based on irrefutable documentation—those of Francisco Mejía and L. Binel—break down when they generalize for the whole country on the basis of the limited mortgage records or tenuous real estate values that they had at their disposal. It is quite another matter, however, to estimate confidently clerical wealth with any greater accuracy—one still ends with too many unknowns, generalizing on the basis of limited evidence.

This writer's calculation is based, if not on exhaustive research, at least on an extensive survey of the materials on the subject. It differs from most earlier efforts since the particular object in mind is to obtain a figure of total wealth subject to disamortization and nationalization to compare with the known property affected by those laws; certain items, therefore, will be disregarded—income from tithes and first fruits, the value of jewels, ornaments, and furniture. This estimate, then, is limited to ecclesiastical real estate and mortgages and the value of religious buildings.

The least disputable aspect in the estimate of the value of corporate wealth is undoubtedly for the regular clergy. The others cited below—reduced to the simplest terms—are more problematical, but probably conservative:

Source	Income
Tithes (one-half of Mora's figure due to end of civil coaction in 1833, continued revolutions, and forced loans)	$ 1,170,576
129 rural properties of monks	147,047
1,738 urban properties of monks	195,553
1,593 urban and rural properties of nuns	436,209
Alms and perquisites	162,192
Capital of regular clergy of $1,464,060 at 5 percent	73,203
Total	$ 2,184,780

The total given by Cuevas for income, excluding tithes, is $1,014,141, while from the figures given, the amount should be $1,014,204.

Source	Value
Regular clergy: real estate;	$ 18,500,000
capital	10,000,000
Chaplaincy endowments	10,000,000
Cofradías and *archicofradías*	5,000,000
Pious works (*obras pías*)	5,000,000
Charities and schools	7,500,000
Religious buildings (convents, churches, chapels, seminaries, *beateríos*, spiritual retreats [*casas de ejercicios*], schools, hospitals)[35]	30,000,000
Other property (real estate and mortgages of cathedrals, parishes, chaplaincy court, *fábrica*)	10,000,000
Total	$ 96,000,000

If, on the other hand, various other estimates are accepted as reasonable—which could be done endlessly—and substituted for items above, much higher amounts can be obtained. Thus, Mora calculated property of the regular clergy at $31,500,000 and that of chaplaincies and pious works at $31,500,000; adding amounts for charities and education, *cofradías*, and religious buildings of $42,500,000 yields a total of $105,500,000. Or accepting the statement of Lucas Alamán—who may yet turn out to be the most accurate—that the clergy owned or held mortgages on one-half of the real estate in New Spain, a total of around $165,000,000 is obtained. This figure, however, depends on acceptance of one of the speculative estimates of real estate values in the Republic.[36]

But tentatively accepting this calculation and turning to various

35. These buildings, though all nationalized, were not all sold; many (notably churches) were left to the service of the Faith; others, such as convents, were devoted to public uses.

36. See *Memoria que el Secretario de Estado y del despacho de Fomento, Colonización, Industria y Comercio de la República Mexicana presenta al congreso de la unión conteniendo documentos hasta el 30 de junio de 1873* (Mexico, 1873), pp. 883–939; and *Memoria de Hacienda, 1869–1870*, p. 995. The former estimated real estate value at $326,750,000, the latter at about the same, although the Minister considered the actual value to be over $510,000,000. Miguel Lerdo's estimate was $1,355,000,000, which he still considered low; see *Cuadro sinóptico*, p. 43.

official reports on disamortization and nationalization, the following conclusion is reached.[37] In the first six months of the operation of the disamortization law, adjudications and sales of ecclesiastical real estate reached over $20,500,000, which the Minister of Finance believed represented less than one-half of the true value of the real estate. The real property submitted for Imperial revision—up to six months prior to the end of that process—was nearly $29,500,000. In addition, in subsequent years, real estate was denounced—over 1,700 properties—for which no value was reported, but $1,000,000 should not be an exaggerated value to assign to these. Doubling these real estate values ($61,000,000), and adding the value of nationalized mortgages reported to the end of the century ($68,600,000), and disregarding the probably considerable value that either evaded operation of the laws or was not included in official statistics yields a total of nearly $130,000,000 in ecclesiastical wealth subjected to nationalization.

With all the tentativeness of the data and shortcomings of the conclusion, the writer is inclined to place the value of ecclesiastical wealth, conservatively, at over $100,000,00 and probably closer to $150,000,000. For reasons noted elsewhere in this study, it seems likely that the elusive but intriguing answer to the question of the value of ecclesiastical holdings will remain unknown. Further research, such as Bazant's, can, however, provide valuable new knowledge on the property question, such as identification of those who acquired the bulk of the property, distribution or concentration of ecclesiastical wealth, and other financial implications of the laws.[38]

37. That is, the *Memorias de Hacienda* for 1857 and subsequent years and revision reports of the Empire.

38. In addition to the work of Bazant, Charles Berry's dissertation, "The Reform in the Central District of Oaxaca, 1856–1867" (University of Texas, 1967), is the result of careful study on the property question. Among many other sources, for statistics on Church wealth in addition to those cited in the summary of estimates in this Appendix, the reader will find especially useful the following: *Memorias* and *Informes de Hacienda* from 1856 to 1900; *Memoria de las operaciones que han tenido lugar en la oficina especial de desamortización del Distrito, desde el 7 de enero en que se abrió, hasta el 5 de dicembre de 1861, en que cesaron sus labores, para continuarlas la Junta Superior de Hacienda* (Mexico, 1862); Luis Alfaro y Piña, *Relación descriptiva de la fundación, dedicación, etc. de las iglesias y conventos de México, con una reseña de la variación que han sufrido durante*

el gobierno de D. Benito Juárez (Mexico, 1863); "Apuntes para la geografía y la estadística del estado de Michoacán, 1849," *Boletín del Instituto Nacional de Geografía y Estadística de la República Mexicana,* 3d ed., vol. 1 (Mexico, 1861); in the *Boletín de la Sociedad de Geografía y Estadística de la República Mexicana* (Mexico), "Documentos para la historia. La desamortización eclesiástica en tiempo de Carlos IV," 2nd epoch, vol. 1 (1869), and Manuel Martínez Gracida, "El estado de Oaxaca y su estadística del culto católico (1881)," 3rd epoch, vol. 6 (1882); in the *Boletín de la Sociedad Mexicana de Geografía y Estadística* (Mexico), Juan María Balbontín, "Notas formadas para la geografía y estadística del departamento de Querétaro," vol. 7 (1859), José Guadalupe Romero, "Noticias para formar la estadística del obispado de Michocán (1860)," vol. 8 (1860), and "Noticias de Nueva España en 1805, publicadas por el tribunal del consulado," 2nd epoch, vol. 2 (1864); Fortino Hipólito Vera, *Itinerario parroquial del arzobispado de México y reseña histórica, geográfica y estadística de las parroquias del mismo arzobispado* (Amecameca, 1880); "Noticia de obras pías . . . ," Archivo General de la Nación de México, Bienes nacionales, leg. 1912, exp. 1; Manuel Rivera Cambas, *Los gobernantes de México* (Mexico, 1873), vol. 2; Jorge Fernando Iturribarría, *Historia de Oaxaca,* vol. 2, *1855 a 1861. La Reforma. La guerra de tres años* (Oaxaca: Imprenta del Gobierno del Estado, 1939); *Anales del Ministerio de Fomento de la República Mexicana, año de 1881* (Mexico, 1881), vol. 5; enclosure with dispatch 1, Corwin to Seward, 29 May 1861 issue of *Mexico Extraordinary* in *Despatches from United States Ministers to Mexico, 1823–1906* (Washington, D.C.: National Archives, Microcopy File no. 97), roll 29, vol. 28; Abad y Queipo, "Escrito presentado a Manuel Sixtos Espinosa . . . ," in *Colección de los escritos más importantes que en diferentes épocas dirigió al gobierno D. Manuel Abad Queipo, obispo electo de Michoacán* (Mexico, 1813); and Miguel Valero Olea, Descripción de el Estado eclesiástico secular y regular del Arzobispado de México Metropoli de esta Nueva España con noticia puntual de la erección y fundación de sus respectivos tribunales, cuerpos académicos, colegios, y casas religiosas de ambos sexos . . . , 1793, Latin American Collection, University of Texas, Austin.

Appendix 2
Value of Nationalized Ecclesiastical Property

	Real Estate	Mortgages	Total
Revisions by the Empire to March 1866[1]	$ 29,405,738	$ 33,020,390	$ 62,426,128
Denunciations, 1867–73[2]			17,500,000
1873–1874	482	2,188,732	
1874–1875	285	1,956,476	
1877–1878	66	641,621	
1878–1879	87	634,669	
1879–1880	125	718,081	
1880–1881	59	716,670	
1882–1883		1,152,025	
1883–1884		651,230	
1884–1885		1,373,693	
1885–1886	34	1,716,296	
1886–1887	92	604,763	
1887–1888	51	1,549,023	
1888–1889	43	1,375,551	
1889–1890	153	1,175,861	
1892–1893	90	842,447	
1893–1894	43	413,931	
1894–1895	51	191,950	
1895–1896		90,000	
1896–1897	34	26,050	
1897–1898		17,490	
1898–1899	15	54,914	
1899–1900	14	19,800	$ 18,111,273
	1,724 properties		$ 98,037,401

1. These figures are from *Informe de Hacienda, 1872–1873*, document 19. In all cases the *centavos* have been omitted.

2. The following figures are taken from various *Memorias de Hacienda*. The value of the real estate denounced is not given; therefore, the figures under "Real Estate" are simply the number of properties denounced. Thus, a considerable amount would have to be added to the total to allow for the value of these properties. However, for the years 1892–1893 and 1893–1894 the value of real estate denounced is apparently included in that of mortgages denounced.

Appendix 3

Income Received by the Government from Disamortization and Nationalization[1]

Years	Amount	Years	Amount
1856	$ 1,083,611	1886–1887	$ 478,879
1861	10,094,184	1887–1888	232,264
1865–1866	2,550,000	1888–1889	218,484
1867–1868	1,027,911	1889–1890	136,377
1868–1869	371,806	1892–1893	93,827*
1869–1870	294,965*	1893–1894	277,044**
1870–1871	779,129	1894–1895	188,304**
1871–1872	729,816	1895–1896	129,338**
1872–1873	734,876	1896–1897	153,970**
1873–1874	562,560	1897–1898	59,738**
1874–1875	453,951	1898–1899	38,447
1875–1876	213,950	1899–1900	74,805**
1876–1877	157,993	1900–1901	33,357**
1877–1878	103,206	1901–1902	3,216
1878–1879	45,407	1902–1903	100,268
1879–1880	17,525*	1905–1906	9,737*
1880–1881	235,699	1906–1907	9,652*
1881–1882	167,833*	1907–1908	2,361*

1. These figures were gleaned principally from *Memorias de Hacienda.* The amount for 1856 represents the *alcabala* payments received by the government as shown in *Memoria presentada al Exmo. Sr. Presidente Sustituto de la República por el C. Miguel Lerdo de Tejada dando cuenta de la marcha que han seguido los negocios de la Hacienda Pública en el tiempo que tuvo a su cargo la Secretaría de este ramo* (Mexico, 1857). The amount for 1861 is from *Memoria de las operaciones que han tenido lugar en la oficina especial de desamortización del Distrito, desde el 7 de enero en que se abrió, hasta el 5 de diciembre de 1861, en que cesaron sus labores, para continuarlas la Junta Superior de Hacienda* (Mexico, 1862). The figure for 1865–66 is from M. Payno, *Cuentas, gastos, acreedores y otros asuntos del tiempo de la intervención francesa y del imperio. Del 1861 a 1867* (Mexico, 1868). In all cases, the *centavos* have been omitted.

Years	Amount	Years	Amount
1882–1883	363,640*	1908–1909	1,129*
1883–1884	75,161*	1909–1910	906*
1884–1885	327,502		
1885–1886	383,688		$ 23,016,516

The "*" indicates that the amount given represents the *líquido*; "**" indicates that it includes stamps of liberation; if there is no indication, the amount is the gross.

Bibliography

This bibliography lists only those sources cited in the footnotes. Excluded, therefore, are studies valuable for background or general information, such as: Wilfrid H. Callcott, *Church and State in Mexico, 1822–1857;* Walter V. Scholes, *Mexican Politics during the Juárez Regime, 1855–1872;* and George M. McBride, *The Land Systems of Mexico;* as well as works useful for contemporary impressions and attitudes, such as: Robert A. Wilson, *Mexico: Its Peasants and Its Priests;* Ignacio M. Altamirano, *Historia y política de México, 1821–1882;* Ignacio Ramírez, *México en pos de la libertad;* and *Mexico: The Country, History, and People.*

Unquestionably, the most important unpublished resources are located in the Latin American Collection of the University of Texas Library and the Archivo General de la Nación de México. The former is also indispensable for published materials on nineteenth-century Mexico. The voluminous Genaro García collection in the Texas library includes important documents and correspondence of leading participants in the tumultuous years of Reform from the 1850s through foreign intervention and Empire and the Restored Republic. The many-volumed series of *Memorias* and *Informes* of different government ministries, particularly of the Finance (Hacienda) Ministry, though incomplete, were a gold mine of statistics, reports, analyses, and opinions. The microfilmed *Despatches of United States Ministers* and *Consuls* were also revealing of conditions in Mexico during the period. Supplementing these documents are the published reports of French ministers to Mexico in the 1850s and 1860s, translated and edited by Lilia Díaz López, *Versión francesa de México.*

Also indispensable were collections of laws, circulars, and resolutions and government manifestos or proclamations located at the University of Texas. Unpublished doctoral dissertations, journal articles, and various issues of the *Boletín de la Sociedad Mexicana de Geografía y Estadística* were other useful resources. Pamphlets and periodicals of the period added another dimension to the study; these included republican and Imperial governmental papers and the significant newspaper *El Siglo Diez y Nueve.* Published court cases dealing with nationalized property provided insights into operations of the laws and problems arising over acquisitions in the unsettled political conditions. The official clerical position was revealed in diverse clerical writings, pastorals, and communications. Congressional debates reflected attitudes, conditions, and problems of the time.

The most useful materials in the Mexican national archives (Archivo General de la Nación in Mexico City) were found in the Ramo de Bienes Nacionales, Ramo de Negocios Eclesiásticos, and the Ramo de Justicia Eclesiástico. Other primary published materials providing insights into conditions were writings, reminiscences or memoirs of contemporaries of the Reform, both prominent and secondary figures, for example, Melchor

Ocampo, Manuel Payno, and Emile de Kératry. Secondary works consulted for this study included multi-volume histories, contemporary polemics, and modern monographs and scholarly articles.

Unpublished Sources

Austin. University of Texas. Latin American Collection. Bazaine, Achille François. Correspondencia, 1862–1867.
———. Comonfort, Ignacio. Correspondencia.
———. Comunicaciones oficiales entre el Gobierno y la Junta suprema de Hacienda creada el 17 de Julio: proyectos de reglamento y presupuestos. 1861.
———. Documentos relativos a la Reforma y a la Intervención, 1850–1867.
———. Intervención francesa. Documentos misceláneos, 1862–1867.
———. Intervención francesa. Miscelánea, 1867–1869.
———. Lares, Teodosio. Correspondencia y otros documentos, 1833–1867.
———. Madrid, Manuel I. Correspondencia, 1840–1859.
———. The Morning Post on the Affairs of Mexico.
———. Ortega, Jesús González. Correspondencia, 1851–1881.
———. Riva Palacio, Mariano. Correspondencia, 1830–1880.
———. Riva Palacio, Vicente. Miscelánea sin fechas.
———. Terán, Jesús. Correspondencia y papeles, 1855–1865.
———. Valero Olea, Miguel. Descripción de el Estado eclesiástico secular y regular del Arzobispado de México Metropoli de esta Nueva España con noticia puntual de la erección y fundación de sus respectivos tribunales, cuerpos académicos, colegios, y casas religiosas de ambos sexos . . . 1793.
———. Villada, José Vicente. Correspondencia, 1871–1879.
Berry, Charles R. "The Reform in the Central District of Oaxaca, 1856–1867. A Case Study." Ph.D. diss., University of Texas, 1967.
Mexico. Archivo General de la Nación de México. Ramos de Bienes Nacionales, Negocios Eclesiásticos, and Justicia Eclesiástico.
Mexico. Archivo Histórico de Hacienda, segundo imperio.
Schmitt, Karl M. "Evolution of Mexican Thought on Church-State Relations, 1876–1911." Ph.D. diss., University of Pennsylvania, 1954.

Published Sources

Abad y Queipo, Manuel. *Colección de los escritos más importantes que en diferentes épocas dirigió al gobierno D. Manuel Abad Queipo, obispo electo de Michoacán.* Mexico, 1813.

Alamán, Lucas. *Historia de México.* 4th ed. Vols. 1 and 5. Mexico: Editorial Jus, 1942.

Alegato de buena prueba que el Licenciado D. Manuel Siliceo, patrono y apoderado del Dr. D. Antonio Fernández Monjardín, ha hecho en el juicio posesorio promovido contra D. José I. Limantour, reclamando el despojo de la casa no. 6 de la calle de la Palma, ante el juez de lo civil Licenciado D. Antonio Aguado. Mexico, 1863.

Alegato presentado a la Suprema Corte de Justicia por el Lic. Ignacio L. Vallarta en representación de los herederos del licenciado Don Jesús Navarro en el amparo promovido por D. Miguel Estrada contra la ejecutoria del tribunal de Michoacán que lo condenó a pagar un capital nacionalizado. Mexico, 1883.

Alfaro y Piña, Luis. *Relación descriptiva de la fundación, dedicación, etc. de las iglesias y conventos de México, con una reseña de la variación que han sufrido durante el gobierno de D. Benito Juárez.* Mexico, 1863.

———. *Relación descriptiva de la fundación, dedicación, situación geográfica, etc. de las catedrales, parroquias, conventos y demás iglesias del arzobispado y obispados de la República Mexicana con una indicación del estado que guardan desde el año de 1861 en adelante.* Mexico, 1863.

Algunas indicaciones acerca de la intervención europea en Méjico, Paris, 1859.

Alvensleven, Baron Maximilian von. *With Maximilian in Mexico.* London, 1867.

Amador, Juan. *Acontecimientos en la Villa de Cós del estado de Zacatecas. El juramento de la Constitución.* Zacatecas, 1857.

Anales del Ministerio de Fomento de la República Mexicana, año de 1881. Vol. 5. Mexico, 1881.

Anderson, William Marshall. *An American in Maximilian's Mexico, 1865–66.* Edited by Ramón Eduardo Ruiz. San Marino, Calif.: The Huntington Library, 1959.

"Apuntes para la geografía y la estadística del estado de Michoacán, 1849." *Boletín del Instituto Nacional de Geografía y Estadística de la República Mexicana.* 3d ed. Vol. 1. Mexico, 1861.

El Archivo Mexicano. Colección de leyes, decretos, circulares y otros documentos. 6 vols. Mexico, 1856–1862.

Archivos privados de D. Benito Juárez y D. Pedro Santacilia. Prologue by J. M. Puig Casauranc. Vol. 1. Mexico: Publicaciones de la Secretaría de Educación Pública, 1928.

Arrangoiz, Francisco de Paula de. *Apuntes para la historia del segundo imperio mejicano.* Madrid, 1869.

———. *Méjico desde 1808 hasta 1867. Relación de los principales acontecimientos políticos que han tenido lugar desde la prisión del virrey Iturrigaray hasta la caída del segundo imperio.* 4 vols. Madrid, 1871–1872.

Arrillaga, Basilio. *Cuartas observaciones sobre el opúsculo entitulado "El imperio y el clero mexicano" del señor Abate Testory (capellán mayor del ejército francés en México).* Mexico, 1865.

Balbontín, Juan María. "Notas formadas para la geografía y estadística del departamento de Querétaro." *Boletín de la Sociedad Mexicana de Geografía y Estadística.* Vol. 7. Mexico, 1859.

Balderrama, Luis C. *El clero y el gobierno de México, apuntes para la historia de la crisis en 1926*. Vol. 1. Mexico: Editorial "Cuauhtemoc," 1927.

Bancroft, Hubert Howe. *The Works of Hubert Howe Bancroft*. Vol. 14, *History of Mexico*; Vol. 6, *1861–1887*. San Francisco, 1888.

Bassols, Narciso. *Leyes de reforma que afectan al clero, publicadas por orden cronológico por Narciso Bassols*. Puebla: Imp. del Convictorio, 1902.

Bazant, Jan. *Alienation of Church Wealth in Mexico. Social and Economic Aspects of the Liberal Revolution, 1856–1875*. Edited and translated by Michael P. Costeloe. Cambridge: The University Press, 1971.

——. "La desamortización de los bienes corporativos de 1856." *Historia Mexicana* 16 (October-December 1966): 193–212.

——. "The Divison of Some Mexican *Haciendas* during the Liberal Revolution, 1856–1862." *Journal of Latin American Studies* 3 (1971): 25–37.

Benson, Nettie Lee, ed. *Mexico and the Spanish Cortes, 1810–1822: Eight Essays*. Austin: University of Texas Press, 1966.

Berry, Charles R. "The Fiction and Fact of the Reform: The Case of the Central District of Oaxaca, 1856–1867." *The Americas* 26 (January 1970): 277–90.

Blumberg, Arnold. "The Mexican Empire and the Vatican, 1863–1867." *The Americas* 28 (July 1971):1–19.

Boletín de las leyes del Imperio Mexicano. Primera parte, tomo II comprende las leyes, decretos y reglamentos generales números del 1 al 176 expedidos por el emperador Maximiliano desde 1° de julio hasta 31 de diciembre de 1865. Mexico, 1866.

Boletín Semestral de la Estadística de la República Mexicana (a cargo del Dr. Antonio Peñafiel, Ministerio de Fomento). No. 1. Mexico, 1888.

Bordonova, Silvestre. *Conducta del obispo de Puebla, Licenciado Don Pelagio Antonio de Lavastida, manifestada en las notas que dirigió al gobierno de Méjico inmediatamente antes y después de su destierro ejecutado el 12 de mayo de 1856*. Paris, 1857.

Buenrostro, Felipe. *Historia del primero y segundo congresos constitucionales de la República Mexicana*. 9 vols. Mexico, 1875–1882.

Burke, Ulick Ralph. *A Life of Benito Juárez, Constitutional President of Mexico*. London, 1894.

Cabrera, Luis. *The Religious Question in Mexico*. New York: Las Novedades, 1915.

Cadenhead, Ivie E., Jr. *Jesús González Ortega and Mexican National Politics*. Fort Worth: Texas Christian University Press, 1972.

Calderón, Francisco R. *La república restaurada: La vida económica*. Vol. 2 of *Historia moderna de México*, edited by Daniel Cosío Villegas. Mexico: Editorial Hermes, 1955.

Calderón de la Barca, Madame Frances. *Life in Mexico, during a Residence of Two Years in That Country*. London, 1843.

Callcott, Wilfrid H. *Liberalism in Mexico, 1857–1929*. Stanford, Calif.: Stanford University Press, 1931.

Cambre, Manuel. *La guerra de tres años, apuntes para la historia de la Reforma*. Guadalajara (?): Biblioteca de Autores Jaliscienses, 1949.

Carreño, Alberto María, ed. *Archivo del General Porfirio Díaz, memorias y documentos.* 30 vols. Mexico: Editorial "Elede," S.A., 1947–1961.

Carta pastoral del Illmo. Sr. Arzobispo de México, Dr. D. Lázaro de la Garza y Ballesteros, dirigida al V. clero y fieles de este arzobispado con motivo de los proyectos contra la Iglesia, publicados en Veracruz por D. Benito Juárez, antiguo presidente del Supremo Tribunal de la nación. Mexico, 1859.

Carta pastoral del Illmo. Sr. Dr. D. Pedro Barajas, Obispo de San Luis Potosí, dirigida a sus diocesanos. San Luis Potosí, 1860.

Carta pastoral que el Illmo. Señor Arzobispo de México Dr. D. Lázaro de la Garza y Ballesteros dirige a sus diocesanos. Mexico, 1858.

Castañeda, Carlos E., ed. *Nuevos documentos inéditos o muy raros para la historia de México.* Vol. 3, *La Guerra de Reforma según el archivo del General D. Manuel Doblado, 1857–1860.* San Antonio, Texas: Casa Editorial Lozano, 1930.

Castillo Negrete, Emilio del. *Apéndice al tomo XXVI de "México en el Siglo XIX."* Mexico, 1892.

Church, George E. *Mexico. Its Revolutions: Are They Evidences of Retrogression or of Progress?* New York, 1866.

Cleven, N. Andrew N. "The Ecclesiastical Policy of Maximilian of Mexico." *Hispanic American Historical Review* 9 (August 1929): 317–60.

Cloud, W. F. *Church and State or Mexican Politics from Cortez to Díaz.* Kansas City, Mo., 1896.

Código de la Reforma, o colección de leyes, decretos, y supremas órdenes, expedidas desde 1856 hasta 1861. Mexico, 1861.

Colección de acuerdos, órdenes y decretos, sobre tierras, casas y solares de los indígenas, bienes de sus comunidades, y fundos legales de los pueblos del estado de Jalisco. 5 vols. Guadalajara, 1849–1880.

Colección de documentos inéditos o muy raros relativos a la reforma en México. 2 vols. Mexico: Instituto Nacional de Antropología e Historia, 1957–1958.

Colección de los aranceles de obvenciones y derechos parroquiales que han estado vigentes en los obispados de la República Mexicana y que se citan en el supremo decreto de 11 de abril de 1857. Mexico, 1857.

Constitución federal de los Estados-Unidos Mexicanos sancionada y jurada por el congreso general constituyente el día 5 de febrero de 1857. Mexico, 1861.

El Constituyente, Periódico Oficial del Gobierno de Oaxaca. Vol. 1. 1856.

Correspondence Relative to the Present Condition of Mexico, communicated to the House of Representatives by the Department of State. Washington, 1862.

Correspondencia de Juárez y Montluc antiguo cónsul general de México. Translated by Alberto G. Bianchi. Mexico: A. Pola, 1905.

Corti, Egon Caesar. *Maximilian and Charlotte of Mexico.* Translated by Catherine Alison Phillips. 2 vols. New York: Alfred A. Knopf, 1928.

Costeloe, Michael P. "Church-State Financial Negotiations in Mexico during the American War, 1846–1847." *Revista de Historia de América,* no. 60 (July–December 1965), pp. 91–123.

———. *Church Wealth in Mexico: A Study of the 'Juzgado de Capellanías' in the*

Archbishopric of Mexico, 1800–1856. Cambridge: The University Press, 1967.

Cotner, Thomas Ewing. *The Military and Political Career of José Joaquín de Herrera, 1792–1854.* Austin: University of Texas Press, 1949. Reprint. New York: Greenwood Press, 1969.

Cruz, Francisco Santiago. *La piqueta de la reforma.* Mexico: Editorial Jus, S.A., 1958.

Cuadro estadístico de las seis provincias que componen la iglesia mexicana el año de 1893. Querétaro, 1893.

Cue Cánovas, Agustín. *Historia social y económica de México.* Vol. 2, *La revolución de independencia y México independiente hasta 1854.* Mexico: Editorial América, 1947.

Cueva, Mario de la et al. *Plan de Ayutla, commemoración de su primer centenario.* ("Ediciones de la Facultad de Derecho, Universidad Nacional Autónoma de México.") Mexico: Talleres de Impresiones Modernas, 1954.

Cuevas, J. de J. *El Imperio, opúsculo sobre la situación actual.* Mexico, 1865.

Cuevas, Mariano. *Historia de la iglesia en México.* Vol. 5. El Paso: Editorial "Revista Católica," 1928.

———. *Historia de la nación mexicana.* 2d ed. 3 vols. Mexico: Buena Prensa, 1952.

Cumberland, Charles C. "An Analysis of the Program of the Mexican Liberal Party, 1906." *The Americas* 4 (January 1948): 294–301.

Despatches from United States Consuls in Mexico City, Mexico, 1822–1906. Washington, D.C.: National Archives, Microcopy File No. 296.

Despatches from United States Consuls in Veracruz, 1822–1906. Washington, D.C.: National Archives, Microcopy File No. 183.

Despatches from United States Ministers to Mexico, 1823–1906. Washington, D.C.: National Archives, Microcopy File No. 97.

Despojo de los bienes eclesiásticos, apuntes interesantes para la historia de la iglesia mexicana. Mexico, 1847.

Diario del Gobierno de la República Mejicana (San Luis Potosí). Vol. 1. 1863.

El Diario del Imperio (Mexico). 5 vols. 1865–1867.

Diario de los debates. Sétimo congreso constitucional de la unión. Vol. 1. Mexico, 1885.

Diario de los debates. Sexto congreso constitucional de la unión. Vol. 4. Mexico, 1887.

Diario Oficial del Gobierno Supremo de la República (Mexico). 1867–1876.

Díaz López, Lilia, ed. and trans. *Versión francesa de México. Informes diplomáticos.* 4 vols. Mexico: El Colegio de México, 1963–1967.

"Documentos para la historia. La desamortización eclesiástica en tiempo de Carlos IV." *Boletín de la Sociedad de Geografía y Estadística de la República Mexicana.* 2nd epoch, vol. 1. Mexico, 1869.

Domenech, Emmanuel. *Le Mexique tel qu'il est. La Vérité sur son climat, ses habitants et son gouvernement.* Paris, 1867.

Dublán, Manuel and Lozano, José María, eds. *Legislación mexicana o colección completa de las disposiciones legislativas expedidas desde la independencia de la república.* Vols. 8, 9, 10, and 12. Mexico, 1878.

Elías, Arturo M. *The Mexican People and the Church.* New York: n.p., 1926(?).

Elton, J. F. *With the French in Mexico.* London, 1867.

Esposición que presentó al respetable consejo de estado el lic. Anastasio Zerecero como representante de la señora Doña Agustina Guerrero de Flores en el espediente sobre revisión de las operaciones de desamortización practicadas sobre la casa no. 1 de la calle de Vergara. Mexico, 1865.

Evans, Albert S. *Our Sister Republic: A Gala Trip through Tropical Mexico in 1869–70.* Hartford, Conn., 1870.

Expediente informativo formado por la sección del gran jurado del congreso de la unión, con motivo de la acusación presentada por D. Juan Andrés Zambrano contra el C. Ministro de Hacienda y Crédito Público, Matías Romero. Mexico, 1868.

Exposición del obispo de León contra el proyecto de elevar a constitucionales las leyes de Reforma. León, 1873.

Exposición dirigida al supremo gobierno por el ciudadano Plácido de Férriz, con motivo del concurso formado a los bienes de la Archicofradía del Santísimo Sacramento, fundada en la parroquia de Santa Catarina Mártir de esta capital. Mexico, 1858.

Exposición que ha presentado al Exmo. Señor Presidente de la República la comisión nombrada por la reunión de compradores de fincas del clero, que tuvo lugar en el Teatro Principal, y acordó representar contra las disposiciones del decreto de 5 de febrero de 1861 (signed 25 February 1861 by Eulalio María Ortega, Ignacio Baz, and Vicente Gómez Parada). Mexico, 1861.

Eyzaguirre, José Ignacio Victor. *Los intereses católicos en América.* Vol. 2. Paris, 1859.

Farriss, N. M. *Crown and Clergy in Colonial Mexico 1759–1821. The Crisis of Ecclesiastical Privilege.* London: The Athalone Press of the University of London, 1968.

Forey, Elié Frèderic. *Manifiesto a la nación mexicana.* Mexico, 12 June 1863.

Frías y Soto, Hilarión. *Juárez glorificado y la Intervención y el Imperio ante la verdad histórica, refutando con documentos la obra del señor Francisco Bulnes entitulada "El verdadero Juárez."* Mexico: Editora Nacional Edinal, S. de R.L., 1957.

Fuero competente en los juicios sobre bienes nacionalizados. Informe a la vista pronunciado por el Lic. Ignacio L. Vallarta en el recurso de súplica interpuesto por D. Atenógenes Llamas contra la sentencia del tribunal de circuito de Guadalajara que declaró incompetente a la jurisdicción federal para conocer de la demanda contra los dueños de la hacienda de Huacasco, sobre pago de un capital nacionalizado. Mexico, 1891.

Gaceta de los tribunales de la República Mexicana, dirigida por el Licenciado Luis Méndez (Mexico). 4 vols. 1860–1863.

Galindo y Galindo, Miguel. *La gran década nacional, o relación histórica de la guerra de reforma, intervención extranjera y gobierno del Archiduque Maximiliano, 1857–1867.* 3 vols. Mexico: Imprenta y Fototipia de la Secretaría de Fomento, 1904–1906.

García, Genaro, ed. *Documentos inéditos o muy raros para la historia de México.* Mexico: Librería de la Viuda de Ch. Bouret, 1905–1910. Vols. 1, 4, and 13, *Correspondencia secreta de los principales Intervencionistas Mexicanas, 1860–62.* Vol. 11, *Don Santos Degollado, sus manifiestos, campañas, destitución militar, enjuiciamiento, rehabilitación, muerte, funerales y honores póstumos.* Vols. 18, 20, 22, and 27, *La intervención francesa en México según el archivo del Mariscal Bazaine.* Vol. 31, *Los gobiernos de Alvarez y Comonfort según el archivo del General Doblado.*

García Cubas, Antonio. *Cuadro geográfico, estadístico, descriptivo e histórico de los Estados Unidos Mexicanos.* Mexico, 1885.

———. *El libro de mis recuerdos.* Mexico: Imprenta de Arturo García Cubas, Sucesores, Hermanos, 1905.

García Granados, Ricardo. *Historia de México desde la restauración de la república en 1867, hasta la caída de Porfirio Díaz.* 4 vols. Mexico: Librería Editorial de Andrés Botas e Hijo, n.d. –1928.

García Icazbalceta, Joaquín. "Informe sobre los establecimientos de beneficencia y corrección de esta capital; su estado actual; noticia de sus fondos; reformas que desde luego necesitan y plan general de su arreglo, presentado por José María Andrade. Méjico, 1864. Escrito póstumo de Don Joaquín García Icazbalceta, publicado por su hijo Luis García Pimentel." *Documentos históricos de Méjico.* Vol. 5. Mexico: Moderna Librería Religiosa, 1907.

García Solorzano, Bulmaro. *Problemas monetarios y del desarrollo económico de México.* Mexico: Taller de Avelar Hnos. Impresores, 1963.

Gaulot, Pablo. *Sueño de imperio.* Translated by Enrique Martínez Sobral. Mexico: A. Pola, editor, 1905.

Geiger, John Lewis. *A Peep at Mexico: Narrative of a Journey across the Republic from the Pacific to the Gulf in December 1873 and January 1874.* London, 1874.

El gobierno constitucional a la nación. (Signed by Juárez, Ocampo, Manuel Ruiz, and Miguel Lerdo de Tejada.) Veracruz, 7 July 1859.

González Navarro, Moisés. *El porfiriato: La vida social.* Vol. 4 of *Historia moderna de México.* Edited by Daniel Cosío Villegas. Mexico: Editorial Hermes, 1957.

———. *Vallarta y su ambiente político jurídico.* Mexico: Talleres Mayela, 1949.

González y González, Luis. "El agrarismo liberal." *Historia Mexicana* 7 (April–June 1958): 469–96.

Gruening, Ernest. *Mexico and Its Heritage.* New York: Century Co., 1928.

Guerrero, Ysidoro. *Unas cuantas palabras a "La Era Nueva" sobre la cuestión de revisión de las ventas de bienes nacionalizados.* Mexico, 1865.

Gutiérrez, Blas José and Alatorre, Flores, eds. *Leyes de Reforma, colección de las disposiciones que se conocen con este nombre publicadas desde el año de 1855 al 1870.* Vol. 2, part 2. Mexico, 1870.

Hale, Charles A. *Mexican Liberalism in the Age of Mora, 1821–1853.* New Haven, Conn.: Yale University Press, 1968.

Hidalgo, José Manuel. *Proyectos de monarquía en México.* Mexico: Editorial Jus, 1962.

Icaza, Mariano de. *Exposición sobre la nulidad de las operaciones practicadas en los años 1861 y 62 con los bienes pertenecientes al Colegio de Niñas y a la corporación que lo fundó.* Mexico, 1864.

Iglesias, José M. *Revistas históricas sobre la intervención francesa en México.* 3 vols. Mexico, 1867–1869.

—— and Prieto, Guillermo. *El Ministerio de Hacienda del 21 de enero al 6 de abril de 1861.* Mexico, 1862.

Informe de Hacienda. 1872–1873, 1873–1874, 1874–1875. Mexico.

Informes y manifiestos de los poderes ejecutivo y legislativo, de 1821 a 1904, publicación hecha por J. A. Castillón de orden del Señor Ministro de Gobernación Don Ramón Corral. 3 vols. Mexico: Imprenta del Gobierno Federal, 1905.

Instrucción pastoral que los Illmos. Sres. Arzobispos de México, Michoacán y Guadalajara dirijen a su venerable clero y a sus fieles con ocasión de la ley orgánica expedida por el Soberano Congreso nacional en 10 de diciembre del año próximo pasado y sancionada por el Supremo Gobierno en 14 del mismo mes. Mexico, 1875.

El Insurgente (Mexico). Vols. 1 and 2. 1908–1909.

Iturribarría, Jorge Fernando. *Historia de Oaxaca.* Vol. 2, *1855 a 1861. La Reforma. La guerra de tres años.* Oaxaca: Imprenta del Gobierno del Estado, 1939.

Johnson, Richard A. *The Mexican Revolution of Ayutla, 1854–1855.* Augustana Library Publications, No. 17. Rock Island, Ill.: Augustana Book Concern, 1939.

Kératry, Emile de. *The Rise and Fall of the Emperor Maximilian: A Narrative of the Mexican Empire, 1861–7, from Authentic Documents with the Imperial Correspondence.* Translated by G. H. Venables. London, 1868.

Knapp, Frank Averill, Jr. *The Life of Sebastián Lerdo de Tejada, 1823–1889: A Study of Influence and Obscurity.* Austin: University of Texas Press, 1951.

——. "Parliamentary Government and the Mexican Constitution of 1857: A Forgotten Phase of Mexican Political History." *Hispanic American Historical Review* 33 (February 1953): 65–87.

Knowlton, Robert J. "Chaplaincies and the Mexican Reform." *Hispanic American Historical Review* 48 (August 1968): 421–37.

——. "Clerical Response to the Mexican Reform, 1855–1875." *Catholic Historical Reivew* 50 (January 1965): 509–28.

——. "Some Practical Effects of Clerical Opposition to the Mexican Reform, 1856–1860." *Hispanic American Historical Review* 45 (May 1965): 246–56.

Labastida, Luis G., ed. *Colección de leyes, decretos, reglamentos, circulares, órdenes y acuerdos relativos a la desamortización de los bienes de corporaciones civiles y religiosas y a la nacionalización de los que administraron las últimas.* Mexico, 1893.

Lara y Pardo, Luis. *De Porfirio Díaz a Francisco Madero: La sucesión dictatorial de 1911.* New York: Polyglot Publishing & Commercial Co., 1912.

Lavrin, Asunción. "The Execution of the Law of *Consolidación* in New Spain: Economic Aims and Results." *Hispanic American Historical Review* 53 (February 1973): 27–49.

———. "Mexican Nunneries from 1835 to 1860: Their Administrative Policies and Relations with the State." *The Americas* 28 (January 1972): 288–310.

Lemprière, Charles. *Notes in Mexico in 1861 and 1862: Politically and Socially Considered.* London, 1862.

Lerdo de Tejada, Miguel M. *Cuadro sinóptico de la República Mexicana en 1856 formado en vista de los últimos datos oficiales y otras noticias fidedignas.* Mexico, 1856.

"Leyes civiles vigentes que se relacionan con la iglesia, y sentencias pronunciadas con arreglo a ellas por los tribunales de la República," in Fortino Hipólito Vera, *Apuntamientos históricos de los concilios provinciales mexicanos y privilegios de América, estudios previos al primer concilio provincial de Antequera.* Mexico, 1893.

Leyes del Imperio, see *Boletín de las leyes del Imperio Mexicano . . . .*

Leyes de Reforma: Gobiernos de Ignacio Comonfort y Benito Juárez (1856–1863). Mexico: Empresas Editoriales, S.A., 1947.

Ligero bosquejo de la actual situación en Méjico. Artículo publicado por "El Veracruzano" en sus números correspondientes a los días 7 y 10 de octubre último. Madrid, 1862.

López Gallo, Manuel. *Economía y política en la historia de México.* Mexico: Ediciones Solidaridad, 1965.

Loza Macías, Manuel. *El pensamiento económico y la Constitución de 1857.* Mexico: Editorial Jus, S.A., 1959.

Macedo, Pablo. *La evolución mercantil. Comunicaciones y obras públicas. La hacienda pública. Tres monografías que dan idea de una parte de la evolución económica de México.* Mexico: J. Ballescá y Cía., Sucesores, Editores, 1905.

Manifestación que hace el gobierno eclesiástico de Guadalajara, contra las disposiciones dictadas en Veracruz. Guadalajara, 1859.

Manifestación que hace el obispo de León a su Venerable Clero, fieles diocesanos y a todo el mundo católico, contra el proyecto de ley orgánica que se discute en el congreso general. León, 1874.

Manifestación que hacen al venerable clero y fieles de sus respectivas diócesis y a todo el mundo católico los Illmos. Sres. Arzobispo de México y obispos de Michoacán, Linares, Guadalajara y El Potosí, y el Sr. Dr. D. Francisco Serrano como representante de la mitra de Puebla. Mexico, 1859.

Manifestaciones que José Ives Limantour, en cumplimiento del decreto de 26 de febrero del presente año, ha dirigido el Exmo. Consejo de Estado, relativas a la casa num. 6 de la calle de la Palma, y a la hacienda de Tenería, situada en jurisdicción de Tenancingo. Mexico, 1865.

Manning, William R., ed. *Diplomatic Correspondence of the United States: Inter-American Affairs, 1831–1860.* Vol. 9, *Mexico, 1848 (mid-year) to 1860.* Washington: Carnegie Endowment for International Peace, 1937.

Martínez Gracida, Manuel. "El estado de Oaxaca y su estadística del culto católico (1881)." *Boletín de la Sociedad de Geografía y Estadística de la República Mexicana.* 3rd epoch, vol. 6. Mexico, 1882.

Masseras, E. *El programa del imperio.* Mexico, 1864.

Mayer, Brantz. *Mexico as It Was and Is.* New York, 1844.

Mecham, J. Lloyd. *Church and State in Latin America: A History of Politico-Ecclesiastical Relations.* Chapel Hill, N.C.: University of North Carolina Press, 1934.

Medina, Hilario, et al. *El liberalismo y la Reforma en México.* Mexico: Editorial Cultura, 1957.

Mejía, Francisco. *Memorias.* Mexico: Ediciones del Boletín Bibliográfico de la Secretaría de Hacienda y Crédito Público, 1958.

Memoria de Hacienda. Various years from 1857 to 1904. Mexico.

Memoria de la corporación municipal que funcionó de agosto a diciembre de 1867. Mexico, 1868.

Memoria de las operaciones que han tenido lugar en la oficina especial de desamortización del Distrito, desde el 7 de enero en que se abrió, hasta el 5 de diciembre de 1861, en que cesaron sus labores, para continuarlas la Junta Superior de Hacienda. Mexico, 1862.

Memoria del Secretario de Estado y del despacho de Justicia e Instrucción Pública, leída a las cámaras del congreso nacional de la República Mexicana en 12 enero de 1844. Mexico, 1844.

Memoria en que el C. General Epitacio Huerta dió cuenta al congreso del estado del uso que hizo de las facultades con que estuvo investido durante su administración dictatorial, que comenzó en 15 de marzo de 1858 y terminó en 1° de mayo de 1861. Morelia, 1861.

Memoria presentada al Exmo. Sr. Presidente Sustituto de la República por el C. Miguel Lerdo de Tejada dando cuenta de la marcha que han seguido los negocios de la Hacienda Pública en el tiempo que tuvo a su cargo la Secretaría de este ramo. Mexico, 1857.

Memoria que el ayuntamiento popular de 1868 presenta a sus comitentes y corresponde al semestre corrido desde el 1 de enero al 30 de junio. Mexico, 1868.

Memoria que el jefe político de Zacualtipan, Felipe Angeles, presenta al C. gobernador del estado sobre los ramos de la administración del distrito por lo relativo al año anterior de 1888. Mexico, 1889.

Memoria que el Secretario de Estado y del despacho de Fomento, Colonización, Industria y Comercio de la República Mexicana presenta al congreso de la unión conteniendo documentos hasta el 30 de junio de 1873. Mexico, 1873.

Memoria que el Secretario de Estado y del despacho de Gobernación presenta al sexto congreso constitucional. Mexico, 1871.

Memorias de Sebastián Lerdo de Tejada. Preliminary study by Leonardo Pasquel. Mexico: Editorial Citlaltépetl, 1959.

Las memorias diplomáticas de Mr. Foster sobre México. Vol. 29 of *Archivo Histórico Diplomático Mexicano.* Mexico: Publicaciones de la Secretaría de Relaciones Exteriores, 1929.

Mendieta y Núñez, Lucio. *El problema agrario de México. Historia. Legislación agraria vigente. Formularios.* 2d ed. Mexico: n.p., 1926.

Menéndez Mena, Rodolfo. *The Work of the Clergy and the Religious Persecution in Mexico.* New York: Latin American News Association, 1916.

"Un Mexicano." *México, el imperio y la intervención.* (2 February 1867) Mexico, n.d.

Miguel Miramón, general de división en gefe del ejército y presidente sustituto de la República Mexicana, a la nación. (12 July 1859) Mexico, n.d.

Moctezuma, Aquiles P. *El conflicto religioso de 1926. Sus orígines. Su desarrollo. Su solución.* 2d ed. Vol. 1. Mexico: Editorial Jus, S.A., 1960.

Molina Enríquez, Andrés. *Juárez y la Reforma.* Mexico: Editora Ibero-Mexicana, 1956.

Mora, José María Luis. *Disertación sobre la naturaleza y aplicación de las rentas y bienes eclesiásticos.* Mexico, 1833. Reprint ed. Mexico: Talleres de la Secretaría de Hacienda y Crédito Público, 1957.

———. *Ensayos, ideas, retratos.* Mexico: Ediciones de la Universidad Nacional Autónoma en la Imprenta Universitaria, 1941.

———. *Obras sueltas.* Vol. 1. Paris, 1837.

Munguía, Clemente de Jesús. *Defensa eclesiástica en el Obispado de Michoacán desde fines de 1855 hasta principios de 1858.* 2 vols. Mexico, 1858.

Murray, Paul V̆. *The Catholic Church in Mexico. Historical Essays for the General Reader.* Vol. 1. Mexico: Editorial E. P. M., Imprenta Aldina, 1965.

La Nacionalidad. Periódico Oficial del Estado de Guanajuato. Vols. 1 and 2. 1855–1856.

Navarro, Juan N. "Mexico of Today." *The National Geographic Magazine* 12 (April 1901): 152; (May 1901): 176; (June 1901): 235.

"El Nigromante" [Ignacio Ramírez]. *El partido liberal y la reforma religiosa en México.* Mexico, 1898.

"Noticias de Nueva España en 1805, publicadas por el tribunal del consulado." *Boletín de la Sociedad Mexicana de Geografía y Estadística.* 2nd epoch, vol. 2. Mexico, 1864.

Observaciones y comentarios a la carta que D. Manuel Payno ha dirigido al señor Gen. Forey. Veracruz, 1863.

Ocampo, Melchor. *Obras completas.* Vol. 2, *Escritos políticos.* Edited by F. Vásquez. Mexico: Imp. y encuadernación de Jesús M. Valdés, 1901.

Ocurso que el doctor Don Antonio Fernández Monjardín presentó en 28 de abril de 1862 al juez 4° de lo civil, Lic. D. Agustín Norma, reclamando el despojo que se le infirió en 24 de mayo de 1861 de una casa de su propiedad, de la que se dió posesión a D. José Ibes Limantour. Mexico, 1862.

Olavarría y Ferrari, Enrique. *México independiente, 1821–1855.* Vol. 4 of *México a través de los siglos,* edited by Vicente Riva Palacio. Mexico, n.d.

La Orquesta (Mexico). 1861, 1864–1866, 1867–1868.

Otero, Mariano. *Ensayo sobre el verdadero estado de la cuestión social y política que se agita en la República Mexicana.* Mexico, 1842.

Pacheco, José Ramón. *Cuestión de Méjico, cartas de D. José Ramón Pacheco al Ministro de Negocios Extranjeros de Napoleón III, M. Drouyn de Lhuys.* Mérida, 1863.

El País. Diario Católico (Mexico). 1909.

Palavicini, Felix F., et al. *México: Historia de su evolución constructiva.* Vol. 3. Mexico: Talleres Tipográficos Modelo, S.A., 1945.

Pallares, Jacinto, ed. *Legislación federal complementaria del derecho civil mexicano.* Mexico, 1897.

Parra, Porfirio. *Sociología de la Reforma.* Mexico: Empresas Editoriales, S.A., 1948.

Payno, Manuel. *Carta que sobre los asuntos de México dirige al señor Gen. Forey.* Mexico, 1862.

———. *Cuentas, gastos, acreedores y otros asuntos del tiempo de la intervención francesa y del imperio. De 1861 a 1867.* Mexico, 1868.

———. *Memoria sobre la revolución de diciembre de 1857 y enero de 1858.* Mexico, 1860.

———, ed. *Colección de las leyes, decretos, circulares y providencias relativas a la desamortización eclesiástica, a la nacionalización de los bienes de corporaciones, y a la reforma de la legislación civil que tenía relación con el culto y con la iglesia.* 2 vols. Mexico, 1861.

Pérez, Juan E. *Almanaque de las oficinas Guía de Forasteros para el año de 1871.* Mexico, 1871.

Pérez Hernández, José María. *Diccionario geográfico, estadístico, histórico, biográfico, de industria y comercio de la República Mexicana.* Vol. 3. Mexico, 1875.

———. *Estadística de la República Mexicana, territorio, población, antigüedades, monumentos, establecimientos públicos, reino vegetal y agricultura, reino animal, reino mineral, industria fabril y manufactura, artes mecánicas y liberales, comercio, navegación, gobierno, hacienda y crédito público, ejército, marina, clero, justicia, instrucción pública, colonias militares y civiles.* Guadalajara, 1862.

Pérez Lugo, J. *La cuestión religiosa en México.* Mexico: Centro Cultural "Cuauhtemoc," 1927.

Pérez Verdía, Luis. *Compendio de la Historia de México.* 11th ed. Guadalajara: Librería Font, 1951.

———. *Historia particular del estado de Jalisco, desde los primeros tiempos de que hay noticia hasta nuestros días.* 3 vols. Guadalajara: Tip. de la Escuela de Artes y Oficios del Estado, 1910–1911.

Peza, Juan de Dios. *Epopeyas de mi patria. Benito Juárez. La Reforma. La interven-ción francesa. El imperio. El triunfo de la República.* Mexico: J. Ballescá y Cía., Sucesores, 1904.

Phipps, Helen. *Some Aspects of the Agrarian Question in Mexico: A Historical Study.* Austin: University of Texas Press, 1925.

Planchet, Regis. *La cuestión religiosa en México o sea vida de Benito Juárez.* Rome: Librería Pontificias de Desclée, Lefebvre & Cía., 1906.

La población del Valle de Teotihuacán. El medio en que se ha desarrollado. Su evolu-ción étnica y social. Iniciativas para procurar su mejoramiento. Por la dirección de Antropología, Manuel Gamio, director. Vol. 2. Mexico: Dirección de Talleres Gráficos, 1922.

La política del General Comonfort y la situación actual de México. Mexico, 1857.

Porras Sánchez, Juan. *Orígenes y evolución de la Reforma en México: Antecedentes ideológicos y legislativos con un apéndice sobre la debatida cuestión del Pa-tronato; 1800–1834.* Puebla: n.p., 1949.

Portes Gil, Emilio. *The Conflict between the Civil Power and the Clergy: Historical and Legal Essay.* Mexico: Press of the Ministry of Foreign Affairs, 1935.

Portilla, Anselmo. *Méjico en 1856 y 1857, gobierno del General Comonfort.* New York, 1858.

Portilla, Juan de la. *Episodio histórico del gobierno dictatorial del Señor Ignacio Comonfort en la República Mexicana, años de 1856 y 1857. Escrito en propia defensa por el Lic. J. de la Portilla.* Mexico, 1861.

Present Condition of Mexico, see Correspondence Relative to . . . .

La prescripción respecto de los bienes nacionalizados. Pedimento fiscal. Apuntes del informe pronunciado por el Lic. Luis G. Labastida y sentencia de segunda instancia que causó ejecutoria en el juicio iniciado por el Sr. Lic. Pedro Azcué, como subrogatorio de la Hacienda Pública Federal, contra los poseedores de la casa esquina de la Plaza del Carmen en San Angel, sobre pago de un capital nacionalizado. Mexico, 1887.

Prieto, Guillermo. *Lecciones de historia patria escritas para los alumnos del Colegio Militar.* 4th ed. Mexico, 1893.

Primer calendario de la guerra estranjera con los principales documentos relativos a ella para el año de 1863. Mexico, 1862 [*sic*].

"Un Progresista." *Los moderados y el estado de México.* Toluca, 1861.

Protesta de los Obispos Católicos contra la intervención francesa. Mexico, 26 De-cember 1863.

Quinta carta pastoral del Illmo. Sr. Arzobispo de Méjico, Dr. D. Lázaro de la Garza y Ballesteros, dirigida al V. clero y fieles de este arzobispado con motivo de los proyectos contra la iglesia, publicados en Veracruz por D. Benito Juárez antiguo presidente del Supremo Tribunal de la nación. Mexico, 1859.

Ramos y Duarte, Feliz. *Diccionario de curiosidades históricas, geográficas, hiero-gráficas, cronológicas, etc. de la República Mejicana.* Mexico, 1899.

La Reforma. Leyes y circulares espedidas por el Supremo Gobierno Constitucional de la República, desde su manifiesto de 7 de julio de 1859. Mexico, 1861.

Rentas eclesiásticas, o sea impugnación de la disertación que sobre la materia se ha publicado de orden del honorable congreso de Zacatecas. Guadalajara, 1834.

Resolución de la Sagrada Congregación acerca de la solicitud que le dirigió un eclesiástico que de buena fe denunció la casa en que vivía con arreglo a la ley de 25 de junio de 1856. Guadalajara, 1858.

Reyes, Ygnacio. *Rectificación de algunas especies vertidas en el cuaderno impreso de Don Joaquín Llaguno sobre el embargo de la hacienda de San Jacinto.* Mexico, 1862.

Reyes Heroles, Jesús. *El liberalismo mexicano.* 3 vols. Mexico: Editorial Cultura, 1957–1961.

Rivera Cambas, Manuel. *Los gobernantes de México.* Vol. 2. Mexico, 1873.

———. *Historia de la intervención europea y norte-americana en México y del imperio de Maximiliano de Hapsburgo.* 3 vols. Mexico, 1888–1895.

———. *Historia de la reforma religiosa, política y social en México.* Vol. 1. Mexico, 1875.

Rivera y Sanromán, Agustín. *Anales mexicanos: La Reforma y el segundo imperio.* 3rd ed. Guadalajara, 1897.

Robertson, William Parish. *A Visit to Mexico, by the West India Islands, Yucatan and United States.* Vol. 2. London, 1853.

Romero, José Guadalupe, "Noticias para formar la estadística del obispado de Michoacán (1860)." *Boletín de la Sociedad Mexicana de Geografía y Estadística.* Vol. 8. Mexico, 1860.

Romero, Matías. "The Philosophy of the Mexican Revolutions." *The North American Review* 162 (1896): 33–47.

Romero de Terreros, Manuel. *La iglesia y convento de San Agustín.* Mexico: Instituto de Investigaciones Estéticas, 1951.

Romero Flores, Jesús. *Anales históricos de la revolución mexicana.* Vol. 1. Mexico: Ediciones "El Nacional," 1939.

———. *Comentarios a la historia de México (1821–1861).* Mexico: Talleres de Imprenta de la Editora B. Costa-Amic, 1958.

Rosa, Agustín de la. *Observaciones sobre las cuestiones que el abate Testory mueve en su opúsculo entitulado "El imperio y el clero mexicano."* Guadalajara, 1865.

Rosa, Luis de la. *Observaciones sobre varios puntos concernientes a la administración pública del estado de Zacatecas.* Baltimore, 1851.

Salado Alvarez, Victoriano. *Episodios nacionales.* Vol. 5, *La Reforma.* Mexico: Colección Málaga, S.A., 1945.

Scholes, Walter V. "A Revolution Falters: Mexico, 1856–1857." *Hispanic American Historical Review* 32 (February 1952): 1–21.

Secretaría de Estado y del despacho de Gobernación. (Re intervention in Puebla Church property; 18 April 1856). Mexico, n.d.

Segura, José Sebastián, ed. *Boletín de las leyes del imperio mexicano, o sea código de la restauración. Colección completa de las leyes y demás disposiciones dictadas por la intervención francesa, por el supremo ejecutivo provisional, y por el imperio mexicano, con un apéndice de los documentos oficiales más notables y curiosos de la época.* 4 vols. Mexico, 1863–1865.

Sentencia pronunciada el día 28 de mayo por el juez 2° de lo civil, Lic. Don José María Barros, en el juicio posesorio promovido por el Dr. D. Antonio Fernández Monjardín contra D. José Ibes Limantour. Mexico, 1863.

Sermonario mexicano o colección de sermones panegíricos, dogmáticos y morales escritos por los oradores mexicanos más notables, ordenados por un eclesiástico de la Mitra de Puebla, coleccionados y publicados por Narciso Bassols. Vol. 3. Mexico, 1890.

Sierra, Justo. *Obras completas del Maestro Justo Sierra.* Vol. 2, *México, su evolución social*; vol. 12, *Evolución política del pueblo mexicano*; vol. 13, *Juárez, su obra y su tiempo.* Mexico: Imp. de Ignacio Escalante and Imp. Universitaria, 1902 and 1948.

El Siglo Diez y Nueve (Mexico). 1856–1858, 1861–1863, and 1867–1870.

Sinkin, Richard N. "The Mexican Constitutional Congress, 1856–1857: A Statistical Analysis." *Hispanic American Historical Review* 53 (February 1973): 1–26.

La Sociedad. Periódico Político y Literario (Mexico). 1857–1859 and 1865–1866.

La Sombra (Mexico). Vol. 1. 1865.

Stevenson, Sara Yorke. *Maximilian in Mexico: A Woman's Reminiscences of the French Intervention, 1862–1867.* New York, 1899.

Testimonio de los autos seguidos por el tesorero de la Muy Ilustre Archicofradía del Santísimo y Soledad de Nuestra Señora, fundada en la parroquia de Santa Cruz de esta ciudad, en el recurso de fuerza en conocer y proceder interpuesto por el mismo, contra el Illmo. Señor Arzobispo de México. Mexico, 1856.

Testory, Abbot. *El imperio y el clero mexicano.* Mexico, 1865.

Toro, Alfonso. *La iglesia y el estado en México, estudio sobre los conflictos entre el clero católico y los gobiernos mexicanos desde la independencia hasta nuestros días.* Mexico: Publicaciones del Archivo General de la Nación, 1931.

Torres, Mariano de Jesús. *Historia civil y eclesiástica de Michoacán desde los tiempos antiguos hasta nuestros días.* Vol. 1. Morelia: Tip. part. del autor, 1914.

Tovar, Pantaleón. *Historia parlamentaria del cuarto congreso constitucional.* 4 vols. Mexico, 1872–1874.

Trueba Urbina, Alberto, ed. *Centenario del Plan de Ayutla.* Mexico: Biblioteca Campechana, Librería de Manuel Porrúa, S.A., 1954.

Undécima pastoral que el Illmo. y Rmo. Sr. Obispo de León, Dr. y Maestro D. José María de Jesús Diez de Sollano y Dávalos, dirige a su Illmo. y V. Cabildo, señores curas y V. clero. León, 1872.

Valadés, José C. *Don Melchor Ocampo, reformador de México.* Mexico: Editorial Patria, S.A., 1954.

———. *El porfirismo, historia de un régimen.* Vol. 1, *El nacimiento, 1876–1884;* vol. 2, *El crecimiento.* Mexico: Antigua Librería Robredo de José Porrúa e Hijos, and Editorial Patria, 1941 and 1948.

Valdés, Manuel. *Memorias de la guerra de reforma.* Mexico: Imp. y Fototipia de la Secretaría de Fomento, 1913.

Vera, Fortino Hipólito. *Apuntamientos históricos* . . . , see "Leyes civiles vigentes
. . . ."

―――. *Catecismo geográfico-histórico-estadístico de la iglesia mexicana.* Amecameca,
1881.

―――. *Itinerario parroquial del arzobispado de México y reseña histórica, geográfica y
estadística de las parroquias del mismo arzobispado.* Amecameca, 1880.

―――, comp. *Colección de documentos eclesiásticos de México, o sea antigua y moderna legislación de la Iglesia Mexicana.* 3 vols. Amecameca, 1887.

Vérgez, José F. *Recuerdos de Méjico.* Barcelona: Imp. de Henrich y Ca., 1902.

La Victoria. Periódico del Gobierno de Oaxaca. Vol. 4. 1863–1864.

Vigil, José M. *La reforma.* Vol. 5 of *México a través de los siglos*, edited by Vicente
Riva Palacio. Mexico, n.d.

Y. O. [Manuel Payno]. *La reforma social de Méjico deducida del aspecto político que
él presenta, y fundada en la esperiencia de cuarenta y cinco años.* Mexico,
1855.

Zamacois, Niceto de. *Historia de Méjico desde sus tiempos más remotos hasta nuestros
días.* Vols. 12–16. Barcelona, 1880–1882.

Zarco, Francisco. *Crónica del congreso extraordinario constituyente, (1856–1857).*
Mexico: El Colegio de México, 1957.

―――. *Historia del congreso estraordinario constituyente de 1856 y 1857.* 2 vols.
Mexico, 1857.

Zayas Enríquez, Rafael de. *Benito Juárez su vida—su obra.* Mexico: Tipografía
de la Viuda de Francisco de León, 1906.

Index